Financial Analysis and the Predictability of Important Economic Events

Financial Analysis and the Predictability of Important Economic Events

AHMED RIAHI-BELKAOUI

QUORUM BOOKS
Westport, Connecticut · London

Library of Congress Cataloging-in-Publication Data

Riahi-Belkaoui, Ahmed, 1943–
    Financial analysis and the predictability of important economic
events / Ahmed Riahi-Belkaoui.
        p.   cm.
    Includes bibliographical references and index.
    ISBN 1–56720–164–4 (alk. paper)
        1. Investment analysis—Mathematical models.   2. Business
Forecasting—Mathematical models.   I. Title.
    HG4529.R5   1998
    658.15'54—dc21   97–32991

British Library Cataloguing in Publication Data is available.

Library of Congress Catalog Card Number: 97–32991
ISBN: 1–56720–164–4

First published in 1998

Quorum Books, 88 Post Road West, Westport, CT 06881
An imprint of Greenwood Publishing Group, Inc.

Printed in the United States of America

∞

The paper used in this book complies with the
Permanent Paper Standard issued by the National
Information Standards Organization (Z39.48–1984).

10 9 8 7 6 5 4 3 2 1

To My Family

Contents

Exhibits

Preface

Financial analysis as based in ratio analysis has been used as a tool for analyzing the financial strengths of corporations. Ratio analysis is generally used as a univariate strategy. The accounting and finance literature has, however, evolved to include in financial analysis multivariate-based models that can be used to explain and/or to predict important economic events. Accordingly this book elaborates on this new aspect of financial analysis and presents specific multi-variate models that have been used and/or can be used for an explanation and/or prediction of economic events of importance to the firm, the managers, and the stockholders. The events to be predicted and/or explained in an explicit mathematical model include:

1. Stock Returns (Chapter 2)
2. Systematic Risk (Chapter 3)
3. Industrial Bond Ratings (Chapter 4)
4. Dual-Labor Theory (Chapter 5)
5. Social Disclosure (Chapter 6)
6. Takeovers (Chapter 7)
7. CEO Compensation (Chapter 8)
8. Corporate Performance (Chapter 9)
9. Corporate Reputation (Chapter 10)
10. Capital Structure (Chapter 11)

Each chapter explicates the economic events and presents an explicit model that can be used in financial analysis aimed at explaining and/or predicting economic events.

This book should be of interest to investors and managers, researchers and students involved in the mathematical application of financial analysis in general, and the use of predictive quantitative models in particular.

Many people helped in the development of this book. Considerable assistance was received from University of Illinois at Chicago students—especially Belia Ortega and Dimitria K. Alvertos. The support of Eric Valentine, publisher of Quorum Books, and John Donohue is greatly appreciated. Finally, to Hedi and Janice Belkaoui, thanks for making "everything" possible and agreeable.

Financial Analysis and the Predictability of Important Economic Events

1

Financial Analysis and the Predictive Approach

INTRODUCTION

Financial analysis is an information processing system used to provide relevant information for decision making. The main source of information is published financial statements. Basically, various accounts from published financial statements are evaluated in relation to each other to form performance indicators, which are then compared to "established" standards. These performance indicators are better known as ratios, and constitute the main tools of conventional financial analysis. Some of the ratios are particularly relevant to the prediction of economic events. It is therefore the purpose of this chapter to elaborate on financial analysis and the predictive approach.

FINANCIAL STATEMENTS AND ACCOUNTING DATA

The financial statements included in annual reports generally include a balance sheet, an income statement, a statement of changes in the financial position, notes to the financial statements, a reconciliation of retained earnings, an auditor's opinion, and supplementary information on the effects of changing prices. These reports are discussed next.

The Balance Sheet

The balance sheet, or statement of financial position, expresses the financial position of a firm at the end of the accounting period, a moment in time. More precisely, it presents both the assets of a firm and claims on those assets (liabilities and owner's equity) at a point in time. Two major questions of interest to the reader are (1) which resources of a firm are recognized as assets and which claims against the firm's assets are recognized as liabilities? and (2) what valuations are placed on these assets and liabilities?

Assets

Four characteristics must be met for a resource (other than cases) to be recognized as an asset: (1) the resource must, singly or in combination with other resources, contribute directly or indirectly to future net cash inflows (or to obviating future net cash outflows); (2) the enterprise must be able to obtain the benefit from the resource and control the access of others to it; (3) the transaction or event giving rise to the enterprise's claim to or control of the benefit must already have occurred; and (4) the future benefit must be quantifiable or measurable in units of money.

The assets are broken down into further, more specific categories by order of decreasing liquidity.

Current assets is "used to designate cash and other assets or resources commonly identified as those that are reasonably expected to be realized in cash or sold or consumed during the normal operating cycle of the business."[1] Current assets consist generally of cash, marketable securities held as short-term investments, accounts and notes receivables net of allowance for uncollectible accounts, inventories of merchandise, raw materials, supplies, work in process and finished goods, and prepared operating costs.

Investments is used to designate the investments in securities of other firms to be held for a long term and whose financial statements have not been consolidated with the parent or investor firm. Long-term investment of 50 percent of the voting stock of a corporation (subsidiary) calls for consolidation of the financial statements of the subsidiary with the parent firm.

Property, plant, and equipment designates the long-lived assets, generally termed fixed assets, acquired for long-term use rather than resale, and generally include land, buildings, machinery, and various equipment. With the exception of land, these assets are carried at original cost less accumulated depreciation.

Intangible assets designates resources that lack physical existence and includes copyrights, patents, trademarks, goodwill, organization costs, franchises, lease holds, and similar items.[2]

Liabilities

Four characteristics must be met before an obligation is recognized as a liability: (1) the obligation must involve a probable future sacrifice of resources—a future transfer of cash goods or services (or a foregoing of a future cash receipt); (2) the obligation must be one of the specific enterprise; (3) the transaction or event giving rise to the enterprise's obligation must already have occurred; and (4) the amount of the obligation and the time of its settlement must be measurable with reasonable accuracy.[3]

The liabilities are further broken down into specific categories.

Current liabilities is "used principally to designate obligations whose liquidation is reasonably expected to require the use of existing resources properly classified as current assets, or the creation of other current liabilities."[4] It includes accounts payables, notes payables, accrued expenses, accrued taxes, and the current portion of long-term debt.

Long-term liabilities designates obligations having due dates or maturities longer than a year. It includes bonds, mortgages, long-term leases, deferred income taxes, and deferred pension obligations.

Owner's Equity

Owner's equity represents the ownership interests in the firm, and includes what was originally invested by them and whatever earnings are "plowed back" in the firm. It includes (1) capital stock, common or preferred, which is the portion of the capital specified in the articles of incorporation at par value;[5] (2) additional paid-in capital, which is the portion paid in excess of the stated or par value; and (3) retained earnings, which represents earnings undistributed and "plowed back" into the firm.

Valuation of Assets and Liabilities

There are four possible valuation methods: (1) acquisition cost or historical cost, which is the amount of cash or other payment made by the firm when it acquired specific assets; (2) current entry value or replacement cost, which is the amount of cash or equivalent necessary to replace the asset by a "similar" asset; (3) current exit value or net realizable value, which is the amount assumed to be realized if the assets were sold in an orderly fashion; and (4) capitalized value, which is present value of future cash flows that can be generated by the asset.

Unfortunately, no single valuation base is used to value all the assets and liabilities. All four valuation bases are used by generally accepted accounting principles. Exhibit 1.1 presents a summary of valuation methods for various assets and liabilities. This situation presents quite an intellectual challenge to those investors who are not versed in the complexities and idiosyncracies of accounting valuations.

The Income Statement

The income statement presents a measure of the financial performance of a firm over an accounting period. The net income is equal to the revenues and gains minus expenses and losses. Let's examine each of these elements of the income statement.

Revenues

Revenues measure the inflow of the net assets resulting from the sales of goods or services. Revenue may be recognized at the time of sale when (1)

Exhibit 1.1
Valuation Bases under Generally Accepted Accounting Principles

ACCOUNTS	VALUATION BASE
Cash	Face or current exchange value (current cash equivalent)
Marketable securities	The porfolio is valued at lower of cost or market (current exit value)
Accounts and notes receivable	Short-term accounts are valued at current cash equivalent, long-term accounts at the present value of the future cash flows (discounted at the historical markets interest rate on date of issue)
Inventories	Lower of cost or market (current entry value)
Investments	Investments in bonds are valued at the present value of the future cash flows. Investments in stocks are valued at lower of cost or market where there is no significant influence and using the equity method where there is "significant influence"
Land	Acquisition cost
Depreciable assets	Acquisition cost (net of accumulated depreciation)
Patents, goodwill, and intangibles	Stated at the amount payable if they are to be paid within the next year, if not, stated at the present value of future cash flows
Nonmonetary liabilities	If arising from transactions where revenues have already been recognized (warranties on product sold), they are stated at the estimated futue cost of the warranty services; if arising from advances from customers for future goods or services, they are stated at the amount of cash received

most of the services to be provided have been performed and (2) some measurable consideration has been received. Revenue may be recognized during the period of production for certain long-term contracts and special order merchandise. Revenue may also be recognized at the time of cash collection for installment sales of merchandise, real estate, or franchises.

Expenses

Expenses measure the outflow of net assets that have been used to generate the revenues. They are therefore recognized in the same period the revenues have been generated.[6] Expenses are composed of cost of goods sold and selling and administrative expenses. The value of the cost of goods sold depends on the cost-flow assumption, either first-in first-out (FIFO), last-in first-out (LIFO), or weighted average. Under the FIFO method, the cost of goods sold is valued at the cost of the earliest units acquired. Under the LIFO method, the cost of goods sold is valued at the cost of the latest units acquired. Under the weighted average method, the cost of goods sold is valued at the average of the costs of all goods available for sale use during the period. There is an important implication to the cost-flow assumptions. FIFO results in lower cost of goods sold and higher income than LIFO when prices are rising. LIFO results in a cost of goods sold figure that is close to current values and in lower cash outlays for income taxes.[7]

Format and Classification within the Income Statement

In general, the income statement contains the following categories:

a. *Income from Continuing Operations*: It is equal to the revenues and gains from the operating areas of the business firm minus the corresponding expenses and losses.

b. *Income, Gains, and Losses from Discontinued Operations*: This section includes the income, gains, and losses resulting from the disposal of a segment of the firm.[8]

c. *Extraordinary Gains and Losses*: This section includes all activities termed extraordinary if they meet all three of the following criteria: (1) unusual in nature, (2) infrequent in occurrence, and (3) material in amount.[9]

d. *Adjustment for Accounting Changes*: This section includes four types of accounting changes, namely, (1) change in accounting estimate, (2) change in accounting principle, (3) change in reporting entity, and (4) correction of errors in prior years' financial statements. According to Accounting Principles Board (APB), *Opinion No. 20*, these changes are to be reflected in the accounts and reported on the financial statements retroactively for a change in accounting entity, prospectively for a change in accounting estimate, and generally, currently for a change in accounting principle.[10]

Earnings per Share

APB *Opinion No. 15* recommends that earnings per share be included in the body of the income statement before receiving an auditor's unqualified opinion.[11] Most firms have a complex capital structure, which includes convertible bonds or convertible preferred stock. To warn about the dilutive effect of such a situation, a dual presentation of primary and fully diluted earnings per share is required. Primary earnings per share represents the earnings applicable to each share of outstanding common stock and common stock equivalent. Common stock equivalents are securities that are likely to be converted into, or exchanged for, common stock instead of their own periodic cash yields over time. Fully diluted earnings per share represent the earnings applicable to each share if besides outstanding common stock, all options, warrants, and convertible securities were exchanged for common stock.

Notes to the Financial Statements and Other Items in the Annual Reports

Notes to the Financial Statements

Given the complexity of the three major financial statements, the balance sheet, income statement, and statement of changes in the financial position, additional information may be needed to guide the annual report user toward a better understanding of the accounting data. This additional information forms the major part of the notes to the financial statements. A high fluency in the accounting language is needed to comprehend the information conveyed by the notes.

Reconciliation of Retained Earnings

This section is used to reconcile the beginning and ending balances in retained earnings.

Auditor's Opinion

This is an important section of the annual report used to express the opinion of the independent certified public accountant on the financial statements, supporting schedules, and notes. The four types of opinions that may result from an independent audit of financial statements are

a. *Unqualified opinion*: when the auditor states that the financial statement "presents fairly" the position and activities of the firm.

b. *Qualified opinion*: when the auditor may feel that the financial statement "presents fairly" the position and activities of the firm, but cannot make one or more of the statements necessary for an unqualified opinion. A qualified opinion is conveyed by the use of "except for" or "subject to" statement in the audit report. "Except for" is used to convey an objection about the financial statements being presented.[12] "Subject to" is used to convey a contingency, uncertainty, or unresolved situations that may affect the financial statements.[13]

c. *Disclaimer of opinion*: when the auditor has been so limited, or there is a serious and material departure from generally accepted accounting principles (GAAP), and as a result, the finding is merely an inability to give an opinion.

d. *Adverse opinion*: when the auditor feels that the audit has shown some serious and material departures from GAAP, and as a result, the financial statements do not present the position and activities of the firm.

Supplementary Information on the Effects of Changing Prices

The Financial Accounting Standards Board (FASB) Statement No. 33, "Financial Reporting and Changing Prices," requires that the company provide supplementary information concerning the effects of inflation on its financial statements. Required disclosures include selected financial information on a constant dollar basis (reflecting the effects of general inflation) as computed using the Consumer Price Index for All Urban Consumers (CPI), and on a current cost basis (reflecting specific price changes of goods and services). The FASB has provided flexibility and encouraged experimentation within the guidelines of the statement. Accordingly, users of annual reports should exercise discretion when considering the supplementary information on the effects of changing prices.

ROLE OF FINANCIAL STATEMENT ANALYSIS

The question of the role of financial statement analysis is important considering the theoretical and empirical evidence supporting the efficiency of the capital market. It is generally assumed that the securities market is efficient. A perfectly efficient market is in continuous equilibrium, so the intrinsic values of securities vibrate randomly and market prices always equal underlying intrinsic values at every instant in time.[14] Applied to the securities market, this assumption implies that market prices "fully reflect" all publicly available information and, by implication, market prices react instantaneously and without bias to new information. Of the three levels of market efficiency, the semi-strong form is the most relevant to the role of financial statement analysis.[15] The semi-strong form of the efficient market hypothesis states that the equilibrium-expected returns (prices) "fully reflect" all publicly available information. In other words, no trading rule based on available information may be used to earn an excess return. The semi-strong form is most relevant to accounting because publicly available information includes financial statements. Tests of the semi-strong hypothesis were concerned with the speed with which prices adjusted to specific kinds of events. Some of the events examined were stock splits, announcements of annual earnings, larger secondary offerings of common stocks, new issues of stocks, announcements of changes in the discount rate, and stock dividends. The results again support the efficient market hypothesis in the sense that prices adjust rather quickly after the first public announcement of information. Which again brings into question the role of financial analysis in such an efficient capital market. There is definitely a role for financial analysis in such an efficient market.

First, the first role results from the two findings that (1) accounting information and stock price movements are significantly associated, even when the effects of other information (e.g., dividend announcements) are taken into account and (2) accounting information appears to be able to assist in the assessment of prospective return and risk. Both findings imply that financial statements analysis may assist in making intelligent investment decisions.

Second, for the first role to be possible, the financial statement analysis must be expertly and quickly done.

Third, a final role of financial statement analysis is to explain and predict economic events that may affect the firm and that are not reflected in some capital market framework. Examples include bond ratings, bankruptcy, takeover, and so forth. The likelihood of these events requires a careful analysis of the financial, operating, and extraordinary dimensions of the affairs of the firm.

FINANCIAL RATIO ANALYSIS

Usefulness of Ratio Analysis

Financial analysis is a methodology designed to provide data for decision-makers. It is intended to be flexible enough to assist different users in their decisions. Financial analysis rests entirely on the use of financial ratios. Financial ratios are more convenient to interpret than financial statement accounts. This convenience is possible because financial ratios represent ''significant relationships'' between various items in financial statements. These financial ratios are then compared to established standard ratios for the firm or other firms in the industry. If the comparison is with similar ratios of the firm over a certain number of years, the analysis is referred to as cross-sectional analysis. Whatever the type of analysis chosen, ratio analysis is intended to evaluate important financial aspects of the firm that depict its financial strengths. Examples include liquidity, leverage, profitability, and turnover dimensions. Some of the types of ratios used to measure these dimensions are presented next. They are classified into four major categories: (1) the firm's ability to meet its short-term obligations, (2) the capital structure of the firm and its ability to meet its long-term obligations, (3) the profitability and efficiency resulting from the use of capital, and (4) the efficiency resulting from the operational use of its assets.

Liquidity Ratios

Liquidity ratios are used to assess the ability of the firm to meet its short-term financial obligations when and as they fall due. These ratios are of prime interest to short-term lenders.

Current Ratio

The current ratios may be expressed as

$$\frac{\text{current assets}}{\text{current liabilities}}$$

Current assets are composed mainly of cash, short-term marketable securities, accounts receivable, inventories, and prepaid expenses. Current liabilities are composed mainly of accounts payable, dividends, taxes payable, and short-term bank loans. The current ratio has long been considered as a good indicator of the firm's liquidity.[16] It is, however, susceptible to "window dressing"; that is, it is susceptible to manipulation intended to approximate a "desirable" current ratio.

Quick (Acid-Test) Ratio

The quick ratio may be expressed as

$$\frac{\text{quick assets}}{\text{current liabilities}}$$

Quick assets are composed of cash, short-term marketable securities, and receivables. The quick ratio is intended to focus on immediate liquidity. Both the quick ratio and the current ratios have been criticized for failure to incorporate information about the timing and magnitude of future cash flows.[17]

Defensive Interval Measure

The defensive interval measure was presented as a better replacement of both the current ratio and the quick ratio:

$$\frac{\text{total defensive assets}}{\text{projected daily operating expenditures}}$$

The total defensive assets have been appropriately defined as follows:

Defensive assets include cash, short-term marketable securities and accounts receivable. Inventories are not included in the total, nor are current liabilities deducted from the total. The denominator includes all projected operating costs requiring the use of defensive assets. Ideally, this would be based on the cash budget for the next year or shorter period. Since this information is unlikely to be available to external analysts, the total of operating expenses on the income statement for the prior period will usually serve as a basis for calculating the projected expenditures. The adjustments must be made to the total expense figure on the statement:

1. Depreciation, deferred taxes and other expenses that do not utilize defensive assets must be subtracted.
2. Adjustments should be made for known changes in planned operations.[18]

Other measures of liquidity based on a fund-flow concept include: (a) the ratio of net working capital to funds provided by operations,[19] (b) the ratio of funds provided from operations to current debt;[20] and (c) a liquidity index based on projected fund flows.[21] Each of these fund-flow-based ratios reflects the idea that liquidity depends on the ability of liquid assets and cash inflows to cover the cash outflow by a material margin.

A measure of future liquidity may be expressed as follows: the five-year cash flow as a percentage of five-year growth needs is equal to the five-year sum of (1) net income available for common stockholders plus (2) depreciation and amortization plus (3) income from discontinued operations and extraordinary items net of taxes, divided by the five-year sum of (1) capital expenditures plus (2) changes in inventories during most recent five years plus (3) common dividends.

Leverage/Capital Structure Ratios

Leverage ratios are used to assess the long-term solvency risk of the firm, that is, its ability to meet interest and principal payments on long-term obligations as they become due. These ratios are of prime interest to long-term lenders and bondholders.

Debt-to-Equity Ratios

There are two possible debt-to-equity ratios:

$$\text{(a) long-term debt to equity} = \frac{\text{long-term debt}}{\text{shareholders' equity}}$$

$$\text{(b) total debt to equity} = \frac{\text{current liabilities} + \text{long-term debt}}{\text{shareholders' equity}}$$

Both debt equity ratios press the degree of leverage in the capital structure of the firm. They are also used as a measure of the financial risk associated with the common stocks of the firm.[22]

Times Interest Earned Ratios

The times interest earned ratio may be expressed as

$$\frac{\text{net income (from continuing operations) before interest and income taxes}}{\text{interest expense}}$$

or

$$\frac{\text{net income plus total interest (adjusted by tax rate)}}{\text{interest expense (adjusted by tax rate)} + \text{preferred dividend requirement}}$$

Profitability Ratios

The profitability ratios portray the ability of the firm to efficiently use the capital committed by stockholders and lenders to generate revenues in excess of expenses. These ratios are consequently of interest to both stockholders and bondholders.

Rate of Return on Assets

The rate of return on assets, also lessen as the rate of return on investment (ROI) is computed as follows:

$$ROI = \frac{\text{net income} + \text{interest expense net of income tax savings} + \text{minority interest in earnings}}{\text{average total assets}}$$

This ratio measures the efficient use of the assets by the firm to generate earnings. One way of explaining the changes in ROI over time is to disaggregate the ratio as follows:

$$ROI = \text{profit margin ratio} \times \text{assets turnover ratio},$$

or

$$ROI = \frac{\text{net income} + \text{interest expense net of income savings} + \text{minority interest in earnings}}{\text{sales}} = \frac{\text{sales}}{\text{average total assets}}$$

where the profit margin ratio reflects the firm's ability to control the level of costs corresponding to the sales realized, and the assets turnover ratio corresponds to the ability to generate sales from the assets used. An improving ROI may be realized by improving either the profit margin ratio or the assets turnover ratio, or by improving both.

Return on Equity

The return on equity is computed as

$$\frac{\text{income available for common stockholders}}{\text{common stockholders' equity}}$$

This ratio indicates how efficiently the capital supplied by the common stockholders was employed within the firm.

Other examples of profitability ratios used by some analysts include the expense-to-revenue ratio, the operating income ratio ([sales cost of goods sold −

selling and administrative expenses]/sales), the earnings per share (presented earlier), the price-earnings ratio (market price of a common stock/earnings per share), the dividends-to-net income or payout ratio, and the operating income-to-operating assets ratio.

Turnover Ratios

Turnover or efficiency ratios are intended to convey various aspects of operational efficiency. They are generally computed on the basis of a sales figure in the numerator and the balance of an asset in the denominator. The previously mentioned total assets turnover ratio is one example of a turnover ratio. Other examples include the following ratios:

Inventory Turnover

The inventory turnover is computed as

$$\frac{\text{cost of goods sold}}{\text{average inventory}}$$

It is used as an indicator of operational efficiency.

Accounts Receivable Turnover

The accounts receivable turnover is computed as

$$\frac{\text{sales}}{\text{average (net) accounts receivable}}$$

By dividing the accounts receivable turnover by 360 days, one also obtains the average collection period for accounts receivable. It is an indicator of the efficiency in the collection efforts of accounts receivable.

Plant Assets Turnover

The plant assets turnover is computed as

$$\frac{\text{sales}}{\text{average plant assets}}$$

It is used as a measure of the relationship between sales and the plant assets used by the firm for its operations.

Adjustments to Financial Statements

Ratio analysis depends to a great extent on data provided by the published financial statements and notes. Because these data may be computed differently from one firm to another due to the choice of different accounting techniques, the analyst may be required to adjust the financial statements to make the ratios from different firms and/or industries comparable. In what follows, some of the most important adjustments are presented.

Comprehensive Income

The first type of adjustment may be to ensure that the computation of income and the classification of recurring and nonrecurring items on income statements are similar. This task may become easier with the eventual adoption of some of the recommendations of the FASB exposure draft on *Reporting Income, Cash Flows, and Financial Position of Business Enterprises*. Among the useful recommendations are the adoption of the term "comprehensive income" to represent the enterprise's total net income from all sources and of the disclosure of the following components of comprehensive income: (a) income from continuing central operations (that is, the basic business and primary source of comprehensive income); (b) income from discontinued operations; (c) income from peripheral or incidental transactions (such as, results of activities that are unusual in nature); and (d) income from price changes, or holding gains and losses (applicable to either a historical cost or current value accounting system).

Inventory-Flow Assumptions

The second type of adjustment is that resulting from the restatement of ratios of different firms to either a FIFO or LIFO flow assumption to make them comparable. This is important since the use of FIFO may generate a higher profit and hence may show a different rate of return on assets than shown under LIFO. This adjustment was made much easier by the IRS regulations issued in early 1981, permitting virtually all types of supplemental LIFO disclosures, in footnotes and in special reports, as long as the disclosures accompany the primary presentation of income on a LIFO basis and they are clearly identified as supplementary to or an explanation of the LIFO presentation.

Depreciation Policy

The third type of adjustment results from the use of an accelerated depreciation method for tax and the straight-line method for book purposes. The choice of different depreciation techniques for tax and book purposes results in the recognition of deferred income taxes in the balance sheet. The analyst may want to convert the depreciation charges to either the accelerated depreciation charges recognized for taxes or the straight-line charges reorganized for book purposes to achieve some comparability from one firm to another.

Deferred Income Taxes

Timing differences arises from the following four sources: (1) revenues included in pretax book income earlier than recognized for tax purposes, (2) revenues included in taxable income earlier than recognized for tax purposes, (3) expenses subtracted in determining pretax book income earlier than deducted in determining taxable income, and (4) expenses deducted in determining taxable income earlier than subtracted in determining pretax book income. APB *Opinion No. 11* requires that comprehensive allocation be followed and that the deferral method be used "since it provides the most useful and practical approach to interperiod tax allocation and the presentation of income taxes in the financial statements."[23] The deferral method requires that the income taxes saved currently because book income exceeds taxable income be set up as a deferred credit in the balance sheet.[24] As a result, the computation of some ratios (ROI and debt equity ratios) would be different from the same ratios computed by firms not deferring taxes. As a result, adjustments may have to be made by the analyst to obtain uniform data for making comparisons.

Use of "Defeasance" Techniques

The adjustments illustrated earlier are some examples of the numerous transformations that can be made to accounting data to make them comparable between firms. The types of adjustments are dictated by the information provided in the financial statements and in the notes regarding the accounting policies exposed by each firm. Given, however, the interest in this book in debt evaluation and rating, a special adjustment is reported here that is needed to offset the use of the defeasance technique. Defeasance has been used by firms to reduce debt on their balance sheet and to increase their reported income. The method takes several forms. In one variation; a company acquires government securities at a discount and places them in a trust, promising to use the future income from the securities to pay off the interest and principal due on its own debt securities as they mature. The company eliminates the debt from its balance sheet. The company also recognizes a profit because the discounted government securities cost less than the cost of redeeming the company's debt at face value. Fortunately, the Securities and Exchange Commission (SEC) issued a release in August 1982 in which it stated that the companies using defeasance techniques should follow a tentative conclusion by the FASB that debt should not be considered as extinguished and that no gain or loss should be recognized, unless the debtor has no further legal obligation with respect to the debt.

SHORTCOMINGS IN FINANCIAL RATIO ANALYSIS

Most of the ratios useful for an effective financial analysis are summarized in Exhibit 1.2. Before using them, however, the rater and/or the analyst should be aware of their limitations.

First, financial statements serve as the primary source of data for the computation of ratios. Given, however, the flexibility in choosing among various generally accepted accounting principles, the ratios among firms may not be comparable unless appropriate adjustments are made to the financial statements. Moreover, comprehensive financial rates analysis is constrained by the lack of standard accepted computational rules. With the exception of the computations of earnings per share, the regulatory agencies have refrained from enacting or suggesting specific guidelines. As a result there is no consensus on the computational methodology of the ratios.[25]

Second, ratio analysis rests on a proper definition of income, especially when income is required in the computation of the ratio. There is actually a big gap between the economic definition of income and the accounting income, as based on a historical cost valuation.[26] Economic income was appropriately defined by Hicks.[27] Basically, he defined a person's personal income as "the maximum amount he can consume during a week, and still *expect* to be as well-off at the end of the week as he was at the beginning."[28] The definition has become the basis of many discussions on the concept of income. One problem raised by such a definition, however, is the lack of consensus on the interpretation of the term "as well-off." The most accepted interpretation is that of capital maintenance, in which case the "Hicksian" income is the maximum amount that may be consumed in a given period and still maintain the capital intact.

There are actually four concepts of capital maintenance: (1) financial capital measured in units of money—money maintenance—which is the concept used to compute accounting income; (2) financial capital measured in units of the same purchasing power—general purchasing power money maintenance—which is the concept used to compute accounting income adjusted for changes in the general price level; (3) physical capital measured in units of money—productive capacity maintenance—which is the concept used to compute current income; and (4) physical capital measured in units of the same purchasing power—general purchasing power productive capacity maintenance—which is the concept used to compute current income adjusted for changes in the general price level.

Which of these incomes is a good surrogate of economic income and should be used in the computation of ratios? The theoretical and sound answer is in favor of the current income adjusted for changes in the general price level. FASB *Statement No. 33* goes one step forward to help the computation of such a figure by requiring the presentation of both general price level and specific price level information.

Third, ratios are generally used to control for the systematic effects of size on the variables under examination. However, Lev and Sunder showed that the ratio form adequately controls for size only under highly restrictive conditions.[29] They sound an important warning:

When these conditions are not met, size is not adequately controlled for, and more seriously, the amount of bias varies with size; it is larger for small firms and relatively small for large firms. Given these problems, the use of ratio analysis in financial analysis and research should be accompanied by a theoretical justification and an empirical analysis of degree to which the data meet the ratio assumptions. In the likely case of deviations from these assumptions, an analysis of the sensitivity of findings to these deviations should be conducted.[30]

Exhibit 1.2
Summary of Main Financial Ratios

RATIO	NUMERATOR	DENOMINATOR
1. Current	Current assets	Current liabilities
2. Quick	Quick assets	Current liabilities
3. Defensive interval measure	Total defensive assets	Projected daily operating expenditures
4. Long-term debt to equity	Long-term debt	Shareholders' equity
5. Total debt to equity	Current liabilities + long-term debt	Shareholders' equity
6. Times interest earned	Net income (from continuing operation) before interest and taxes	Interest expense
7. Times interest earned	Net income + total interest expense (adjusted by tax rate)	Interest expense (adjusted by tax rate) + preferred dividend requirement

8. Rate of return on assets	Net income + interest expense net of income tax savings + minority interest in earnings	Average total assets
9. Return on equity	Income available for common stockholders	Common stockholders' equity
10. Inventory turnover	Cost of goods sold	Average inventory
11. Accounts receivable turnover	Sales	Average (net) accounts receivable
12. Plant assets turnover	Sales	Average plant assets
13. Five-year cash flow as percentage of five-year growth needs	Five-year sum of (1) net income available for common stockholders + (2) depreciation and amortization + (3) income from discontinued operations and extraordinary items net of taxes	Five-year sum of (1) capital expenditures, + (2) change in inventories during most recent five years + (3) common dividends

The second major issue examined in the article is the choice of the size variable, where the choice should be justified on theoretical grounds, or "information should be provided on the degree of substitutability of the different measures, and the sensitivity of the findings to alternative measures."[31]

Finally, ratio analysis relies mostly on the comparison of the specific ratios of a specific firm with an industry average. Knowledge on the industry's average and standard deviations is crucial for inferences based on the ratio analysis. However, not only measures of dispersion of the ratio distribution are rarely communicated to users, but also the findings are that, in general, financial ratios are not normally distributed and that skewness exists.[32] To approximate normality some transformation of financial ratios may be necessary. Examples of possible transformations include the logarithmic and the power and square root transformations.

THE NATURE OF THE PREDICTIVE APPROACH

The predictive approach arose from the need to solve the difficult problem of evaluating alternative methods of accounting measurement and from the search for a criterion on which to base the choice between measurement alternatives. The predictive approach to the formulation of an accounting theory utilizes the criterion of predictive ability, in which the choice among different accounting options depends on the ability of a particular method to predict events that are of interest to users. More specifically, "the measure with the greatest predictive power with respect to a given event is considered to be the 'best' method for that particular purpose."[33]

The criterion of predictive ability follows from the emphasis on relevance as the primary criterion of financial reporting.[34] Relevance connotes a concern with information about future events. Relevance data, therefore, are characterized by an ability to predict future events.

The criterion of predictive ability is also well accepted in the natural and physical sciences as a method of choosing among competing hypotheses. Beaver and others,[35] by showing that alternative accounting measures have the properties of competing hypotheses, have rationalized the use of predictive ability in accounting. An obvious advantage of the predictive approach is that it allows us to evaluate alternative accounting measurements empirically and to make a clear choice on the basis of a discriminatory criterion.

Predictive ability is also a purposive criterion that can easily be related to one purpose of gathering accounting data—the facilitation of decision making. The accounting literature has always held that accounting data must facilitate decision making. As soon as the "facilitation of decision making" is introduced, however, two problems arise. First, it is difficult to identify and define all the decision models employed by accounting information users, because most of the models are descriptive rather than normative. Second, even when the decision model is well defined, a criterion for the choice of relevant information is missing. Intended to resolve this second problem, the criterion of predictive ability allows us to determine which accounting measure produces the better decisions. Let us note here the fundamental distinction between prediction and the decision. It is possible to predict without making a decision, but it is not possible to make a decision without a prediction.

It appears then that the predictive method may suffer from a failure to identify and define the decision models of users and types of events that ought to be predicted. Even if a given theoretical structure were developed to identify items or events that ought to be predicted, the problem remains of specifying a theory that will link those events to the accounting measures in terms of an explanatory and predictive relationship.

A growing body of empirical accounting research has evolved from the predictive approach. Two streams may be identified. One is concerned with the ability of accounting data to explain and predict economic events; the other is concerned with the ability of accounting data to explain and predict market reaction to disclosure.

PREDICTION OF AN ECONOMIC EVENT

One general objective of accounting is to provide information that can be used to predict business events. In the perspective of the predictive approach to the formulation of an accounting theory, alternative accounting measurements should be evaluated on the basis of their ability to predict economic or business events. In general, the predictive value criterion is a probability relationship between economic events of interest to the decision-maker and relevant predictor variables derived in part from accounting information.

Time-Series Analysis

Time-series analysis is a structural methodological approach by which temporal statistical dependencies in a data set may be examined.[36] Past values of a single data set are used to give clues regarding future realizations of the same data set. Time-series analysis research focuses mainly in (1) time-series properties of reported earnings and (2) prediction issues in time-series analysis. Each is examined next.

Time-Series Properties of Reported Earnings

Knowledge of the properties of reported earnings may enhance their information content, predictive ability, and feedback value. The application of statistical procedures to the study of the time-series properties of accounting variables stems from the thesis that accounting variables can best be described as random variables. The research has examined the behavior of reported earnings and models that describe quarterly earnings:[37]

1. With respect to the *annual-earnings series*, findings present a *moving-average process* or a *submartingale*. What results is a continuous debate over which time-series model or models should be applied to observed accounting numbers. Fortunately, a new line of research may provide some closure on the debate. It consists of first modeling the observed time series, and then using the method to test the fit of the derived models.[38,39] In any case, this type of research would be of more use and more interest to policy-makers if it were applied to determine the effect of accounting policy changes on probabilistic models of earnings behavior.[40]

2. With respect to the *quarterly-earnings series*, findings seem to show that the quarterly-earnings process is not totally random in character. It appears to follow an *autoregressive process* characterized by seasonal and quarter-to-quarter components.[41,42]

Predicting Future Accounting Earnings

The reported earnings number is an aggregate number in two dimensions: one dimension is temporal, in that annual earnings are an aggregate of four individual quarterly earnings; one dimension is compositional, in that annual earnings are an aggregate of time-equivalent subseries, such as sales and cost of goods sold.[43] Accounting time-series-based research has considered the predictive ability of past annual earnings, past quarterly earnings, and earnings components:

1. With respect to the use of *past annual earnings* to predict future earnings, studies show that sophisticated autoregressive (or moving-average) processes developed using Box and Jenkins' procedures do not appear to forecast significantly better than the random-walk model.[44,45]

2. With respect to the use of *past quarterly earnings* to predict future earnings, studies show a better predictive ability of the models of quarterly earnings compared with annual models and more comprehensive Box and Jenkins' "individually identified" models.[46]

3. With respect to the use of *earnings components* to predict future earnings, evidence is in favor of good forecasting ability of disaggregated sales and earning data,[47] but this is not demonstrated for models based on components such as interest expense, depreciation expense, and operating income before depreciation.[48] More work needs to be done before closure can be achieved on the subject.

Relevance of Earnings Forecasts

Earnings forecasts are becoming increasingly popular and important to an efficient functioning of capital markets. These forecasts are assumed to be particularly useful to users of accounting information. Earnings forecasts may be provided by analysts, management, or statistical models. The relevance of these forecasts rests to a great extent on their reasonable accuracy; the investors, in particular, and the capital markets, in general, would have no confidence in inaccurate earnings forecasts, and consequently would not utilize them. An important question centers then on the predictive accuracy of each type of forecast. Given that both analysts and managers use more information in forecasting earnings per share than historically based mechanical models, the question centers more specifically on comparing the accuracy of each of the three types of forecasts. Accordingly, various studies have examined the research question, ''Are forecasts of earnings by analysts or management superior to statistical models?''

At this stage of the research, there seems to be disagreement as to whether earnings forecasts made by analysts and/or management are more accurate than forecasts based on a statistical analysis of the pattern in historical annual-earnings and quarterly-earnings time-series models. In addition, industry variables seem to make ''a difference'' in the ability to forecast a firm's earnings. It is too early to have closure on the subject. Various issues remain unanswered, and the research to date suffers from various limitations. Abdel-Khalik and Thompson identify the following unanswered issues:

the relevance of forecasted data, the value of nonaccounting information in forecasting, the randomness of earnings time series, the cost of alternative forecasting procedures, and the respective motives of management and security analysts in making forecasts.[49]

Similarly, Griffin identifies the following caveats of the research:

First, the results are typically based on an ''average'' firm or a firm at the median position in a cross section. Such average results may have application in specific contexts. Second, analysis by industry, size, risk, and other possible explanatory variables has received only scant attention so far in developing statistical models. Third, most studies use rather naive models and thus do not recognize recent research on the properties of accounting earnings. This suggest that they are potentially biased in favor of the superiority of the published forecasts.

Finally, the finding that managers and analysts have about the same degree of forecasting success is probably not unreasonable given the present institutional setting. Company investor-relations programs and analysts' periodic meetings with management suggests that, insofar as the earnings forecast is concerned, the overlap of information accessible to management and analysts is considerable.[50]

Distress Prediction

The most relevant applications of the predictive approach are attempts made to seek empirically validated characteristics that distinguish financially distressed from nondistressed firms. Both univariate and multivariate models have been used to help an auditor determine when a firm is approaching default. Scott provides the following brief overview of the process:

Most bankruptcy-prediction models are derived using paired-sample technique. Part of the sample contains data from firms that eventually failed; the other part contains contemporaneous data from firms that did not fail. A number of plausible and traditional financial ratios are calculated from financial statements that were published before failure. Next, the researchers search for a formula based either on a single ratio or a combination

of ratios, that best discriminates between firms that eventually failed and firms that re-
mained solvent. A careful researcher also tests the resulting formula both on the original
sample and a holdout sample that was not used to derive the formula.[51]

In Beaver's univariate study,[52] which tested a set of accounting ratios to predict corporate failure, the most noticeable result was the superior predictive
ability of cash flow-to-total debt ratios, followed by net income to total assets.
Among the multivariate studies, Altman's use of a multiple discriminant analysis
for the prediction of corporate failure[53] resulted in a discriminant model that
contained five variables: (1) working capital/total assets (liquidity), (2) retained
earnings/total assets (age of firm and cumulative profitability), (3) earnings before interest and taxes/total assets (profitability), (4) market value of equity/book
value of debt (financial structure), and (5) sales/total assets (capital turnover).
Altman was able to classify more than 90 percent of the firms in his sample
correctly. The discriminant analysis technique for the prediction of distress has
been used successfully in other studies to demonstrate the information value of
various types of accounting data. The results of this research have led to the
acceptance of the ZETA discriminant analysis model of Altman, Haldeman, and
Narayanan[54] by over three dozen financial institutions.[55]

The major limitation of the research and distress prediction arises from the
absence of an articulated economic theory of financial distress. Witness the
following statement made by Ohlson:

This paper presents some empirical results of a study predicting corporate failure as
evidence by the event of bankruptcy. . . . One might ask a basic and possibly embarrass-
ing question: Why forecast bankruptcy? This is a difficult question, and no answer or
justification is given here . . . Most of the analysis should simply be viewed as descriptive
statistics—which may, to some extent, include estimated prediction error rates—and no
"theories" of bankruptcy or usefulness of financial ratios are tested.[56]

Despite the absence of economic theory of distress, the discriminant-analysis-
based models can be very helpful in a variety of practical decision context. For
example, "(i) they can process information quicker and at a lower cost than do
individual loan officers and bank examiners, (ii) they can process information
in a more consistent manner, and (iii) they can facilitate decisions about loss
function being made at more senior levels of management."[57]

Various limitations are associated with research on corporate distress prediction.[58] The first limitation arises from the absence of a general economic theory
of financial distress that can be used to specify the variables to be included in
the models.

A second limitation relates to the different definition of the event of interest.
All of the studies examined observable events, such as legal bankruptcy, loan
default, and omission of preferred dividend rather than financial distress per se.
Finally, the results of the superior predictive ability of some accounting ratios

may not be generalized to permit the formulation of an accounting theory based on consistent predictors of corporate failure.

Prediction of Bond Premiums and Bond Ratings

The following four factors are assumed to create bond risks and consequently to affect the yields to maturity of bonds:

1. Default risk: the inability of a firm to meet part or all bond interest and principal payments.
2. Marketability risk: the possibility of learning to dispose of the bonds at a loss.
3. Purchasing-power risk: the loss incurred by bondholders due to changes in the general price level.
4. Interest-rate risk: the effect of unexpected changes in the interest rates on the market value of bonds.

Fisher examined the power of a four-factor model to explain differences in the risk premiums of industrial corporate bonds.[59] The following four variables are included in the model:

1. Earnings variability, measured as the coefficient of variation on after-tax earnings of the most recent nine years.
2. Solvency, or reliability in meeting obligations, measured as the length of time since the latest of the following events occurred: the firm was founded, the firm emerged from bankruptcy, or a compromise was made in which creditors settled for less than 100 percent of their claim.
3. Capital structure, measured by the market value of the firm's equity/par value of its debt.
4. Total value of the market of the firm's bonds.

The first three represent different proxies for default risk; the fourth variable represents a proxy for marketable risk. The four variables account for 75 percent of the variation in the risk premiums on bonds.

The bond ratings issued by the three rating agencies in the United States (Fitch Investors' Service, Moody's Investors' Service, and Standard & Poor's Corporation) are judgments about the investment quality of long-term obligations. Each rating is an aggregation of default probability. Despite the claims by these agencies that their ratings cannot be empirically explained and predicted, various studies have attempted to develop models to predict the rating categories assigned to industrial bonds,[60] electric utility bonds,[61] and general-obligation municipal bonds.[62]

All of these studies tried in the first stage to develop a bond-ratings model from an experimental sample of bond ratings on the basis of a selected list of

accounting and financial variables, using either regression, dichotomous probability function, or multiple discriminant or multivariate probit analysis. In the
second stage, the obtained model was applied to a holdout sample to test the
predictive ability of the model. Despite the general success of such models,
some unresolved problems may limit their usefulness:

1. With one exception, these models suffer from the lack of an explicit and testable
   statement of what a bond rating represents and the absence of an ''economic rationale'' for the variable to be included.
2. None of these models accounts for possible differences in the accounting treatments
   used by individual companies
3. The studies among the regression models treat the dependent variables as if they were
   on an interval scale. In other words, the assumption is that the risk differential between
   an AAA and an AA bond is the same as the risk differential between a BB and a B
   bond.
4. With one exception, all of the studies confused ex ante predictive power with ex post
   discrimination. When a given discriminant model is developed on the basis of a
   sample A_1 and tested on a time coincident sample A_2, the authors claim predictive
   success but actually demonstrate only ex post discriminant success. Testing on A_2
   implies only that the inference about the importance of the independent variables in
   the discriminant function is warranted. Prediction requires intertemporal validation.
   Ex ante prediction means using the discriminant model developed on the basis of A_1
   from time dimension t_1 on a sample B from time dimension $t + 1$.[63]

Predictive Ability of Information Decomposition Measures

Information theory is concerned with the problem of measuring changes in
knowledge.[64] Theil applied information theory and the related entropy concept
to the development of a set of measures for financial statement analysis.[65] These
information decomposition measures are assumed to express the degree of stability over time in financial statement decomposition. In studies investigating
their predictive ability, information decomposition measures have been associated with corporate bankruptcy[66] and corporate takeover.[67] Initial results point
to the usefulness of the entropy concept in financial analysis and suggest opportunities for future research.

Explaining Corporate Restructuring Behavior

Corporate restructuring behavior includes such mechanisms as mergers, con-
solidations, acquisitions, divestitures, going private, leveraged buyouts (LBOs),
and spinoffs. They are undertaken to either (a) maximize the market value of
equities held by existing shareholders or (b) maximize the welfare of existing
management.[68] Research focused on the characteristics of acquired and nonacquired firms, and covered two areas: (a) ex post classificatory analysis and (b)

ex ante predictive analysis, using either univariate or multivariate models.[69] All the studies point to the relevance of various accounting ratios in classifying or predicting takeovers. The limitations of these studies are similar to those advanced in the case of distress prediction.

Credit and Bank-Lending Decisions

Trade and bank-lending decisions constitute another example of economic events that may be explained and/or predicted on the basis of accounting and other financial information.

Various organizations, such as Dun & Bradstreet, Inc., the National Credit Office, the National Association of Credit Management, the Robert Morris Associates, and various industry trade associations, engage in some form of trade-credit analysis. From the perspective of the predictive approach, the research consists of replicating or predicting the credit evaluation or change therein on the basis of accounting and other financial information. For example, Ewert evaluates, with some success, the extent to which financial ratios can be used to differentiate good from bad accounts, where bad accounts are either placed in collection or written off as uncollectible.[70] On the other hand, Backer and Gosman have had less success in predicting the firms that would be likely to be downgraded by Dun & Bradstreet on the basis of financial ratios.[71]

The bank-lending decision has also been the subject of empirical and predictive research. Three areas of research may be identified:

1. The first are deals with efforts to simulate aspects of a bank's investment and lending processes. The investment decision is the subject of simulation analysis by Clarkson[72] and Cohen, Gilmore, and Singer.[73] The results imply that financial information plays a major role in the decision.

2. The second area deals with a prediction of the loan-classification decision. Orgler uses, with minor success, a multiple regression model to replicate the Federal Deposit Insurance Corporation's classification of bank loans into "criticized" and "uncriticized" categories.[74] However, Dietrich and Kaplan have been more successful in using a statistical "logit" model to explain and predict four classes of loans from "current/in good standing" to "doubtful."[75]

3. The third area deals with the estimation and prediction of commercial bank financial distress. These studies have examined the feasibility of predicting bank financial distress on the basis of accounting data. Sinkey has been able to predict a large proportion of failures based on a model that includes two variables: (a) operating expenses to operating income and (b) investments to assets.[76] Similarly, Pettaway and Sinkey have continued the same line of research using both market- and accounting-based screening models.[77] The accounting screen has been found to provide valuable lead time that regulators can use to carry out their statutory responsibilities more effectively.

CONCLUSIONS

Financial analysis relies on either a univariate approach to ratio analysis generally advocated in textbooks or a multivariate approach to ratio analysis. The multivariate approach generates quantitative models that can be used to explain and predict various economic events. Accordingly, the next chapters will introduce multivariate models that can help explain and/or predict the following economic events:

a. Stock returns

b. Systematic risk

c. Industrial bond ratings

d. Dual labor sector

e. Social disclosure

f. Takeover

g. CEO compensation

h. Corporate reputation

i. Corporate performance

j. Capital structure

NOTES

1. *Accounting Research Bulletin No. 43*, AICPA (1953), chap. 3A.

2. A precise definition is lacking. For example, *Accounting Principles Board Opinion No. 17* is devoted entirely to intangibles but never defines the term.

3. Financial Accounting Standards Board, *Statement of Financial Concepts No. 3*, paragraphs 17 and 29.

4. *Accounting Research Bulletin No. 43*, AICPA (1953), chap. 3A.

5. While common shares have only a residual claim, preferred shares are granted special privileges entitling their holder to dividends at a certain rate that must be paid before dividends to common shareholders. Preferred shares may be participating, which entitles their holders to also participate in the distribution of the residual left to common shareholders, or they may be convertible, which entitles their owner to convert them into a specified amount of common shares at specified times. Most preferred dividends are cumulative, entitling their holder to eventually receive all postponed dividends. Finally, most preferred shares are callable, which entitles the corporation to reacquire them at specified prices.

6. The accounting principles governing this treatment is the matching principle. Basically, it holds that expenses should be recognized in the same period as the associated revenue. That is, revenues are recognized in a given period according to the realization principle and then the related expenses are recognized. The association is best accomplished when it reflects the "cause-and-effect" relationship between cost and revenues. Operationally, it consists of a two-stage process of accounting for expenses. First, costs are capitalized as assets representing bundles of service potential or benefits. Second,

these assets are written off as expenses to recognize the proportion of the asset's service potential that has expired in the generation of revenues during the period.

7. It seems, however, that for some companies, FIFO accounting makes more sense. M. H. Granof and D. G. Short asked the controllers of 380 corporations that have not adopted LIFO why they haven't. They found that most non-LIFO companies are *not* incurring a tax penalty. Other reasons included the following:

a. FIFO is preferable for those firms using tax loss or tax credit forwards.

b. LIFO prevents these companies from taking advantage of the "lower of cost or market."

c. A company may now report the results of a subsidiary in its financial statements based on any inventory method, even though the subsidiary used LIFO to compute taxable income. The court of appeals held that Insilco Corporation did not violate the LIFO conformity requirement when, as a parent corporation, it issued consolidated financial statements in which inventories were priced at an average cost method, even though the consolidated inventories included the inventories of three subsidiaries that reported to the parent on a LIFO basis.

d. Various drawbacks of LIFO could outweigh possible tax benefits. For more information see M. H. Granof and D. G. Short, "For Some Companies, FIFO Accounting Makes Sense," *Wall Street Journal*, August 30, 1982, p. 10.

8. Accounting Principles Board, *Opinion No. 30* (1973), paragraph 15, recommends the recognition of the net income, gains, and losses (net of income tax effects) at the measurement date if it is loss and at the time of realization if it is a gain. This treatment follows the well-known *conservatism principle*, which recommends recognizing losses as soon as possible and postponing the recognition of gains until realization.

9. Accounting Principles Board, *Opinion No. 30* (1973); Financial Accounting Standards Board, *Statement of Financial Accounting Standards No. 4* (1975).

10. Accounting Principles Board, *Opinion No. 20* (1970).

11. Accounting Principles Board, *Opinion No. 15* (May, 1969).

12. "Except for" is used if (1) the scope of the audit has been limited, (2) the financial statements contain a departure from GAAP, (3) GAAP were not consistently applied.

13. The Canadian Institute of Chartered Accountants dropped the "subject to" opinion requirement effective November 1980.

14. P. Samuelson, "Proof that Properly Discounted Present Values of Assets Vibrate Randomly," *Bell Journal of Economics and Management Science* (Autumn, 1973), pp. 369–374.

15. E. Fama, "Efficient Capital Markets: A Review of Theory and Empirical Work," *Journal of Finance* (May, 1970), pp. 383–447. Fama also presented the weak and strong forms of the efficient market hypothesis. The weak form of the efficient market hypothesis states that the equilibrium-expected returns (prices) "fully reflect" the sequence of past returns (prices). In other words, historical price and volume data for securities contain no information that may be used to earn a profit superior to a simple "buy-and-hold" strategy. This form of the hypothesis began with the theory that price changes follow a true "random walk." This school, though, is naturally challenged by "technical analysts" or "chartists," who believe that their rule based on past information can earn greater-than-normal profits. Filter rules, serial correlation, and run tests have tested the weak form of the efficient market hypothesis. The results support the hypothesis, particularly for returns longer than a day. The strong form of the efficient market hypothesis states that the equilibrium-expected returns (prices) fully reflect all information (not just

publicly available information). In other words, no trading rules based on any information including inside information may be used to earn an excess return. Evidence on the strong form of the efficient market hypothesis is not conclusive. While one study was able to show that mutual funds do not have any superior consistent performance over time, given a presumed access to special information, another study argued for the possibility of superior returns, given access to specialists' outlook.

16. R. A. Foulke, *Practical Financial Statement Analysis*, 6th ed. (New York: McGraw-Hill, 1968).

17. J. E. Walter, "Determination of Technical Solvency," *Journal of Business* (January, 1957), pp. 30–43; K. W. Lemke, "The Evaluation of Liquidity: An Analytical Study," *Journal of Accounting Research* (Spring, 1970), pp. 47–77.

18. S. Davidson, G. H. Sorter, and H. Kalle, "Measuring the Defensive Position of a Firm," *Financial Analyst Journal* (January–February, 1964), p. 23.

19. H. Bierman, Jr., "Measuring Financial Liquidity," *The Accounting Review* (October, 1960), pp. 628–632.

20. Walter, "Determination of Technical Solvency," pp. 30–43.

21. Lemke, "The Evaluation of Liquidity: An Analytical Study," pp. 47–77.

22. Financial risk is generally defined in terms of the volatility of the earnings streams that accrue to common stockholders. In general, the higher the proportion of debt in the capital structure, the higher the volatility of earnings and the higher the financial risk of the firm.

23. Accounting Principles Board, *Opinion No. 11* (1967), paragraph 34.

24. Edward E. Williams and M. Chapman Findlay III, *Investment Analysis* (Englewood Cliffs, N.J.: Prentice-Hall, 1974), p. 154.

25. Although there is a lack of consensus on how the financial ratios should be computed, empirical evidence seems to show that there is agreement on which ratios are important. For more information see Charles H. Gibson, "How Industry Perceives Financial Ratios," *Management Accountants* (April, 1982), pp. 13–19.

26. Ahmed Belkaoui, *Accounting Theory* (San Diego, Calif.: Harcourt Brace Jovanovich, 1981), p. 143.

27. Accounting income is operationally defined as the difference between the realized revenues arising from the transactions of the period and the corresponding historical costs. It suffers from the following limitations: (a) it fails to recognize unrealized increases in values of assets held in a given period because of the application of the historical cost and the realization principles; (b) it relies on the historical cost principle, making comparability difficult, given the different acceptable methods of computing "cost" (for example, the different inventory costing methods) and the different acceptable methods of cost allocation generally deemed arbitrary and incorrigible; and (c) it relies on the historical cost principle, which may give the impression to users that the balance sheet represents an approximation of value rather than merely a statement of unallocated cost balances. Besides, the emphasis on an income determination led to a resolution of controversial issues based on their impact on the income statement, thereby creating in the balance sheet a mixture of items that are quite hard to define, for example, deferred tax allocation debits and credits.

28. J. R. Hicks, *Value and Capital*, 2nd ed. (Oxford: Clarendon Press, 1946), p. 172. Hicks' "week" refers to a specified period of time rather than a week.

29. They stated that a ratio is an adequate instrument for size control when the variable under examination, y, is strictly proportional to the size of the operations. For more

information see B. Lev and S. Sunder, "Methodological Issues in the Use of Financial Ratios," *Journal of Accounting and Economics* (December, 1979), p. 190.

30. Ibid., pp. 193–134.

31. Ibid., p. 198.

32. Paul Barnes shows that where financial ratios are non-normally distributed, the comparison of a financial ratio with an industry average is likely to misinform. However, he also shows that where financial ratios are input to certain statistical models (regression and multiple discriminant analysis) normality is irrelevant. Paul Barnes, "Methodological Implications of Non-Normally Distributed Financial Ratios," *The Journal of Business Finance and Accounting* (Spring, 1982), pp. 51–62.

33. W. H. Beaver, J. W. Kennelly, and W. M. Voss, "Predictive Ability as a Criterion for the Evaluation of Accounting Data," *The Accounting Review* (October, 1968), p. 675.

34. *A Statement of Basic Accounting Theory*, chap. 3 (New York: American Accounting Association, 1966).

35. Beaver, Kennelly, and Voss, "Predictive Ability as a Criterion for the Evaluation of Accounting Data," p. 676.

36. Charles R. Nelson, *Applied Time Series Analysis for Managerial Forecasting* (New York: Holden-Day, 1973).

37. Surveys of literature include A. R. Abdel-Khalik, "Three Generations of Research on Quarterly Reports: Some Thoughts on the Research Process," in R. D. Nair and T. H. Williams, eds., *Perspectives on Research* (Madison: University of Wisconsin, 1980); K. S. Lorek, R. Kee, and W. H. Van, "Time-Series Properties of Annual Earnings Data: The State of the Art," *Quarterly Review of Economics and Business* (Spring, 1981), pp. 97–113.

38. K. Cogger, "A Time-Series Analytic Approach to Aggregation Issues in Accounting Data," *Journal of Accounting Research* (Autumn, 1981), pp. 285–298.

39. B. C. Dharan, "Identification and Estimation Issues for a Casual Earnings Model," *Journal of Accounting Research* (Spring, 1983), pp. 18–41.

40. N. Dopuch and R. L. Watts, "Using Time-Series Models to Assess the Significance of Accounting Changes," *Journal of Accounting Research* (Spring, 1972), pp. 180–194.

41. G. Foster, "Quarterly Accounting Data: Time-Series Properties and Predictive Ability Results," *The Accounting Review* (January, 1977), pp. 1–21.

42. P. A. Griffin, "The Time-Series Behavior of Quarterly Earnings: Preliminary Evidence," *Journal of Accounting Research* (Spring, 1977), pp. 71–83.

43. Ray Ball and George Foster, "Corporate Financing Reporting: A Methodological Review of Empirical Research," *Journal of Accounting Research, Studies on Current Research Methodologies in Accounting: A Critical Evaluation* 20 (Supplement, 1982), p. 209.

44. R. L. Watts and R. W. Leftwich, "The Time-Series of Annual Accounting Earnings," *Journal of Accounting Research* (Autumn, 1977), pp. 253–271.

45. W. S. Albrecht, L. L. Lookabill, and J. C. McKeown, "The Time-Series Properties of Annual Accounting Earnings," *Journal of Accounting Research* (Autumn, 1977), pp. 226–244.

46. W. A. Collins and W. S. Hopwood, "A Multivariate Analysis of Annual Earnings Forecasts Generated form Quarterly Forecasts of Financial Analysts and Univariate Time-Series Models," *Journal of Accounting Research* (Autumn, 1980), pp. 390–406.

47. D. W l. Collins, "Predicting Earnings with Subentity Data: Some Further Evidence," *Journal of Accounting Research* (Spring, 1976), pp. 163–177.

48. J. G. Manegold, "Time-Series Properties of Earnings: A Comparison of Extrapolative and Component Models," *Journal of Accounting Research* (Autumn, 1981), pp. 360–373.

49. A. R. Abdel-Khalik and R. B. Thompson, "Research on Earnings Forecasts: The State of the Art," *The Accounting Journal* (Winter, 1977–1978), p. 192.

50. P. A. Griffin, "Usefulness to Investors and Creditors of Information Provided by Financial Reporting: A Review of Empirical Accounting Research," *Research Report* (Stamford, Conn.: Financial Accounting Standards Board, 1982), p. 83.

51. J. Scott, "The Probability of Bankruptcy: A Comparison of Empirical Predictions and Theoretical Models," *Journal of Banking and Finance* (September, 1981), p. 320.

52. W. H. Beaver, "Financial Ratios and Predictors of Failure," *Empirical Research in Accounting: Selected Studies, Journal of Accounting Research* 4 (Supplement, 1966), pp. 71–111.

53. E. I. Altman, "Predicting Railroad Bankruptcies in America," *Bell Journal of Economics and Management Science* (Spring, 1973), pp. 184–211.

54. E. I. Altman, R. G. Halderman, and P. Narayanan, "ZETA Analysis," *Journal of Banking and Finance* (June, 1977), pp. 29–54.

55. E. Altman, *Corporate Financial Distress* (New York: John Wiley & Sons, 1983).

56. J. A. Ohlson, "Financial Ratios and Probabilistic Prediction of Bankruptcy," *Journal of Accounting Research* (Spring, 1980), pp. 109–131.

57. Ball and Foster, "Corporate Financial Reporting," p. 218.

58. Frederick L. Jones, "Current Techniques in Bankruptcy Predictions," *Journal of Accounting Literature* 6 (1987), pp. 131–164.

59. L. Fisher, "Determinants of Risk Premium on Corporate Bonds," *Journal of Political Economy* (June, 1959), pp. 217–237.

60. J. O. Horrigan, "The Determination of Long-Term Credit Standing with Financial Ratios," *Empirical Research in Accounting: Selected Studies, Journal of Accounting Research* 4 (Supplement, 1966), pp. 44–62; G. E. Pinches and K. A. Mingo, "A Multivariate Analysis of Industrial Bond Ratings," *Journal of Finance* (March, 1973), pp. 1–18; A. Belkaoui, "Industrial Bond Ratings: A Discriminant Analysis Approach," *Financial Management* (Autumn, 1980), pp. 44–51; A. Belkaoui, *Industrial Bonds and the Rating Process* (Westport, Conn.: Greenwood Press, 1984).

61. E. I. Altman and S. Katz, "Statistical Bond-Rating Classification Using Financial and Accounting Data," *Proceedings of the Conference on Topical Research in Accounting,* M. Schiff and G. H. Sorteer, eds. (New York: New York University Press, 1976), pp. 205–239.

62. J. J. Horton, "Statistical Classification of Municipal Bonds," *Journal of Bank Research* (Autumn, 1970), pp. 29–40.

63. Belkaoui, *Industrial Bonds and the Rating Process.*

64. S. Kullback, *Information Theory and Statistics* (New York: John Wiley & Sons, 1959), p. 7.

65. H. Theil, "On the Use of Information Theory Concepts in the Analysis of Financial Statements," *Management Science* (May, 1969), pp. 459–480.

66. B. Lev, *Accounting and Information Theory* (Evanston, Ill.: American Accounting Association, 1969), pp. 18–34.

67. A. Belkaoui, "The Entropy Law, Information Decomposition Measures, and Cor-

porate Takeover," *Journal of Business Finance and Accounting* (Autumn, 1976), pp. 41–52.

68. George Foster, *Financial Statement Analysis*, 2nd ed. (Englewood Cliffs, N.J.: Prentice-Hall, 1986), p. 461.

69. Examples of studies include K. G. Palpepu, "Predicting Takeover Targets: A Methodological and Empirical Analysis," *Journal of Accounting and Economics* (March, 1986), pp. 3–36; A. Belkaoui, "Financial Ratios as Predictors of Canadian Takeovers," *Journal of Business Finance and Accounting* (Spring, 1978), pp. 93–107; and U. P. Rege, "Accounting Ratios to Locate Takeover Targets," *Journal of Business Finance and Accounting* (Autumn, 1984), pp. 301–311.

70. D. C. Ewert, "Trade Credit Management: Selection of Accounts Receivable Using a Statistical Model," Research Monograph No. 79 (Atlanta: Georgia State University, 1980).

71. M. Backer and M. L. Gosman, *Financial Reporting and Business Liquidity* (New York: National Association of Accountants, 1978).

72. G. P. E. Clarkson, *Portfolio Selection: A Simulation of Trust Investment* (Englewood Cliffs, N.J.: Prentice-Hall, 1962).

73. K. J. Cohen, T. C. Gilmore, and F. A. Singer, "Bank Procedures for Analyzing Business-Loan Applications," in K. J. Cohen and F. S. Hammer, eds., *Analytical Methods in Banking* (Homewood, Ill.: Richard D. Irwin, 1966).

74. Yuir E. Orgler, "A Credit-Scoring Model for Commercial Loans," *Journal of Money, Credit and Banking* 2 (November, 1970), pp. 435–445.

75. J. R. Dietrich and Robert S. Kaplan "Empirical Analysis of Commercial-Loan Classification Decisions," *The Accounting Review* (January, 1982), pp. 18–38.

76. J. F. Sinkey, Jr., "A Multivariate Statistical Analysis of the Characteristics of Problem Banks," *Journal of Finance* (March, 1975), pp. 21–36.

77. R. H. Pettaway and J. F. Sinkey, Jr., "Establishing On-Site Bank Examination Priorities: An Early-Warning System Using Accounting and Market Information," *Journal of Finance* (March, 1980), pp. 137–150.

SUGGESTED READINGS

Altman, E. I. "Financial Ratios, Discrminant Analysis and the Prediction of Corporate Bankruptcy." *Journal of Finance* (September, 1968), pp. 585–609.

Altman, E. I., R. G. Halderman, and P. Narayanan. "ZETA Analysis: A New Model to Identify Bankruptcy Risk of Corporations." *Journal of Banking and Finance* (June, 1977), pp. 29–54.

Ashton, R. H. "The Predictive Ability Criterion and User-Prediction Models." *The Accounting Review* (October, 1974), pp. 719–732.

Ball, R., and R. L. Watts. "Some Time-Series Properties of Accounting Income Numbers." *Journal of Finance* (June, 1972), pp. 663–681.

Beaver, W. H. "Alternative Accounting Measures as Predictors of Failure." *The Accounting Review* (January, 1968), pp. 113–122.

Beaver, W. H., J. W. Kennelly, and W. M. Voss. "Predictive Ability as a Criterion for the Evaluation of Accounting Data." *The Accounting Review* (October, 1968), pp. 675–683.

Belkaoui, A. "The Entropy Law, Information Decomposition Measures, and Corporate

Takeover." *Journal of Business Finance and Accounting* (Autumn, 1976), pp. 41–52.

Belkaoui, A. "Financial Ratios as Predictors of Canadian Takeovers." *Journal of Business Finance and Accounting* (Spring, 1978), pp. 93–107.

Belkaoui, A. "The Impact of the Disclosure of the Environment Effects of Organizational Behavior on the Market." *Financial Management* (Winter, 1976), pp. 26–31.

Belkaoui, A. "Industrial Bond Ratings: A Discriminant Analysis Approach." *Financial Management* (Autumn, 1980), pp. 44–51.

Belkaoui, A. *Industrial Bonds and the Rating Process*. Westport, Conn.: Greenwood Press, 1984.

Brown, L. D., and M. S. Rozeff. "Univariate Time-Series Models of Quarterly Earnings per Share: A Proposed Model." *Journal of Accounting Research* (Spring, 1979), pp. 179–189.

Elton, E. J., and M. J. Gruber. "Earnings Estimate and the Accuracy of Expectational Data." *Management Science* (April, 1972), pp. 409–424.

Ruland, W. "The Accuracy of Forecasts by Management and Financial Analysts." *The Accounting Review* (April, 1978), pp. 439–447.

Sinkey, J. F., Jr. "A Multivariate Statistical Analysis of the Characteristics of Problem Banks." *Journal of Finance* (March, 1975), pp. 21–36.

Watts, R. L., and R. W. Leftwich. "The Time-Series of Annual Accounting Earnings." *Journal of Accounting Research* (Autumn, 1977), pp. 253–271.

2

The Prediction of Stock Returns Using Popular Financial Ratios

INTRODUCTION[1]

Fundamental information analysis, or financial statement analysis, seeks the valuation of corporate securities by the evaluation of value-relevant accounting fundamentals. Various studies have identified value-relevant fundamentals in the context of a return-fundamentals relation.[2-4] While Ou and Penman[5] used a statistical search procedure in the determination of candidate fundamentals, Lev and Thiagarajan[6] relied on a guided search procedure based on analysts' claim of usefulness in security valuation.

This chapter builds on previous research in the examination of value-relevant fundamentals by relying on a return-fundamentals relation. The search for fundamentals is however, different, focusing on a set of financial variables (fundamentals) popularized in the "textbook" literature as useful in security valuation.

SUPPORT FOR THE USE OF POPULAR RATIOS

This chapter relies instead on a search for fundamentals guided by the "popularity" of financial ratios in major financial analysis texts. Various reasons may support this choice.

First, the inclusion of these "popular" ratios in financial analysis texts is generally based on their theoretical explanations of fundamental relationships and signals experienced by the firms. For example, liquidity ratios refer to the ability of the firm to meet its short-term financial obligations when and as they fall due; capital structure ratios provide information about the extent to which nonequity capital is used to finance the assets of the firms; profitability ratios

Exhibit 2.1
Definition of Popular Financial Ratios Used in This Study for Value Relevance

Signal	Measured as
1. Profitability	Earnings per share (EPS)
2. Profitability	Net Income/Sales (NI/S)
3. Profitability	Earnings Before Taxes/Total Worth (EBT/TW)
4. Liquidity	Current Assets/Current Liabilities (CA/CL)
5. Liquidity	Cash and Marketable Securites/Sales (CMS/S)
6. Liquidity	Cash Flow From Operations/Total Assets (CFFO/TA)
7. Capital Structure	Long-term Liabilities/Shareholders' Equity (LTL/SE)
8. Debt Service Coverage	Earnings Before Taxes/Interest (EBT/I)
9. Turnover	Sales/Total Assets (S/TA)
10. Turnover	Sales/Account Receivables (S/AR)
11. Turnover	Cost of Goods Sold/Inventory (COGS/I)

refer to the ability of a firm to generate revenues in excess of expenses; and turnover ratios indicate various aspects of efficiency with which assets are utilized.

Second, these popular ratios are also the most frequently cited in published annual reports, showing some selectivity in the choice of these ratios and even an outcome of the "vested self-interest" of management in these ratios.

Third, surveys of the preferences of chief executive officers and other senior executives concerning the ratios and other indicators that they use regularly for various types of decision making show the importance of "popular" financial ratios.

Based on these arguments, this chapter examines the role of "popular" financial ratios in security valuation.

POPULAR FINANCIAL RATIOS

To identify popular financial ratios claimed to be useful in security valuation, we searched major financial analysis texts. The comparison of different signals and the way they are measured in the various texts led to the identification of different financial ratios summarized in Exhibit 2.1. They are the popular measures of known fundamental signals. These signals include profitability, liquidity, capital structure, debt service coverage, and turnover. The a priori rationales for these popular ratios and their signals is that (a) profitability and turnover are positively related to market returns, while (b) liquidity, capital structure, and debt service coverage are negatively related to market returns.

METHODOLOGY

Two cross-sectional regressions were used. The first regression is a returns-earnings regression as follows:

$$Ri = ai + b\Delta Ei + Ui; \; i = 1, 2, \ldots, n, \text{ number of firms} \tag{1}$$

where

Ri = Annual stock return of firm i, computed as the sum of the end of the year stock price and dividends divided by the beginning of the year stock price

ΔEi = Annual change in EPS (primary, excluding extraordinary items), deflated by beginning-of-year share price.

The second regression includes the fundamentals:

$$Ri = ai + \sum_{j=1}^{12} bj \; Sji + Vi \tag{2}$$

where

Si = fundamental signals outlined in Exhibit 2.1; $j = 1, \ldots, 11$.

The regression in Equation (2) is compared to the benchmark set by the regression in Equation (1).

SAMPLE SELECTION

The sample is selected for the period 1973–1991 using the criteria: (1) data needed for the computation of the 11 signals are available on the 1991 Compustat Primary, Secondary, Tertiary and Full Coverage Annual Industrial File and (2) security price and the factor to adjust for stock splits and stock dividends are available on the Center for Research in Security Prices (CRSP) file. Firms with data available ranged from 156 to 212 firms per year.

GENERAL RESULTS

The correlation matrix (Pearson and Spearman) for all the variables used in the study is shown in Exhibit 2.2. Four relatively large coefficients appear in the table. The net income/sales is correlated with current assets/current liabilities (0.17), cash plus marketable securities/sales (-0.31), cash flow from operations/ total assets (0.36), and sale/total assets (-0.17). In addition, the cash plus marketable securities/sales is correlated with cost of goods sold/inventory (-0.21). However, in all cross-sectional regressions, the condition indices are less than 19. This suggests that multicollinearity is not a serious problem.

The regression models in Equations (1) and (2) are estimated for each of the years 1973 to 1991. The results are shown in Exhibit 2.3. Columns 14 and 15 show, respectively, the adjusted R^2 of the model based on Equation (2) and the adjusted R^2 of the model based on Equation (1) (used as benchmark). The results

Exhibit 2.2
Correlation Matrix

	EPS	CA/CL	EBT/I	EBT/TW	CMS/S	CFFO/TA	LTL/SE	NI/S	S/TA	S/AR	COGS/I
EPS	1.000										
CA/CL	0.0270	1.000									
EBT/I	0.0054	-0.0969*	1.000								
EBT/TW	0.0068	0.0090	-0.0003	1.000							
CMS/S	-0.0004	0.0660*	-0.0414	-0.0009	1.000						
CFFO/TA	0.0635*	0.0125	0.0233	-0.0037	0.0159	1.000					
LTL/SE	-0.0011	-0.0297	-0.0047	0.0080	0.0073	-0.0541*	1.000				
NI/S	0.0960*	0.1718*	0.0231	-0.0034	-0.3176*	0.3651*	-0.076*	1.000			
S/TA	0.0241	0.0431*	-0.0645*	0.0168	-0.1241*	-0.0410*	-0.017	0.1733*	1.000		
S/AR	-0.0038	-0.0055	0.1149*	-0.0015	0.0007	0.0012	0.0105	0.0103	-0.111*	1.000	
COGS/I	0.0028	-0.1114*	0.0939*	-0.0009	-0.2147*	0.0273	-0.013	-0.0020	0.123*	0.012	1.000

Note: *Significant at $\alpha=0.01$.

Exhibit 2.3
Value Relevance of Popular Financial Ratios

Year	Intercpt	EPS	CACL	EBTI	EBIT/TW	CMS/S	CFFO/TA	LTL/SE	N/S	S/TA	S/AR	COGS/I	F	R²	R̄²	N
1973	-0.2604**	0.0138	-0.0029	-1.00006*	0.2296	0.1145	0.0183	-0.0091	3.8064*	-0.0013	-0.0074	-0.0004	4.723*	93.5%	0.5%	180
1974	-0.4868*	0.0892*	-0.0123*	-0.00015*	0.1855**	-0.2867	0.1769	-0.0347*	0.2460	0.1015**	-0.0016	0.0008*	2.969*	16.04%	0.7%	182
1975	0.4969	0.0480*	-0.091*	-0.00009**	0.2140	3.5348*	-1.3233**	-0.1786	3.1935**	0.0873	0.0016*	0.0046	3.128*	15.75%	0.3%	195
1976	0.3562*	0.0114**	-0.0205	0.0001	0.1637	0.0905	0.3621*	-0.0275	-0.5252	-0.0055	-0.0010*	-0.0029*	1.901**	7.51%	0.3%	209
1977	-0.5578*	0.0037	-0.0336	0.00003	0.3139	0.3890	-0.1443*	-0.1615*	1.8912*	0.1975*	-0.0042*	0.0006	4.848*	20.9%	0.3%	212
1978	-0.8117*	0.0118	-0.0204*	0.0008**	0.4530*	0.8788*	0.1657*	-0.2262*	0.0130	0.0795	-0.0013	-0.0021	4.555*	19.41%	0.4%	219
1979	0.1909	-0.0056	-0.0519	-0.0005*	-0.3407*	0.1198*	0.1358	-0.0018	0.5731	0.0230*	-0.038*	-0.0032**	3.647*	16.10%	0.4%	220
1980	0.2190	0.0593*	-0.1365*	-0.0007*	0.5047*	0.9090*	-1.0239**	-0.0205	2.5970*	0.1307*	-0.0027	-0.0006*	4.937*	21.44%	2%	210
1981	-0.2862*	0.0056*	-0.0481*	0.0008	0.0613	-0.3566*	0.4844	-0.0360	1.3976**	0.0249	0.0026**	-0.0017	2.354*	11.99%	1.3%	201
1982	0.04811	0.0663*	-0.0492	-0.0002*	0.0364	1.0261*	0.0003	-0.0241*	0.7537	0.1483*	0.0030	0.0035*	2.801*	14.43%	1.6%	194
1983	0.0261	0.0062*	-0.0734*	-0.0010	0.0479*	-0.5921	0.8746**	-0.0348*	0.1486	0.0672*	0.0018**	0.0009	3.335*	17.33%	0.8%	186
1984	-0.1193**	0.1019*	-0.0146	-0.00009	0.1306*	-0.5049*	0.5737*	-0.0947*	0.9360*	-0.0036*	0.0009	-0.0012*	8.093*	34.10%	8.1%	183
1985	0.1525*	0.0971*	-0.0584*	0.0003*	0.5363*	0.1136	0.9718*	-0.0373	0.9829*	0.0979*	-0.0026*	-0.0007	5.561*	26.23%	3.7%	183
1986	-0.0573	0.0579	0.0102*	-0.00003	0.1141	-0.8639**	0.9938*	-0.1719*	9.757*	-0.0187	-0.0001*	-0.0014*	5.201*	26.34%	0.5%	171
1987	0.0811	0.1669*	-0.0131*	-0.0005**	0.0017*	-0.0318	0.4275	-0.0269**	0.5909*	-0.0075	0.0002	-0.0019**	1.521**	9.59%	1.13%	176
1988	-0.0033	0.0509*	-0.0661**	-0.00001*	0.0003*	-0.3077*	0.9647*	-0.0007*	0.3366	0.1135*	-0.0007*	-0.0004*	2.406*	13.97%	0.5%	174
1989	0.1400	0.0157*	0.057*	-0.0002	0.008*	-0.1516	0.0399*	-0.0276*	1.0260*	-0.045*	0.0006*	0.00003	1.651**	10.19%	1.2%	171
1990	-0.2180*	0.0078*	-0.0430**	-0.0003*	-0.0277*	0.9143**	0.2563*	0.0066*	2.0490**	0.0095*	0.0005*	-0.0022*	8.344*	36.31%	3%	172
1991	0.2904*	0.1310*	-0.0460*	-0.0006**	0.0180*	0.3266*	-0.8452**	-0.0088*	1.1639*	0.1114*	-0.016*	-0.0012*	1.916**	11.52%	1.4%	156
Across-Years T-Value	0.535*	0.894**	-1.958*	-.0342	0.703	3.587*	4.050*	-1.545	7.853*	4.288*	0.167	-0.913				

Notes: *Significant at α=0.01.
**Significant at α=0.05.

Source: Ahmed Riahi-Belkaoui, "Value Relevance of Popular Financial Ratios," *Advances in Quantitative Analysis of Finance and Accounting* 5 (1997), p. 198. Reprinted with permission of the publisher.

Exhibit 2.4
Classification of Firms into Categories of Inflation and Growth Level

Categories	Low	Medium	High
Inflation	1983 (3.2),[1] 1985 (3.6)	1973 (6.2), 1976 (5.8)	1974 (11.0), 1975 (9.1)
	1986 (1.9), 1987 (3.6)	1977 (6.5), 1982 (6.2)	1978 (7.0), 1979 (11.3)
	1988 (4.1), 1991 (4.2)	1984 (4.3), 1989 (4.8)	1980 (13.5), 1981 (10.3)
		1990 (5.4)	
GNP Growth	1974 (-0.5),[2] 1975 (-1.1)	1979 (2.8), 1981 (1.6)	1973 (5.4), 1976 (5.1)
	1980 (-0.6), 1982 (-2.3)	1983 (3.8), 1985 (8.9)	1977 (4.6), 1978 (4.8)
		1986 (2.8), 1987 (3.0)	1984 (6.0), 1988 (4.0)
	1990 (1.3), 1991 (-0.9)	1989 (2.7)	

Notes: [1]The numbers between parentheses are the changes in Consumer Price Index.
[2]The numbers between parentheses are the changes in GNP.

show a drastic improvement in R^2 for each year, indicating the "popular" fundamental signals contributed significantly to the explanation of the annual market return beyond reported earnings. The yearly coefficients of each of the 11 fundamental variables are statistically significant in at least 12 years out of the 19 years examined. In addition, the across-year significance test, first suggested by Bernard (1987), indicates that the earnings per share, current assets/current liabilities, cash + marketable securities/sales, net income/sales, and sales total assets signals are significant at $\alpha = 0.01$.

As expected, the signals of current assets/current liabilities, earnings before interest and taxes/interest, the cash + marketable securities/sales, the long-term liabilities/stockholders' equity, and the cost of goods sold/inventory are negative. Also as expected, the signals of earnings per share, the profit before tax/total worth, and net income over sales have a positive sign. The sign of cash flow from operations/total assets, sale/total assets, and sales/accounts receivables are, however, mixed.

IMPACT OF INFLATION AND GROWTH

Similarly to other studies on the value-relevance of accounting data, this chapter extended the analysis to evaluate the impact of changes in the macroeconomic variables of inflation and GNP growth. The inflation and growth levels were measured, respectively, by (a) the annual change in the Consumer Price Index and (b) the annual change in real GNP. The sample was divided into three levels of inflation rate and GNP growth rate. The classification is shown in Exhibit 2.4. Exhibit 2.5 shows the results of the regression model in Equation (2) for each of the three levels of inflation and GNP growth. The results show that the significance of several "popular" signals is conditioned by the levels of inflation and/or GNP growth.

Exhibit 2.5

Value Relevance of Popular Financial Ratios Conditioned on Level of Inflation and GNP Growth

Independent Variable	Inflation Ratio			GNP Growth		
	High	Medium	Low	High	Medium	Low
Intercept	−0.01240	−0.9162**	0.07482**	−0.15504*	0.03068	0.01356
EPS = X_1	0.00145*	0.01252*	0.00124*	0.00579**	0.00133*	0.04443*
CA/CL = X_2	−0.02030	−0.00330	−0.002880*	−0.00452	−0.01309	−0.04206**
EBT/I = X_3	−0.00006	−0.00006*	−0.00007	−0.00002*	−0.00003	−0.00001*
EBT/TW = X_4	0.15066*	0.01282	0.00040*	0.00020	0.00819*	0.04684
CMS/S = X_5	−1.04327*	−0.2272**	−0.13769*	−0.24307*	−0.09301	−1.41319*
CFFO/TA = X_6	−0.28689	0.35829*	0.69789*	0.65075*	0.58523*	−0.17693
LTL/SE = X_7	−0.00471	−0.01645**	−0.00323	−0.03758*	−0.01431	−0.00949*
NI/S = X_8	1.1943*	1.15657*	0.74290*	0.96440*	1.00027*	1.14773*
S/TA = X_9	0.06807**	0.06518*	0.04089**	0.07739*	0.02908	0.10898*
S/AR = X_{10}	−0.00065	0.00049*	0.00002	−0.00065*	0.00016	0.00010*
COGS/I = X_{11}	−0.00035	−0.00016*	−0.00021	−0.00052*	−0.00045	−0.00037*
F	5.801*	10.387*	7.755*	9.091*	8.978*	6.993*
R^2	4.97%	7.99%	6.53%	7.87%	7.04%	6.52%

Notes: *Significant at $\alpha = 0.01$.
**Significant at $\alpha = 0.05$.

CONCLUSIONS

This chapter shows the value-relevance of popular financial ratios in both a noncontextual setting and a setting conditioned by levels of inflation of growth. The popularity of these ratios in conventional texts and prediction ability models seems justified by the results of this study. Compared to similar studies examining the value relevance of analysts' favorite ratios, this chapter shows that the return-fundamentals relation is best explained by consideration of "popular" financial ratios.

NOTES

1. This chapter has been adapted with permission of the publisher from Ahmed Riahi-Belkaoui, "Value Relevance of Popular Financial Ratios," *Advances in Quantitative Analysis of Finance and Accounting* 5 (1997), pp. 193–201.

2. R. W. Holthausen and D. F. Larcker, "The Prediction of Stock Return Using Financial Statement Information," *Journal of Accounting and Economics* (June–September, 1992), pp. 337–412.

3. B. Lev and S. R. Thiagarajan, "Fundamental Information Analysis," *Journal of Accounting Research* (Autumn, 1993), pp. 190–215.

4. J. Ou and S. Perman, "Financial Statement Analysis and the Prediction of Stock Returns," *Journal of Accounting and Economics* (November, 1989), pp. 295–329.

5. Ibid.

6. Lev and Thiagarajan, "Fundamental Information Analysis," pp. 190–215.

SUGGESTED READINGS

Belseley, D., E. Kuh, and R. Welsh. *Regression Diagnostics: Identifying Influential Data and Source of Collinearity.* New York: Wiley, 1980.

Bernard, V., and T. Sober. "The Nature and Amount of Information in Cash Flows and Accruals." *The Accounting Review* (October, 1989), pp. 624–657.

Bernard, V. "Cross-Sectional Dependence and Problems in Influences in Market-Based Accounting Research." *Journal of Accounting Research* (Spring, 1987), pp. 1–48.

Foster, G. *Financial Statement Analysis: A New Approach.* Englewood Cliffs, N.J.: Prentice-Hall, 1974.

Frishkoff, P. *Reporting of Summary Indicators: An Investigation of Research and Practice.* Stamford, Conn.: FASB, 1981.

Gibson, C. H. "How Industry Perceives Financial Ratios." *Management Accounting* (April, 1982), pp. 13–19.

Gibson, C. H. "Financial Ratios in Annual Reports." *The CPA Journal* (September, 1982), pp. 18–29.

Holtausen, R. W., and D. F. Larcker. "The Prediction of Stock Return Using Financial Statement Information." *Journal of Accounting and Economics* (June–September, 1992), pp. 373–412.

Lev, B. *Financial Statement Analysis: A New Approach.* Englewood Cliffs, N.J.: Prentice-Hall, 1974.

Lev, B., and S. R. Thiagarajan. "Fundamental Information Analysis." *Journal of Accounting Research* (Autumn, 1993), pp. 190–215.

Ou, J., and S. Penman. "Financial Statement Analysis and the Prediction of Stock Returns." *Journal of Accounting and Economics* (November, 1989), pp. 295–329.

Walsh, F. J. *Measuring Business Performance.* New York: The Conference Board, 1984.

Williamson, R. W. "Evidence on the Selective Reporting of Financial Ratios." *The Accounting Review* (April, 1984), pp. 296–299.

Wilson, P. "The Relative Information Content of Accruals and Cash Flows: Combined Evidence at the Earnings Announcement and Annual Report Release Date." *Journal of Accounting Research* (Supplement, 1986), pp. 165–200.

3

The Prediction of Systematic Risk

INTRODUCTION[1]

The literature of finance theory and particularly work with the capital-asset-pricing model has identified a systematic or market risk and a specific or diversifiable risk. One interesting research question has been the degree of association between the common stock systematic risk and accounting-determined risk measures. Different conceptual studies argue that differences in systematic risk between firms may be due to differences in the corporate financial decision. In other words, it is thought that corporate risk variables derived from accounting data resulting from corporate decisions may convey information about the magnitude of the systematic risk of a common stock. Empirical evidence, mainly for the U.S. market, is still inconclusive. Similar evidence for the Canadian market is either rare or suffers from serious methodological shortcomings.[2] Consequently, the purpose of this chapter is to provide some Canadian empirical evidence on the relationships between accounting-determined and market-determined measures of risk. With a knowledge of the accounting determinants of the systematic risk or beta, business managers may be able better to assess the relevance of their particular corporate decisions. Similarly, the investing public may be able better to predict any future variations in the firm's systematic risk on the basis of published accounting numbers. Finally, a positive association between beta and accounting risk measures will provide evidence for the semi-strong efficient market hypothesis for the Canadian market in the sense that market prices reflect all publicly available information. In other words, any association will lend support to the hypothesis that accounting data reflect the events that (1) determine a security's riskiness and (2) are also reflected in its market price. The issue is of major importance to all users basing their valuation models on accounting numbers.

RELATED RESEARCH

The study of the association of an individual firm's risk with its underlying accounting characteristics started with the seminal study of Beaver, Kettler, and Scholes,[3] which discovered significant relationships between β and divided payout, financial leverage, and earnings yield instability measures. Gonedes,[4] however, did not find a strong relationship between the regression parameters of his accounting model and the risk coefficient of the market model. He explained the difference between both studies on the basis of the differences of the accounting ratios used. He scaled income numbers by another accounting number, namely, total assets, while Beaver, Kettler, and Scholes scaled income numbers with market prices. Using his words:

I suppose that "The significant associations" reported by Beaver, Kettler, and Scholes are direct results of the fact that their so-called "accounting-based" estimates of earnings covariability are actually functions of market prices because they used market prices to scale income numbers.[5]

However, in another study, Derstine and Huefner[6] using both market and accounting scaled data, found significant correlation. The objectives of their study were, however, different. First, they found that alternative accounting methods (specifically LIFO and FIFO) did not affect intercompany comparisons of accounting ratios. Second, in ranking companies on the basis of accounting data and market-determined risk, the LIFO-FIFO choice did not create a significant difference.

The results of Beaver, Kettler, and Scholes were verified using a similar set of explanatory variables on cross-sectional monthly regressions by Breen and Lerner.[7] In their study, only the regression coefficients of the stability of earnings growth, size, payout, earnings growth rate, and numbers of shares traded had the expected sign and were statistically significant. Their results on the instability of the sign, magnitude and statistical significance of the leverage factor contradicted the results of Hamada's study,[8] which concluded that leverage accounts for 21 percent to 24 percent of the systematic risk. Along the same lines, other different studies focused on the link between beta and financial data. Rosenberg and McKibben[9] found that 13 out of 32 variables examined were significant. Louge and Merville[10] found financial leverage, return assets, and asset size variables to be significant. Most recently, Beaver and Manegold,[11] Bildersee,[12] Melicher,[13] Melicher and Rush,[14] and Thompson[15] reported results supporting the association between accounting-determined and market-determined risk measures.

The present chapter differs from previous studies in several respects:

1. Contrary to previous studies, all of which employ U.S. data, this chapter is restricted to Canadian firms.

2. This chapter uses factor analysis to identify the main financial dimensions.

3. To correct for the short-term instability of individuals, a single four-year market period, January 1, 1971, to December 31, 1974, was chosen as the period of analysis.

4. Similarly, most of the previous research focuses on the University of Chicago Center for Research in Security Price File ending December 1968, which might be biased by the bull market of the 1960s and hence does not portray the economic environment of the 1970s.

RISK MEASURES EMPLOYED

Systematic Risk

The capital-asset-pricing model asserts that in equilibrium, and under certain conditions, the risk premium for an individual security, $E(\tilde{R}_i) - E(\tilde{R}_F)$ is related to the risk premium of the market, $E(\tilde{R}_m) - E(\tilde{R}_F)$ by the expression:

$$E(\tilde{R}_i) - E(\tilde{R}_F) = [E(\tilde{R}_m) - E(\tilde{R}_F)]\beta i$$

where

$E(\tilde{R}_F)$ = risk-free rate

$E(\tilde{R}_m)$ = expected return on a market factor

$\beta i = \text{cov}(\tilde{R}_i, \tilde{R}_m)/\text{var}(\tilde{R}_m)$

and βi is a measure of the systematic or nondiversificable risk. Its estimation is operationally possible using the one-factor market model, which asserts a linear relationship between the rate of return on security i, R_{it}, and the market rate of return, R_{mt}, for a period t. It is expressed in this study as follows:

$$r_{it} = \alpha_i + \beta r_{mt} + e_{it},$$
$$E\{e_{it}\} = O,$$
$$E\{e^2_{it}\} = N^o,$$
$$E\{e_{it} \cdot e_{ik}\} = O, \forall k \neq t,$$
$$E\{e_{st} \cdot e_{it}\} = O, \forall s \neq i,$$
$$E\{\ln\{r^2_m\} \cdot e_{it}\} = O$$

where

r_{it} = continuously compounded rate of return of security i at period t

= $\log_e (1 + R_{it})$

= $\log_e [(P_t + D_t)/P_{t-1}]$

R_{it} = non-compounded single period return of security i in period t,
r_m = market factor in period t $\log_e$ (TSEI/TSEI$_{t-1}$),
TSEI = Toronto Stock Exchange Index,
e_{it} = logarithm of the residual term,
D_{it} = cash divided per share,
α_i, β_i = parameters of the least-squares regression

Here r_{it} is used instead of R_{it} because it is admitted that, first, r_{it} has fewer outliers in its relative frequency distribution and therefore will yield more efficient risk statistics than R_{it}, and second, r_{it} is distributed more symmetrically than the positively skewed R_{it} variable. Besides, the results of the model are not changed by restating them in terms of r_{it} instead of R_{it}.

Accounting-Based Measures of Risk

Although most accounting ratios are not defined in terms of covariance of returns, they may be perceived by financial users as a reflection of the uncertainty of the earnings stream of a firm. This rationale for the perception of accounting ratios as surrogates for the total variability of return of common stocks may lie in the socialization and learning process. Most finance textbooks and most techniques of financial analysis and share valuation rely on ratio analysis for decision making and resource allocation. An a priori belief is created, whether in the classroom or in the marketplace, in the presumed usefulness of accounting ratios as determinants of systematic risk. In other words, the users have been socialized into thinking of accounting ratios as surrogates for the total variability of return of common stocks.

A more conceptual rationale for the perception of accounting ratios as surrogates for systematic risk may also be implied by the capital-asset-pricing model. It may be said on the basis of the implications of the capital-asset-pricing model that the systematic risk of common stock is related directly to financial leverage and inversely to liquidity, profitability, and activity. So, accordingly, the ratios, chosen as a group, measured financial qualities such as profitability, liquidity, leverage, and activity and are listed in Exhibit 3.1. These variables are presumed to reflect the results of the main corporate decisions most likely to be associated with the systematic risk of the firm. All the 15 variables were based on the arithmetic averages of the four-year period 1971–1974.

DATA AND METHODOLOGY

Fifty-five Canadian companies were employed in this study (see Appendix 3.A). The selection criteria were (1) all the stocks were continuously listed on the Toronto Stock Exchange for the period of analysis, January 1, 1971 to December 31, 1974, and (2) besides the availability of continuous accounting data, firms were chosen so as to achieve a wide representation of industries.

Exhibit 3.1
List of Ratios

1. Common Stock
   Total Assets
2. Net Working Capital
   Total Assets
3. Operating Income + Extraordinary Gains and Losses
   Total Assets
4. Cost of Sales
   Total Assets
5. Cash Dividends
   Income for Common
6. Current Assets
   Current Liabilities
7. Long-Term Debt
   Common Equity
8. Long-Term Debt
   Total Assets
9. Total Liabilities + Preferred Stock
   Common Equity
10. Net Income Flow Through Base
    Net Share Equity
11. Net Income Deferred Credit Base
    Net Share Equity
12. Net Income Flow Through Base
    Sales
13. Net Working Deferred Credit Base
    Sales
14. Net Working Capital
    Sales
15. Cost of Sales
    Inventory

An important problem ignored in most previous studies is the possibility of multicollinearity between the accounting data. This produces possible biases. Consequently, the following methodology was used:

1. The β of the group of firms was estimated by regressing a time-series of historical returns from the Canadian stock on returns from The Toronto Stock Exchange Industrial Index.
2. A factor-analytic procedure enabled the identification of basic financial dimensions represented by the accounting ratios.
3. The β of the group of firms was finally regressed against the reduced accounting ratio set obtained in step 2.

EMPIRICAL RESULTS

Stationarity of Common Stock Systematic Risk

Exhibit 3.2 lists the distribution of beta for seven periods: 1971, 1972, 1973, 1974, 1971–1972, 1973–1974, and 1971–1974. They were computed from bi-

Exhibit 3.2
Distribution of Beta Coefficients

Period	Mean	Standard Deviation	Number of Betas > 0	Number of Betas > 0	Low	Fractiles					High
						0.10	0.25	0.50	0.75	0.90	
1971	0.3714	0.6410	50	12	-2.8412	-0.1188	0.1099	0.3559	0.7621	1.1548	1.5033
1972	0.7384	0.8252	47	15	-0.54933	-0.2864	0.06113	0.73818	1.3083	1.9197	3.2623
1973	0.6029	0.8956	50	12	-1.8982	-0.24307	0.2023	0.6336	1.1914	1.6556	2.6561
1974	0.6180	0.8479	51	11	-2.374	-0.3689	0.1801	0.6800	1.1229	1.8118	2.804
1971-72	0.5080	0.5751	52	10	-1.6708	-0.1424	0.09811	0.5342	0.8069	1.3577	1.723
1973-74	0.6269	0.7065	53	9	-1.0992	0.1689	0.1815	0.6797	1.0666	1.4644	2.6912
1971-74	0.5681	0.5183	55	7	-1.1993	-0.03675	0.2618	0.53731	0.8858	1.2893	2.0383

Exhibit 3.3
Correlation Coefficients for Successive Betas

Periods	Correlation Coefficient β
1971 × 1972	0.3835 (2.828)*
1972 × 1973	0.5888 (4.7764)*
1973 × 1974	0.27385 (2.0178)*
1971-72 × 1973-74	0.4786 (5.340)*

t values in parentheses.
*Significant at 0.01 level.

weekly return data. This table summarizes the distribution of betas in each of the seven periods in terms of high, low, mean, medium, standard deviations, and quartile points. The number of the betas less than zero is also presented. Over the period of interest to this study, 1971–1974, the mean was 0.5681, the median was 0.5373, and the first fourth quartile points, respectively, were 0.03675 and 1.2893. It is also appropriate to note that during the same period only seven companies, or 11.29 percent, have betas less than zero.

To examine the stationarity of betas, correlation tests examined the association between beta values in successive market periods, thus performing four correlation studies, 1971 and 1972, 1972 and 1973, 1973 and 1974, 1974 and 1971–1972, and 1973–1974. Exhibit 3.3 lists the correlation coefficients between the successive betas. The beta correlation coefficients were significant at 0.01 level for three periods out of four.

Factor Analysis Phase

Although the multivariate approach to the study of the determinants of the systematic risk presents intuitive appeal by allowing the consideration of more than one explanatory variable, there is always the risk that the accounting ratios as independent variables may be mutually correlated. This departure from one of the assumptions of the linear model, known as multicollinearity, may impair the results. An efficient way to resolve the problem is to submit the original ratio set to a factor-analytic procedure, both to simplify and to group patterns in the data. Factor analysis is a generic name for a class of techniques that permits

Exhibit 3.4
Summary of Factor Analysis for 15 Ratios

Factor	Eigenvalue	Percent Variance Explained	Cumulative Proportion of Total Variance Explained
1	3.35217	0.223	0.223
2	2.344	0.156	0.379
3	1.976	0.132	0.511
4	1.679	0.112	0.623
5	1.417	0.094	0.717
6	0.899	0.074	0.791
7	0.753	0.050	0.841
8	0.567	0.038	0.879
9	0.542	0.036	0.915
10	0.443	0.030	0.945
11	0.388	0.025	0.970
12	0.227	0.016	0.986
13	0.117	0.007	0.993
14	0.074	0.005	0.998
15	0.0165	0.001	0.999

data reduction and summarization without appreciable loss of information. It reduces the number of variables in terms of new, uncorrelated factors. The factor patterns explain parsimoniously the observed data and retain the most important information contained in the original data matrix. Since multicollinearity problems were experienced in this study, the original set of ratios was factored into five distinct and orthogonal dimensions, with each dimension being a linear combination of the original 15 ratios. The first five factors shown in Exhibit 3.4 were retained as the main dimensions by applying a decision rule that required an eigenvalue of at least 1.00 for a factor to be retained. These five factors accounted for 71.7 percent of total variance. Information about the grouping of 15 ratios with each factor is presented in the factors loading matrix in Exhibit 3.5. Only the highest factor-loadings ratios per ratio are shown.

An examination of the grouping of certain ratios with the factors and their corresponding factor loadings lead to the labeling of the five factors as (1) profitability, (2) leverage, (3) liquidity, (4) activity, and (5) dividend policy. The factor analysis reduced the original set of fifteen mutually correlated ratios into five uncorrelated dimensions. The decision was made to choose from each of these five factors the ratio showing the highest loading on the factor, to form the reduced set of accounting ratios for the next phase of the analysis.

Multiple Regression Phase

The basic evolutionary relationship of this study was

Exhibit 3.5
Factor Patterns among the Ratios of Canadian Firms*

	1	2	3	4	5
Accounting Ratios			*Factor Loading*		
1. Common stock/total assets		-0.414			
2. Net working capital/total assets					0.662
3. Operating income - extraordinary gains and losses/total assets	0.692				
4. Cost of sales/total assets				0.881**	
5. Cash dividends/income for common stock					0.783**
6. Current assets/current liabilities			0.762**		
7. Long-term debt/common equity		0.941**			
8. Long-term debt/total assets		-0.446			
9. Total liabilities + preferred stock/common equity		0.929			
10. Net income flow through/net share equity	0.917				
11. Net income deferred credit base/ net share equity	0.935**				
12. Net income flow through base/sales				-0.802	
13. Net income deferred credit base/sales				-0.742	
14. Net working capital/sales			0.649		
15. Cost of sales/inventory					0.806

*The highest factor loadings per ratio is shown.
**The highest factor loadings per factor.

$$\beta = a + b_1x_1 + b_2x_2 + b_3x_3 + b_4x_4 + b_5x_5 + M$$

As indicated earlier the independent variables finally chosen were those ratios having the highest factor loadings on each of the five dimensions identified in the factor-analytic phase. They are as follows:

x_1 = Cost of sales/total assets

x_2 = Cash dividends/income for common stock

x_3 = Current assets/current liabilities

x_4 = Long-term debt/common equity

x_5 = Net income deferred credit base/net share equity

The parameters of the equation were estimated by ordinary least-squares regression, the results of which are reported in Exhibit 3.6. The results are interesting on two points:

Exhibit 3.6
Stepwise Regression Results (with t values in parentheses)

$y = 0.5338 - \quad 0.0090\,x_1 - \quad 0.1016\,x_2 + \quad 0.0915\,x_3 + \quad 0.00321\,x_4 - \quad 1.3806\,x_5$
$\qquad\qquad\qquad (-1.276)^{***} \quad (-1.610)^{**} \quad (2.894)^{*} \quad (1.290)^{***} \quad (-2.057)^{**}$

F value = 8.352

$\qquad R^2 = 0.3410$

where y = Beta

$\qquad x_1$ = Cost of sales/total assets

$\qquad x_2$ = Cash dividends/income for common stocks

$\qquad x_3$ = Current assets/current liabilities

$\qquad x_4$ = Long-term debt/common equity

$\qquad x_5$ = Net income deferred credit base/net share equity

*Significant at the 0.01 level.
**Significant at the 0.05 level.
***Significant at the 0.10 level.

1. All the variables showed significant relationships with the estimated beta. Systematic risk for Canadian firms as measured by their betas is negatively related to their measures of activity, dividend payout, and profitability and positively related to their leverage and liquidity. Noteworthy is the choice of 0.10 confidence level to infer a significant relationship with beta for both the leverage and the activity ratios. It might be due, as suggested in other studies, to a misspecification of the true relationship between beta and both the leverage and activity ratios. A linear relationship was maintained in the study because of the lack of conceptual justification for a nonlinear or quadratic relationship.

2. The empirical results are all in the direction implied theoretically by the capital-asset-pricing model (CAPM) except for the liquidity ratio. A significant positive relationship is found between the current ratio and estimated beta, contradicting established belief of a negative relationship. Intuitively, one might infer that although increased liquid assets holdings reduce the risk of technical insolvency and lower the firm's beta, the current ratio, contrary to popular beliefs, is not a good measure of liquidity. Current assets, as a numerator to the current ratio, includes not only cash and short-term negotiable instruments but also accounts receivables and inventory amounts. Although the cash and short-term negotiable assets may be considered similar to holdings of risk-free assets, accounts receivables and inventory amounts are far from being risk free. Consequently, the current ratio, as a measure of the shift from liquid assets to current operating assets, will have a positive relationship with the systematic risk of a firm. The results in this study seem to verify this point.

CONCLUSION

The Canadian evidence based on examination of the data of 55 Canadian firms supports the contention that accounting-based measures of risk are impounded in the systematic risk of common stocks. A significant positive relationship was found between both the current ratio and the long-term debt-to-common equity and the systematic risk. A significant negative relationship was also found between the cost of sales to total assets, the cash dividends to income for common stocks, and the net income deferred credit base to net share equity and systematic risk. In conclusion, both conceptually and empirically it may be stated that the systematic risk of Canadian common stocks is related directly to financial leverage and inversely to profitability and activity; and, contrary to conceptual findings, liquidity as expressed by the current ratio was found to be directly related to the systematic risk.

Although restricted to a small sample of Canadian firms and to only a four-year period of analysis, the results may be of help to those financial managers speculating about the impact of their financial policies in the systematic risk of their firms' common stock.

APPENDIX 3.A SAMPLE FIRMS USED

List of Companies

1. Acklands
2. Woodward Stores
3. Crush International
4. Dominion Stores
5. Molson
6. Gulf Oil
7. Metropolitan Stores
8. Moore Corporation
9. BC Sugar
10. Canadian Marconi
11. Labatt
12. Transair
13. Becker Milk
14. Atlo Industries
15. Silverwood Industries
16. Bell Canada
17. Loblaws
18. Hayes Dana
19. Union Gas
20. Revelstoke Co.
21. Bow Valley
22. Greyhound
23. Kelly Douglas
24. Selkirk Holdings
25. Metropolitan Gas
26. Consumer Gas
27. Brascan
28. Thompson Newspapers
29. R. L. Crain Ltd.
30. Southam Press
31. Simpson Sears Ltd.
32. ITL Industries
33. Hudson Bay
34. Abitibi Paper Co.
35. Russel Hugh
36. Versatile Manufacturing
37. BC Forest Products
38. Canadian Tire
39. Interprovincial Steel and Pipe
40. Steel Company of Canada
41. Massey Ferguson
42. Loeb M.
43. Algoma Steel Corporation
44. CAE Industries Ltd.

45. Alcan
46. Canadian Corporate Management Co. Ltd.
47. Zellers
48. Steinberg Ltd.
49. Slater Steel Industries

50. Rothams
51. Leigh Instruments
52. Great Lakes Paper and Pulp
53. EMCO
54. Asbestos Corporation Ltd.
55. Oshawa Group Ltd.

NOTES

1. This chapter has been adapted with permission of the editor from Ahmed Belkaoui, "Accounting Determinants of Systematic Risk in Canadian Common Stock: A Multivariate Approach," *Accounting and Business Research* (Winter, 1978), pp. 3–10.

2. Ahmed Belkaoui, "Canadian Evidence of Heteroscedasticity in the Market Model," *Journal of Finance* (September, 1977), pp. 1320–1324.

3. W. Beaver, P. Kettler, and M. Scholes, "The Association between Market-Determined and Accounting-Determined Risk Measures," *The Accounting Review* (October, 1970), pp. 654–682.

4. Nicholas J. Gonedes, "Evidence of the Information Content of Accounting Numbers: Accounting-Based and Market-Based Estimates of Systematic Risk," *Journal of Financial and Quantitative Analysis* (June, 1973), pp. 407–443.

5. Ibid, p. 436.

6. Robert P. Derstine and Ronald J. Huefner, "LIFO-FIFO, Accounting Ratios and Market Risk," *Journal of Accounting Research* (Autumn, 1974), pp. 216–234.

7. William J. Breen and Eugene M. Lerner, "Corporate Financial Strategies and Market Measures of Risk and Return," *Journal of Finance* (May, 1973), pp. 339–351.

8. Robert S. Hamada, "The Effect of the Firm's Capital Structure on the Systematic Risk of Common Stocks," *Journal of Finance* (May, 1972), pp. 435–452.

9. Barr Rosenberg and Walt McKibben, "The Prediction of Systematic and Unsystematic Risk," *Journal of Financial and Quantitative Analysis* (March, 1973), pp. 317–333.

10. Dennis E. Logue and Larry J. Merville, "Corporate Financial Strategies and Market Measures of Risk and Return," *Journal of Finance* (May, 1973), pp. 339–351.

11. William Beaver and James Manegold, "The Association between Market-Determined and Accounting-Determined Measures of Systematic Risk: Some Further Evidence," *Journal of Financial and Quantitative Analysis* (June, 1975), pp. 231–284.

12. John S. Bildersee, "Market-Determined and Alternative Measures of Risk," *Accounting Review* (January, 1975), pp. 31–98.

13. Ronald W. Melicher, "Financial Factors which Influence Beta Variations within an Homogeneous Industry Environment," *Journal of Financial and Quantitative Analysis* (March, 1974), pp. 231–241.

14. Ronald W. Melicher and David F. Rush, "Systematic Risk, Financial Data, and Bond Rating Relationships in a Regulated Industry Environment," *Journal of Finance* (May, 1974), pp. 534–544.

15. Donald J. Thompson II, "Sources of Systematic Risk in Common Stocks," *Journal of Business* (April, 1976), pp. 173–188.

SUGGESTED READINGS

Beaver, William, and James Manegold. "The Association between Market-Determined and Accounting-Determined Measures of Systematic Risk: Some Further Evidence." *Journal of Financial and Quantitative Analysis* (June, 1975), pp. 231–284.

Beaver, W., P. Kettler, and M. Scholes. "The Association between Market-Determined and Accounting-Determined Risk Measures." *Accounting Review* (October, 1970), pp. 654–682.

Belkaoui, Ahmed. "Canadian Evidence of Heteroscedasticity in the Market Model." *Journal of Finance* (September, 1997).

Belkaoui, Ahmed. "The Market Model Applied to Canadian Common Stocks: Some Empirical Evidence." Working Paper 76–20, Faculty of Management Sciences, University of Ottawa.

Bildersee, John S. "Market-Determined and Alternative Measures of Risk." *Accounting Review* (January, 1975), pp. 31–98.

Breen, William J., and Eugene M. Lerner. "Corporate Financial Strategies and Market Measures of Risk and Return." *Journal of Finance* (May, 1973), pp. 339–351.

Derstine, Robert P., and Ronald J. Huefner. "LIFO-FIFO, Accounting Ratios and Market Risk." *Journal of Accounting Research* (Autumn, 1974), pp. 216–234.

Dixon, W. J., ed. *Biomedical Computer Programs*. Berkeley and Los Angeles: University of California Press, 1974, pp. 255–264.

Falk, H., and L. A. Gordon. "The Relationship between Accounting Industry Risk Measurement and Industrial Betas." *Proceedings of the Canadian Association of Administrative Sciences*, produced by the School of Business, Queen's University at Kingston, 1976, Section 2–50.

Fama, E. F. "Efficient Capital Market: A Review of Theory and Empirical Work." *Journal of Finance* (May, 1970), pp. 383–417.

Fama, Eugene F. "Risk, Return and Equilibrium: Some Clarifying Comments." *Journal of Finance* (March, 1968), pp. 312–322.

Francis, J. C. "Skewness and Investor Decisions." *Journal of Financial and Quantitative Analysis* (March, 1975), pp. 215–232.

Gonedes, Nicholas J. "Evidence on the Information Content of Accounting Numbers: Accounting-Based and Market-Based Estimates of Systematic Risk." *Journal of Financial and Quantitative Analysis* (June, 1973), pp. 407–443.

Hamada, Robert S. "The Effect of the Firm's Capital Structure on the Systematic Risk of Common Stocks." *Journal of Finance* (May, 1972), pp. 435–452.

Logue, Dennis E., and Larry J. Merville. "Corporate Financial Strategies and Market Measures of Risk and Return." *Journal of Finance* (May, 1973), pp. 339–351.

Lintner, John. "The Valuation of the Risk Assets and the Selection of Risky Investments in Stock Portfolio and Capital Budgets." *Review of Economics and Statistics* (February, 1965), pp. 125–132.

McCallum, J. S., and W. Vierra. "The Association between Accounting and Market Determined Measures of Risk: The Canadian Evidence." *Proceedings of The Canadian Association of Administrative Sciences*, produced by the School of Business, Queen's University at Kingston, 1976, Section 2–86.

Melicher, Ronald W. "Financial Factors which Influence Beta Variations within an Homogeneous Industry Environment.'' *Journal of Financial and Quantitative Analysis* (March, 1974), pp. 231–241.

Melicher, Ronald W., and David F. Rush. ''Systematic Risk, Financial Data, and Bond Ratings Relationships in a Regulated Industry Environment.'' *Journal of Finance* (May, 1974), pp. 534–544.

Rosenberg, Barr, and Walt McKibben. ''The Prediction of Systematic and Unsystematic Risk.'' *Journal of Financial and Quantitative Analysis* (March, 1973), pp. 317–333.

Rummel, Ralph J. *Applied Factor Analysis*. Evanston, Ill.: Northwestern University Press, 1970.

Thompson, Donald J., II. ''Sources of Systematic Risk in Common Stocks.'' *Journal of Business* (April, 1976), pp. 173–188.

4

The Prediction of Industrial Bond Ratings

INTRODUCTION

The best-known measures of prospective bond quality are the bond ratings assigned by the three agencies: Moody's, Standard & Poor's, and Fitch. Their ratings provide a judgment of the investment quality of a long-term obligation and a measure of default risk. Accordingly, they may affect the interest rate an organization pays on its bonds. Although each rating agency has defined the meaning of its ratings, the agencies have not explicitly specified the process they use to arrive at these ratings. Given the importance of ratings, various authors have attempted to explain and predict them based on the financial and/or statistical characteristics of the bonds and issuing firms. These rating-prediction studies were reviewed in the previous chapter. Although the models derived do an adequate job of capturing the human judgments of bond raters, they suffer from (a) a diversity of approaches used in selecting independent variables for the regression, discriminant, or multivariate probit models; (b) a lack of an "economic rationale" underlying the choice of these variables;[1] (c) a failure to account for the differences among the companies in their accounting for long-term leases; and (d) the confusion of ex ante predictive power with ex post discrimination. Consequently this study will correct for the above limitations to develop a multiple-discrimination bond-rating model.

ECONOMIC RATIONALE[2]

A bond rating is primarily a judgment of the investment quality of a firm's long-term obligation. It reflects the raters' expectations and estimates of the relevant characteristics of the quality of the investment. To capture the determinants of bond ratings, these characteristics of the investment quality must be identified and rationalized on an economic basis.

The investment quality of a bond is determined by the interaction among three general variables: firm-, market-, and indenture-related variables.

The firm-related variables depict the ability of the firm to provide adequate protection for bondholders. This ability depend on both size and coverage factors. The size factor allows rating of the bonds in terms of the security they provide. The security itself is a function of the firm's command over total resources. Going from the most aggregate to the least aggregate expression, the command over total resources depends on (1) the total size of the firm, (2) the total size of the debt, (3) the long-term capital intensiveness, and (4) the short-term capital intensiveness. Thus, variables expressing each of these determinants of the size factor should be included in a bond-rating model.

The coverage factor allows rating of bonds in terms of the ability of the firm to service the financial changes. Thus, while the size factor is concerned with stock considerations, the coverage factor is concerned with bond considerations, the ability of the firm to service the financial resources. Going from the most aggregate to the least aggregate, the flow of financial resources depends on (1) the total actual liquidity of the firm, (2) the debt coverage, and (3) the future liquidity of the firm. Thus, variables expressing each of these determinants of the coverage factor should be included in any bond-rating model.

The market-related variables depict the ability of the firm to create a favorable market response to all its securities. They reflect the investors' expectations in the aggregate about the firm's performance. Thus, variables expressing measures of investors' expectations about the firm's profitability should be included in any bond-rating model.

The indenture-related variables depict the relevant covenants and terms of the indenture that is the basic legal document constituting the contract between the bondholders and the bond issuer. They are deemed very important in bond rating.[3] In spite of the possible difficulties of operationalizing them, variables expressing relevant covenants of the indenture should also be included in any bond-rating model.

DEVELOPMENT OF THE MODEL

Method

To avoid the limitations of the studies surveyed in Chapter 3, the following methodology will be used.

First, the bond-rating model will be based on a multiple-discriminant model. Because bonds convey ordinal information (an AAA bond is more secured than an AA bond, which is more secure than an A bond, etc.) the multiple-discriminant and the multivariate probit models are more appropriate than the regression model. And as seen in the Kaplan and Urwitz study,[4] the regression model seems more robust than the multivariate probit model, which leaves the multiple discriminant model as the most appropriate.

Second, to avoid confusion between tests of validation or classification efficiency and tests of prediction the following steps will be used.[5]

The first step is to "fit" a discriminant function over a sample of firms A_1 from the data collected in 1981. This sample is the analysis sample.

The second step is to use the linear discrimination function obtained in the first step to classify firms of a time-coincident holdout, or validation sample A_2. This sample A_2 of firms with data collected in 1981 is the validation sample. This step has been confused in other studies with prediction. Ex post discrimination may provide a useful foundation for explanation of the past, but it does not provide sufficient evidence for concluding that the future can be predicted.[6]

Assuming successful ex post discrimination, the explanatory significance of the financial variables (independent variables) is investigated using both samples A_1 and A_2 from 1981 data. That is, the sample are recombined to form an estimating sample, and a new linear discriminant model for the total 1981 sample is estimated. This involves merely a reestimation of the coefficients and not a search for variables.

The next step is to use the linear discriminant model, obtained as just explained, to classify sample B observations from another year, and in this case from 1980. As stated correctly: "Prediction thus requires intertemporal validation whereas explanation requires only cross validation."[7]

Both cross-validation (the second step) and intertemporal validation (preceding paragraph) will yield a classification matrix showing the hit rate for the model. Similarly to all the previous studies, the success of the prediction will be measured by the hit rate, that is, the percentage of industrial bonds correctly classified.

Samples Selection

As explained in the preceding sections, four randomly selected samples of industrial bonds rated B or above by Standard & Poor's will be used.[8]

1. An analysis sample of 266 industrial bonds rated B or above by Standard & Poor's in 1981.

2. A validation sample of 115 industrial bonds rated B or above by Standard & Poor's in 1981.

3. An estimating sample of 381 industrial bonds rated B or above by Standard & Poor's in 1981. The estimating sample is a combination of the analysis and validation samples. The year 1981 was used to ensure that all firm's represented have a uniform accounting treatment of financial leases following the Financial Accounting Standard Board Statement 13, "Accounting for Leases," effective since 1976.

4. A control sample of 388 industrial bonds rated B or above by Standard & Poor's in 1980.[9]

Exhibit 4.1 provides a brief summary of the exact composition of the total sample. Thirty-seven industries were represented in each of the samples (aerospace, airlines, appliances, automotive, beverages, building materials, chemicals, conglomerates, containers, drugs, electrical and electronics, food processing, food and lodging, general machinery, instruments, leisure time industries, metals and mining, miscellaneous manufacturing, natural resources [fuel], office equipment and computers, oil service and supply, paper, personal care products, publishing, radio and television broadcasting, railroads, real estate and housing, retailing [food], retailing [nonfood], service industries, special machinery, steel textiles and apparel, tire and rubber, tobacco, trucking, and utilities).

Variables in the Multiple Discriminant Model

Nine variables were selected to be included in the multiple discriminant model as representative of the factors identified in the economic rationale section.

X_1 = *Total assets*, included as representative of the total size of the firm.

X_2 = *Total debt*, included as a measure of the total indebtedness of the firm.

X_3 = *Long-term debt/total invested capital*, included as a measure of the long-term capital intensiveness of the firm. Here invested capital means the sum of the total debt, preferred stock, and common equity (which includes common stocks, capital surplus, and retained earnings).

X_4 = *Short-term debt/total invested capital*, included as a measure of the short-term capital intensiveness of the firm.

X_5 = *Current assets/current liabilities*, included as a measure of the total liquidity of the firm.

X_6 = *Fixed charge coverage ratio*, net income plus total interest expense (adjusted by tax rate)/interest expense (adjusted by tax rate) plus preferred dividend requirement, included as a measure of debt coverage.

X_7 = *Five-year cash flow as percentage of five-year growth needs*. Five-year sum of (1) net income available for common stockholders, plus (2) depreciation and amortization, plus (3) income from discontinued operations and extraordinary items net of taxes divided by five-year sum of (1) capital expenditures, plus (2) change in inventories during most recent five years (except utilities), plus (3) common dividends; included as a measure of future liquidity.

X_8 = *Stock price/common equity per share*, included as a measure of investors' expectations.

X_9 = *Subordination* (0–1), included as a measure of the most relevant covenant in the indenture.

These nine variables are, in general, different from the variables used in previous corporate industrial bond-rating models. Exhibit 4.2 presents a comparative analysis of the variables used in these studies. Most of the variables and

Exhibit 4.1
Sample Size of Industrial Corporate Bonds

RATINGS	ANALYSIS SAMPLE 1981		VALIDATION SAMPLE 1981		ESTIMATING SAMPLE 1981		CONTROL SAMPLE 1980	
	Numbers	%	Numbers	%	Numbers	%	Numbers	%
AAA	13	4.88	6	5.21	19	4.98	20	5.15
AA	51	19.17	17	14.78	68	17.84	99	25.51
A	112	42.10	35	30.43	147	38.58	140	36.08
BBB	51	19.17	30	26.08	81	21.25	50	12.88
BB	9	3.38	20	17.39	29	7.61	40	10.30
B	30	11.27	7	6.08	37	9.71	39	10.05
Total	266	100	115	100	381	100	388	100

Exhibit 4.2
Comparative Analysis of Variables Used in Bond Rating Models

RATIO	THIS STUDY	HORRIGAN	WEST	PINCHES AND MINGO	KAPLAN AND URWITZ
1. Total size of the firm	Total assets	Total assets	Not used	Not used	Total assets
2. Total size of the debt	Total debt	Not used	Bonds outstanding	Not used	Not used
3. Long-term capital intensiveness	Long-term debt as a percentage of total invested capital	Net worth over total debt	Debt equity ratio	Long-term debt over total assets	a. Long-term debt over total assets b. Long-term debt over net worth
4. Short-term capital intensiveness	Short-term debt as a percentage of total invested capital	Not used	Not used	Not used	Not used
5. Actual liquidity	Current ratio	Working capital over sales	Not used	Not used	Not used
6. Debt coverage	Fixed charge coverage ratio	Not used	Not used	Five-year mean of net income plus interest charge over interest charge	a. Cash flow before interest and taxes over interest b. Cash flow

					before interest and taxes over total debt
7. Future liquidity	Five-year cash flow as a percentage of five-year growth needs	Not used	Not used	Not used	Not used
8. Investors' expectations	Stock price as a percentage of book value	Not used	Not used	Not used	Accounting and market betas
9. Indenture provision	Subordination status	Subordination status	Not used	Subordination status	Subordination status
10. Others	Not used	Sales over net worth	Period of solving	Years of consecutive dividends	Net income over total assets
11. Others	Not used	Net operating profit	Nine-year earnings	Net income over total assets	Coefficients of variations of total assets
12. Others	Not used	Not used	Not used	Issue size	Issue size
13. Others	Not used	Not used	Not used	Not used	Coefficient of variations of net income

factors used in this study are absent in the other models due mainly to the absence of an economic rationale in their choice of variables. For example, measures of investors' expectations and short-term capital intensiveness are used in only two model (this study); short-term capital intensiveness is used only in this study; actual liquidity is used in only two models (this study and Horrigan's); future liquidity is used only in this study; only long-term capital intensiveness is used in all models.

Discriminant Analysis Results on the Analysis Sample

The overall discriminating power of the model using the analysis sample was accomplished by testing for differences in the group centroids. The overall F value for the model, $F = 20.25$ ($p < 0.001$), permits rejection of the null hypothesis that the differences in the group centroids of the six bond-rating groups was zero. This result justifies an examination of the discriminating power of each of the nine independent variables. Exhibit 4.3 presents the means and univariate F ratios for all nine variables by bond-rating groups. All the variables were significant. From a univariate point of view and on the basis of the magnitude of the F ratio, it may be stated that subordination status is the most important variables followed by short-term debt over invested capital, total assets, fixed change coverage ratio, total debt, long-term debt over total invested capital, stock price over book value, and five-year cash flow over five-year growth needs.

The independent variables were examined for multicollinearity. Exhibit 4.4 shows the correlation matrix for all the variables. The intercorrelations (average $r = 0.0146$) are not judged large enough to produce a basis in the estimation of the parameters of the model.

A stepwise multiple discriminant analysis was used to determine the discriminant functions. The BMDP7M program was used for the task.[10] Exhibit 4.5 shows the obtained six functions. Based on Wilks' lambda and its associated chi square, the six functions were found to be significant. Exhibit 4.6 presents the pairs of values for the test of significance of the Mahalanobias distance between groups.[11] All the F values were significant, which permits one to reject the null hypothesis that the pairs of group centroids are equal at the 0.01 level.

To determine the relative importance of the variables in the model, four criteria were used.[12] The rank ordering of the nine variables according to the univariate F ratio, the forward and backward stepwise methods, and the scale-weighted method are shown in Exhibit 4.7. The univariate F ratio and the stepwise forward method show subordination to be the most important and future liquidity ratio to be the least important. The stepwise backward method shows the long-term debt ratio to be the most important, followed by subordination, and the total assets to be the least important. Finally, the scale-weighted method shows the subordination to be the most important, followed by the current ratio, and the total debt to be the least important. Before evaluating the classification

Exhibit 4.3
Variable Means and Tests of Significance (Analysis Sample)*

VARIABLE	BOND RATING						
	AAA	AA	A	BBB	BB	B	F**
X_1	18433.72	5447.61	2056.82	2263.99	716.43	609.71	29.48
X_2	5655.25	1143.26	533.93	757.16	257.67	277.62	8.01
X_3	15.50	20.40	29.33	37.77	37.59	48.81	6.92
X_4	5.33	9.00	4.35	8.93	4.45	6.03	31.21
X_5	1.65	1.60	1.92	1.61	1.98	1.89	2.92
X_6	19.76	8.75	6.93	4.70	5.91	3.79	14.38
X_7	88.19	83.03	82.26	72.36	58.42	69.55	2.88
X_8	132.28	149.13	108.62	89.74	200.37	148.40	5.90
X_9	1.00	1.00	0.99	0.80	0.11	0.00	157.55

*$\alpha = 9.260$.

**All the F values are significant at the 0.05 level of significance.

Exhibit 4.4
Correlation Coefficients over the Nine Variables (Analysis Sample)

VARIABLE	X_1	X_2	X_3	X_4	X_5	X_6	X_7	X_8	X_9
X_1	1.000								
X_2	0.739	1.000							
X_3	-0.068	0.094	1.000						
X_4	0.078	0.002	-0.200	1.000					
X_5	-0.261	-0.202	-0.356	-0.216	1.000				
X_6	-0.030	-0.090	-0.534	-0.203	0.350	1.000			
X_7	0.044	-0.055	-0.346	0.046	0.316	0.304	1.000		
X_8	-0.054	-0.051	-0.048	0.007	0.218	0.291	-0.050	1.000	
X_9	0.206	0.069	-0.358	-0.008	-0.143	0.141	0.163	-0.226	1.000

64

Exhibit 4.5
Discriminant Functions (Analysis Sample)

VARIABLE	BOND RATING					
	AAA	AA	A	BBB	BB	B
X_1	0.00091	0.00039	0.00025	0.00024	0.00026	0.00024
X_2	0.00028	-0.000020	-0.000022	-0.00009	-0.00015	-0.00024
X_3	0.48955	0.49510	0.59913	0.73207	0.75037	0.92494
X_4	0.68989	0.72489	0.65544	0.86627	0.73371	0.87970
X_5	7.69142	6.89274	8.15657	8.52282	9.35400	10.20789
X_6	1.03822	0.66162	0.64337	0.68019	0.54337	0.58578
X_7	0.02869	0.04225	0.04496	0.04496	0.04309	0.06080
X_8	0.01764	0.02030	0.01049	0.00378	0.01593	0.00386
X_9	28.47068	26.72795	25.09872	18.84681	0.38142	-4.60076
Constant	-48.13343	-34.42768	-36.42350	-35.75230	-129.57942	-38.46189

Exhibit 4.6
Pairs of *F* Values for the Test of Significance of the Mahalanobis Distance between Groups (Analysis Sample)

GROUP	AAA	AA	A	BBB	BB
AA	13.81				
A	24.14	9.85			
BBB	29.25	19.35	11.91		
BB	29.46	24.36	21.30	12.28	
B	67.91	91.85	91.45	43.87	2.54

Degrees of freedom (9,252).

accuracy of the model, the equality of the covariance matrices among the six bond rating groups was tested, using Box's M and its associated F test.[13] The resulting F value of 1.03 is not significant at the 0.05 level, resulting in the acceptance of the null hypothesis of equal covariance matrices and supporting the use of linear rather than quadratic classification rules. Similarly, we employed equal prior probabilities for classification, based on the belief that the distribution of bonds in the population is either unstable or unknown and that the main objective is evaluation of the importance of the variables included in the model without any consideration of prior probabilities.

Finally, the multiple discrimination model was used to classify the experimental group of bonds from which it was developed, based on the probability of group membership. The classification matrix for the analysis sample is shown in Exhibit 4.8. The total number of correctly classified bonds is obtained by summing the upper left-lower right diagonal of the classification matrix in Exhibit 4.8. It shows that the multiple discriminant analysis classified correctly 72.93 percent (194/266) of the firms. The model performs better for some of the individual categories, AAA (76.92 percent), AA (74.51 percent), A (80.36 percent), BBB (54.90 percent), BB (66.67 percent), and B (73.33 percent).

Validation

As stated earlier, ex post discrimination or cross-validation consists in classifying firms of a time-coincident holdout or validation sample using the discriminant functions obtained from the analysis sample. Another reason for validation is the need to check for possible biases due to sampling errors and search. Thus, the multiple-discriminant model obtained with the analysis sample of 1981 was used to classify firms from a validation sample of 1981. The classified results are shown in Exhibit 4.9. The model correctly rated 67.8 percent of the firms in the validation sample. Using the Z statistic of Mosteller and Bush,[14] the null hypothesis that the results are due to chance is rejected, con-

Exhibit 4.7
Variable Importance Ranked According to Different Criteria

VARIABLE	UNIVARIATE F RATIO	STEPWISE FORWARD	STEPWISE BACKWARD	SCALE WEIGHTED
X_1	3	2	9	8
X_2	5	8	3	9
X_3	2	3	1	5
X_4	6	4	5	4
X_5	8	7	6	2
X_6	4	5	4	3
X_7	9	9	8	2
X_8	7	6	7	7
X_9	1	1	2	1

Exhibit 4.8
Classification Table (Analysis Sample)

FROM GROUP	NUMBER OF OBSERVATIONS (AND PERCENTAGES) CLASSIFIED INTO GROUPS						
	AAA	AA	A	BBB	BB	B	TOTAL
AAA	10 (76.92)	2 (15.38)	1 (7.69)	0 (0.00)	0 (0.00)	0 (0.00)	13 (100.00)
AA	6 (11.76)	38 (74.51)	7 (13.73)	0 (0.00)	0 (0.00)	0 (0.00)	51 (100.00)
A	1 (0.89)	10 (8.93)	90 (80.36)	10 (8.93)	1 (0.89)	0 (0.00)	112 (100.00)
BBB	1 (1.96)	1 (1.96)	12 (23.53)	28 (54.90)	6 (11.76)	3 (5.88)	51 (100.00)
BB	0 (0.00)	0 (0.00)	0 (0.00)	2 (22.22)	5 (66.67)	2 (22.22)	9 (100.00)
B	0 (0.00)	0 (0.00)	0 (0.00)	0 (0.00)	8 (26.67)	22 (73.33)	30 (100.00)

Exhibit 4.9
Classification Table (Validation Sample)

FROM GROUP	NUMBER OF OBSERVATIONS (AND PERCENTAGES) CLASSIFIED INTO GROUPS						
	AAA	AA	A	BBB	BB	B	TOTAL
AAA	2 (0.33)	4 (0.67)	0 (0.00)	0 (0.00)	0 (0.00)	0 (0.00)	6 (1.00)
AA	5 (0.29)	12 (0.71)	0 (0.00)	0 (0.00)	0 (0.00)	0 (0.00)	17 (1.00)
A	0 (0.00)	0 (0.00)	25 (0.71)	0 (0.00)	10 (0.28)	0 (0.00)	35 (1.00)
BBB	0 (0.00)	0 (0.00)	3 (0.10)	21 (0.70)	6 (0.20)	0 (0.00)	30 (1.00)
BB	0 (0.00)	0 (0.00)	0 (0.00)	4 (0.20)	13 (0.65)	3 (0.15)	20 (1.00)
B	0 (0.00)	0 (0.00)	0 (0.00)	0 (0.00)	2 (0.28)	5 (0.71)	7 (1.00)

Exhibit 4.10
Comparison of the Validation Classification

STUDY	% CORRECT VALIDATION SAMPLE
Pinches and Mingo	65 and 56
Horrigan	59
West	60
Belkaoui	65.9
This study	67.8

firming the previous discriminating power results of the model. Exhibit 4.8 shows the hit rate for the nine categories. A final interesting result appearing in Exhibit 4.10 is the higher validation results presented by this study approach. As stated earlier, validation should not be confused with prediction. It merely provides sufficient evidence for concluding that the future can be predicted. Accordingly, in what follows, the discriminant model is reestimated on the basis of the total sample of 1981 (analysis plus validation samples) and then applied to a sample of 1980 to test its predictive ability.

Estimating the Model's Linear Discriminant Functions

Given the successful ex post discrimination, the explanatory significance of the independent variables in investigated, using both the analysis and the validation sample from 1981. That is, the samples are recombined to form a total 1981 sample, and new linear discriminant functions are fitted. This step is merely a reestimation of the coefficients and not a new search for variables.

The overall discrimination power of the model based on the total 1981 sample was accomplished by testing for differences in the group centroids. The overall F value for the model of $F = 20.32$ ($p < 0.001$) permits rejection of the null hypothesis that the difference in the group centroids of the six bond-rating groups was zero. This result justifies again an examination of the discriminating power of each of the nine independent variables. Exhibit 4.11 presents the means and univariate F ratios for all nine variables by bond-rating group.

All the variables were found to be significant. The nine dependent variables were again examined for multicollinearity. Exhibit 4.12 shows the correlations matrix for all variables. The intercorrelations (average $r = 0.021$) are not judged large enough to produce a bias in the estimation of the parameters of the model.

A stepwise discriminant analysis based on the BMDP7M program was again used to determine the discriminant functions. Exhibit 4.13 shows the multiple discriminant functions for each rating group. Based on Wilks' lambda and its associated chi square, the six functions were found to be significant. Exhibit 4.14 presents the pairs of F values for the test of significance of the Mahalan-

Exhibit 4.11
Variable Means and Tests of Significance (Estimating Sample)

VARIABLE	BOND RATING						F VALUE
	AAA	AA	A	BBB	BB	B	
X_1	13632.415	5541.445	2100.367	1746.706	1084.565	696.059	25.164
X_2	4009.726	1097.522	554.030	581.456	367.962	987.135	7.359
X_3	13.963	18.954	28.224	37.165	41.775	47.856	50.471
X_4	5.952	8.414	4.419	7.816	6.324	5.808	6.250
X_5	1.778	1.564	1.962	1.781	1.962	1.856	2.214
X_6	17.589	10.817	7.099	4.720	4.100	3.775	15.943
X_7	89.373	85.539	81.278	76.912	63.765	67.348	3.302
X_8	144.494	147.080	110.247	102.406	155.813	141.427	4.132
X_9	0.947	0.985	0.911	0.617	0.344	0.054	58.732

DF = 5,375.
F values significant at $\alpha = 0.05$.

Exhibit 4.12
Correlation Coefficients over the Nine Variables (Estimating Sample)

VARIABLE	X_1	X_2	X_3	X_4	X_5	X_6	X_7	X_8	X_9
X_1	1.000								
X_2	0.063	1.000							
X_3	-0.137	0.063	1.000						
X_4	0.051	0.028	-0.155	1.000					
X_5	-0.259	-0.215	-0.271	-0.215	1.000				
X_6	0.102	-0.045	-0.513	-0.184	0.152	1.000			
X_7	0.020	-0.055	-0.361	0.042	0.284	0.251	1.000		
X_8	-0.088	-0.060	-0.022	-0.035	0.074	0.206	-0.0008	1.000	
X_9	0.206	0.108	-0.280	0.069	-0.079	0.008	0.101	-0.185	1.000

Exhibit 4.13
Discriminant Functions (Estimating Sample)

VARIABLE	FUNCTIONS					
	AAA	AA	A	BBB	BB	B
X_1	0.000737	0.000431	0.00269	0.000250	0.000265	0.000242
X_2	0.000119	-0.000147	-0.000149	-0.000233	-0.000295	-0.000357
X_3	0.44234	0.48229	0.58069	0.71530	0.76589	0.85499
X_4	0.62823	0.67906	0.60516	0.79864	0.80544	0.84459
X_5	7.26898	6.80279	7.832642	8.35763	9.15411	9.24043
X_6	0.68425	0.54641	0.48850	0.50766	0.48010	0.49208
X_7	0.06102	0.06600	0.06777	0.07116	0.05952	0.06970
X_8	0.01802	0.01687	0.00809	0.00235	0.00705	0.00099
X_9	10.26302	9.76648	8.78782	4.27079	1.69732	-1.73660
Constant	-31.6004	-26.0425	-26.1304	-29.3824	-31.3397	-34.8229

F statistic = 16.492.

Exhibit 4.14
**Pairs of *F* Values for the Test of Significance of the Mahalanobias Distance
between Groups (Estimating Sample)**

GROUP	AAA	AA	A	BBB	BB
AA	7.32				
A	19.86	13.79			
BBB	30.86	31.89	16.51		
BB	30.80	29.63	17.71	3.47	
B	48.50	59.90	44.72	13.45	2.51

DF = 9,367.

obias distance between groups. All the *F* values were significant, which permits one to reject again the null hypothesis that the pairs of group centroids are equal to the 0.01 level.

To determine the relative importance of the variables in the models, four criteria were again used. The rank ordering of the nine variables according to the univariate *F* ratio, the forward and backward stepwise methods, and the scale-weighted method are shown in Exhibit 4.15. Similarly to the analysis performed on the experimental sample, the rank ordering of the nine variables differs from one method to another. Before evaluating the classification accuracy of the model, the equality of the covariance matrices among the six bond-rating groups was tested using Box's *M* and its associated *F* test. The resulting *F* value of 1.05 is not significant at the 0.05 level, leading to the acceptance of the null hypothesis of equal covariance matrices and supporting the use of linear rather than quadratic classification rules. Similarly, we employed equal probabilities for classification.

Finally, the multiple discriminant model was used to classify the total estimating sample of bonds from which it was developed, based on the probability of group membership. The classification matrix for the estimating sample is shown in Exhibit 4.16. The total number of correctly classified bonds is obtained by summing the upper left-lower right diagonal of the classified matrix in Exhibit 4.16. It shows that the multiple discriminant analysis classification correctly rated 67.19 percent (256/381) of the firms. The model performs differently for the individual categories, AAA (47.37 percent), AA (66 percent), A (80.27 percent), BBB (53 percent), BB (51 percent), and B (70.27 percent).

Prediction

Whereas explanation required only cross-validation, prediction requires intertemporal validation. That is to say, the discriminant model obtained from the total sample of 1981 must be used to classify a control sample of bonds from

Exhibit 4.15
Variable Importance Ranked According to Different Criteria (Estimating Sample)

VARIABLE	UNIVARIATE F RATIO	STEPWISE FORWARD	STEPWISE BACKWARD	SCALE WEIGHTED
X_1	3	3	3	8
X_2	5	8	4	9
X_3	2	2	2	5
X_4	6	4	7	4
X_5	9	6	9	2
X_6	4	7	5	3
X_7	8	9	6	6
X_8	7	5	8	7
X_9	1	1	1	1

Exhibit 4.16
Classification Table (Estimating Sample)

FROM GROUP	NUMBER OF OBSERVATIONS (AND PERCENTAGES) CLASSIFIED INTO GROUPS						TOTAL
	AAA	AA	A	BBB	BB	B	
AAA	9 (.47)	10 (.52)	0 (0.00)	0 (0.00)	0 (0.00)	0 (0.00)	19 (1.00)
AA	11 (0.16)	45 (0.66)	11 (0.16)	0 (0.00)	0 (0.00)	0 (0.00)	68 (1.00)
A	1 (0.0068)	13 (0.088)	118 (0.80)	9 (0.061)	5 (0.034)	1 (0.0068)	147 (1.00)
BBB	0 (0.00)	0 (0.00)	15 (0.18)	43 (0.53)	8 (0.098)	15 (0.18)	81 (1.00)
BB	0 (0.00)	0 (0.00)	0 (0.00)	7 (0.34)	15 (0.51)	7 (0.24)	29 (1.00)
B	0 (0.00)	0 (0.00)	1 (0.027)	4 (0.108)	6 (0.16)	26 (0.70)	37 (1.00)

another year in order to test the predictive ability of the model. The control sample chosen was a sample of bonds from 1980. Thus, the multiple discriminant model obtained from the total 1981 estimating sample (Exhibit 4.12) was used to classify firms from the control sample of 1980. The classification or prediction results are shown in Exhibit 4.17. The model correctly rated 63.65 percent of the firms in the control sample. Using again the Z statistic of Mosteller and Bush, the null hypothesis that the results are due to chance is rejected, confirming the previous discriminating power of the model and establishing the predictive power of the model.

USING THE BOND-RATING MODEL

Model Performance

The methodology used was discriminant analysis to avoid some of the pitfalls of the other techniques. Based on an economic rationale, the discrimination analysis model developed in this study correctly rated 72.93 percent of the ratings in an analysis sample (1981), 67 percent of the ratings in a validation sample (1981), 67.19 percent of the ratings in a total estimating sample (1981), and 63.65 percent of the ratings in a control sample. Both validation and predictive ability of the model were significant. Besides, two results are noteworthy. First, most misclassified firms were classified in categories adjacent to the true ratings. Second, an examination of the *Credit Watch* list published by Standard & Poor's for five consecutive weeks following the availability of the information on which the study is based showed that seven of the firms put on the list correspond to five of the misclassified firms (see Exhibit 4.18).

The Discriminant Functions

The discriminant model based on the estimating 1981 sample yields a discriminant function for each of the five rating groups. These discriminant functions may be used to explain and/or predict bond ratings. They are as follows:
For an AAA rating:

$$Z = -\ 31.6004 + 0.000737X_1 + 0.000119X_2 + 0.44234X_3$$
$$+\ 0.62823X_4 + 7.26898X_5 + 0.68425X_6 + 0.06102X_7$$
$$+\ 0.01802X_8 + 10.26302X_9$$

For an AA rating:

$$Z = -\ 26.0425 + 0.000431X_1 + 0.000147X_2 + 0.48299X_3$$
$$+\ 0.67906X_4 + 6.80279X_5 + 0.54641X_6 + 0.06600X_7$$
$$+\ 0.01687X_8 + 9.76648X_9$$

Exhibit 4.17
Classification Table (Control Sample)

FROM GROUP	NUMBER OBSERVATIONS (AND PERCENTAGES) CLASSIFIED INTO GROUPS						TOTAL
	AAA	AA	A	BBB	BB	B	
AAA	9 (.45)	8 (.40)	3 (.15)	0 (0.00)	0 (0.00)	0 (0.00)	20 (1.00)
AA	7 (0.07)	62 (0.62)	30 (0.30)	0 (0.00)	0 (0.00)	0 (0.00)	99 (1.00)
A	0 (0.00)	31 (0.22)	99 (0.70)	10 (0.07)	0 (0.00)	0 (0.00)	140 (1.00)
BBB	0 (0.00)	0 (0.00)	12 (0.24)	35 (0.70)	3 (0.06)	0 (0.00)	50 (1.00)
BB	0 (0.00)	0 (0.00)	0 (0.00)	7 (0.17)	18 (0.45)	15 (0.37)	40 (1.00)
B	0 (0.00)	0 (0.00)	0 (0.00)	0 (0.00)	15 (0.38)	24 (0.61)	39 (1.00)

Exhibit 4.18

Firms Misclassified and Also on the *Credit Watch* List

	Sample(s) in Which Misclassification Occurred	CREDIT WATCH RATING				
		March 29, 1982	April 5, 1982	April 12, 1982	April 19, 1982	April 26, 1982
Utilities, transportation						
Arizona Public Service Company	Analysis sample	/	/	/	/	Negative
Industrial retailing						
Brunswick Corp.	Estimating sample / Validation sample	Negative	Negative	Negative	Negative	Negative
Coca–Cola Co.	Estimating sample / Validation sample	Negative	Negative	Negative		
Columbia Pictures Inds. Inc.	Estimating sample / Validation sample	Positive	Positive	Positive	Positive	Positive
Lone Star Industries Inc.	Estimating sample / Validation sample	Negative	Negative	Negative	Negative	Negative
Murphy (G.C.) Co.	Estimating sample / Validation sample	Negative	Negative	/	/	/
Resorts International Inc.	Estimating sample / Validation sample	Negative	Negative	Negative	/	/

For an A rating:

$$Z = -26.1304 + 0.000269X_1 - 0.000149\ X_2 + 0.58069X_3$$
$$+ 0.60516X_4 + 7.83642X_5 + 0.48850X_6 + 0.06777X_7$$
$$+ 0.00809X_8 + 8.18782X_9$$

For a BBB rating:

$$Z = -29.3824 + 0.000250X_1 - 0.000233X_2 + 0.71530X_3$$
$$+ 0.79864X_4 + 8.35763X_5 + 0.50766X_6 + 0.07116X_7$$
$$+ 0.00235X_8 + 4.27079X_9$$

For a BB rating:

$$Z = -31.3397 + 0.000265X_1 - 0.000295X_2 + 0.76589X_3$$
$$+ 0.80544X_4 + 9.15411X_5 + 0.48010X_6 + 0.05952X_7$$
$$+ 0.00705X_8 + 1.69732X_9$$

For a B rating:

$$Z = -34.8229 + 0.000242X_1 - 0.000357X_2 + 0.85499X_3$$
$$+ 0.84459X_4 + 9.24043X_5 + 0.49208X_6 + 0.06970X_7$$
$$+ 0.00099X_8 - 1.73660X_9$$

where

X_1 = *Total assets*, included as a representative of the total size of the firm (in millions).

X_2 = *Total debt*, included as a measure of the total indebtness of the firm (in millions).

X_3 = *Long-term/total invested capital*, included as a measure of the long-term capital intensiveness of the firm. By invested capital is meant the sum of the total debt, preferred stock and common equity (which includes common stock, capital surplus, and retained earnings).

X_4 = *Short-term debt/total invested capital*, included as a measure of the short-term capital intensiveness of the firm.

X_5 = *Current assets/current liabilities*, included as a measure of the total liquidity of the firm.

X_6 = *Fixed charge coverage ratio*, included as a measure of debt coverage.

X_7 = *Five-year cash flow as a percentage of five-year growth needs*, included as a measure of future liquidity.

X_8 = *Stock price/common equity share*, included as a measure of investors' expectations.

X_9 = *Subordination*, 1 for subordination, 0 for others; included as a measure of the most relevant covenant in the indenture.

The Classification Procedure

The classification method consists simply of using the discriminant functions on new data as follows: For each firm that needs to be classified into a bond rating category, compute the classification score for each rating category from the discriminant function coefficients (multiply the data by the coefficients and add the constant term). The firm is then classified into the group for which the classification score is highest.

To illustrate the classification procedure, let's use the following 1980 data for Frontier Airlines (the rating given by Standard & Poor's was B).

X_1 = \$312.8 (in millions)

X_2 = \$116.1 (in millions)

X_3 = 48.7

X_4 = 4.1

X_5 = 0.9

X_6 = 3.5

X_7 = 52.8

X_8 = 104.7

X_9 = 1 (subordinated debt)

The classification scores for each rating category from the discriminant functions obtained by multiplying the coefficients by the data and adding the constant term are the following:

Z_{AAA} = 18.50916

Z_{AA} = 26.208

Z_A = 30.37737

Z_{BBB} = 38.72666

Z_{BB} = 41.09244

Z_B = 43.51933

Given that Z_B gives the highest classification score, the firm is classified by the model in the bond-rating category B.

Given the sample classification procedure outlined in the previous paragraphs, the model may be useful to all those interested in explaining, predicting, and/or justifying bond ratings and evaluating the investment quality of bonds.

The issuing firm may use the classification procedure to explain the ratings assigned to its industrial bonds. Firms may be at a loss as to why their bonds have been assigned a given rating. The classification procedure provides a direct and easy way to check on their ratings. Conflicts between the ratings assigned by the rating agencies and this book's classification procedure may indicate that the rating agencies are concerned about qualitative factors not impounded in the model. Examples of factors include quality of management, growth plans, and so forth.

The issuing firm may use the classification procedure to predict the ratings that may be assigned to a new issue. Firms are generally at a loss when attempting to determine these ratings. The classification procedure outlined in this chapter provides a first idea of the ratings that may be assigned to them. Based on the results of the classification, firms may elect to go on with the new issue or attempt to first improve their financial conditions.

Investors may use the classification procedure to assess the investment quality of bonds. The model provides a direct and inexpensive way to classify bonds into five possible categories without resorting to the cumbersome and time-consuming univariate analysis. The issuing firm may use the classification procedure to continuously check on their investment quality and to prevent being put on the *Credit Watch* list.

CONCLUSIONS

Based on the economic rationale, the discriminant analysis model developed in this study correctly rated 72.93 percent of the ratings in an analysis sample, 67 percent of the ratings in a validation sample, 67.19 percent of the ratings in a total estimating sample, and 63.65 percent of the ratings in a control sample. Both validation and predictive ability of the model were significant. Most misclassified firms were rated in adjacent categories to the true ratings. Such a model may be useful to the rating agencies themselves if it helps them to reduce inconsistencies among individual ratings, to form a preliminary rating of a bond, or to capture and evaluate the judgments of their raters. The model may be useful to investors when corporate bonds are not rated by Fitch, Moody's, and/or Standard & Poor's. Above all, the findings should be useful to those who pay to have bonds rated. Hence, managers may form an opinion of the eventual ratings and take sound actions to improve some of the financial dimensions outlined in this study in order to achieve a better rating. The implementations of the model are briefly explained in the next chapter.

NOTES

1. George Foster, *Financial Statement Analysis* (Englewood Cliffs, N.J.: Prentice-Hall, 1978), p. 443. One exception is provided in Stewart C. Meyers, "Determinants of Corporate Borrowing," *Journal of Financial Economics* (November, 1977), pp. 147–176. Meyers argues that corporate borrowing is inversely related to the proportion of market value accounted for by "real opportunities or growth opportunities." These growth opportunities are contingent on discretionary future investment by the firm. So, issuing risky debt reduces the present market value of a firm holding growth opportunity by inducing a suboptimal investment strategy or by leading the firm and its creditor to bear

the costs of avoiding the suboptimal strategy. As Meyers admits, however, a general measure of this concept is difficult to derive from accounting data.

2. This economic rationale was first presented in Ahmed Belkaoui, "Industrial Bond Ratings: A New Look," *Financial Management* (Autumn, 1980), pp. 45–46.

3. H. C. Sherwood, *How Corporate and Municipal Debt Is Rated* (New York: John Wiley & Sons, 1976).

4. Robert S. Kaplan and Gabriel Urwitz, "Statistical Models of Bond Ratings: A Methodological Inquiry," *The Journal of Business* 52, no. 2 (1979), pp. 231–261.

5. This procedure was suggested in O. Maurice Joy and John O. Tollefson, "On the Financial Applications of Discriminant Analysis," *Journal of Financial and Quantitative Analysis* (December, 1975), pp. 726–727.

6. Ibid., p. 727.

7. Ibid., p. 728.

8. The C ratings were not included because of difficulties of ensuring adequate and sufficient representation (and also to reduce the number of categories to a manageable level).

9. The reader may be interested in testing the model on a control sample of industrial bonds rated B or above in future years, whenever information on the independent variables in those years becomes available.

10. W. J. Dixon, *BMDP Statistical Software 1981* (Berkeley and Los Angeles: University of California Press, 1981).

11. B. J. Winer, *Statistical Principles in Experimental Design*, 2nd ed. (New York: McGraw-Hill, 1971), p. 845.

12. Robert A. Eisenbeis, Gary G. Gilbert, and Robert B. Avery, "Investigating the Relative Importance of Individual Variables and Variable Subsets in Discriminant Analysis," *Communications in Statistics* (September, 1973), pp. 205–219.

13. William M. Cooley and P. R. Lohnes, *Multivariate Data Analysis* (New York: John Wiley & Sons, 1971).

14. F. Mosteller and R. R. Bush, "Selecting Quantitative Techniques," in G. Undzey, ed., *Handbook of Social Psychology*, vol. I (Reading, Mass.: Addison-Wesley, 1954), pp. 289–334.

SUGGESTED READINGS

Belkaoui, Ahmed. *Accounting Theory*. New York: Harcourt Brace Jovanovich, 1981.
———. "Industrial Bond Ratings: A New Look." *Financial Management* (Autumn, 1980), pp. 44–51.
Belkaoui, Ahmed. *Industrial Bonds and the Ratings Process*. Westport, Conn.: Greenwood, 1983.
Cooley, William M., and P. R. Lohnes. *Multivariate Data Analysis*. New York: John Wiley & Sons, 1971.
Dixon, W. J. *BMDP Statistical Software 1981*. Berkeley and Los Angeles: University of California Press, 1981.
Eisenbeis, Robert A., Gary G. Gilbert, and Robert B. Avery. "Investigating the Relative Importance of Individual Variables and Variable Subsets in Discriminant Analysis." *Communications in Statistics* (September, 1973), pp. 205–219.
Foster, George. *Financial Statement Analysis*. Englewood Cliffs, N.J.: Prentice-Hall, 1978.

Horrigan, J. O. "The Determinant of Long-Term Credit Standing with Financial Ratios." *Empirical Research in Accounting: Selected Studies*, 1966. Supplement to *Journal of Accounting Research* (1966), pp. 44–62.

Joy, O. Maurice, and John O. Toffelson. "On the Financial Applications of Discriminant Analysis." *Journal of Financial and Quantitative Analysis* (December, 1975), pp. 783–793.

Kaplan, Robert S., and Gabriel Urwitz. "Statistical Models of Bond Ratings: A Methodological Inquiry." *Journal of Business* 52, no. 2 (1979), pp. 231–261.

Mosteller, F., and R. R. Bush. "Selecting Quantitative Techniques." In G. Undzey, ed., *Handbook of Social Psychology*, vol. I. Reading, Mass.: Addison-Wesley, 1954, pp. 289–334.

Pinches, G. E., and K. A. Mingo. "A Multivariate Analysis of Industrial Bond Ratings." *Journal of Finance* (March, 1973), pp. 1–18.

West, R. R. "An Alternative Approach to Predicting Corporate Bond Ratings." *Journal of Accounting Research* (Spring, 1970), pp. 118–127.

Winer, B. J. *Statistical Principles in Experimental Design*, 2nd ed. New York: McGraw-Hill, 1971.

5

The Accounting Validation of the Dual-Labor Theory

INTRODUCTION

The dual-economy and the dual-labor-market paradigms are often included within the broadly defined field of radical economics. This umbrella term describes a discipline that focuses on those phenomena contaminating what others see as the economic order. Seven examples of these phenomena include (1) unequal distribution of income, wealth, and power within individual countries; (2) maldistribution of resources within individual countries; (3) failure to internalize the set of social costs involved in the term "quality of life"; (4) militarism or racial discrimination; (5) "economic imperialism" and "neo-colonialism"; (6) an inefficient reward system paying better for virtuoso solutions to the "wrong" (primary technical) problems than for thinking seriously about the dangerous ones; and (7) an erroneous "one-dimensional" view of human nature as producing, consuming, and nothing more.[1]

The dual-economy paradigm with its emphasis on the differences in economic organization within social structures is not a very recent phenomenon. One may cite J. H. Boeke's model of economic dualism contrasting Western capitalist and traditional agricultural societies and stressing the function of such economic dualism for colonial economic development,[2] Furnivall's portrayal of social and economic segmentation in the Far Eastern colonies as a "plural society,"[3,4] and more recently, a set of studies of local urban labor markets conducted in advanced capitalist societies where labor markets are defined as either "primary" or "secondary."[5-8]

The two major components of the paradigm refer either to the economic organization of firms, as in the dual-economy theory, or to the description of the labor force and labor-market characteristics as in the dual-labor market. The

relationship between both generally relies on the assumption that the features of
the economic organization of firms are reflected in labor-market outcomes.

This sectorial view of the economy was introduced as a vehicle to address
persistent social problems that have not vanished in spite of the so-called attempts at resolving them. In advanced capitalist societies, these social problems
are considered structural features of the general system and include the persistence of large numbers of people living below the poverty level; gender and
racial inequalities, despite the existence of legislation and education and training
spending; and the degree of alienation in both blue-collar and white-collar workers. The dual model is a distinct analytical construct derived from two hypotheses: one locates its roots in the flux and uncertainty inherent in the economic
system and in the uneven impact of these parameters on various factors of
production and different groups of workers; the other hypothesis is based on the
outgrowth of the process of the division of labor.[9] Dualism, in fact, encompasses
three main characteristics: namely, the existence of a dual economy reflecting
the organization of capital, the existence of dual-labor market in thin capital
structures, and a set of outcomes facing the workers as a result of these duali-
ties.[10]

Most dual-economy validation attempts take place within economic and/or
sociological frameworks and focus on industry as the level of analysis. This
chapter proposes an accounting test that combines both univariate and multivariate tests, uses the firm as the unit of analysis, and uses accounting financial
variables as the dimensions most likely to delineate between firms in the core
and peripheral sectors. Before providing the results of both univariate and multivariate accounting tests, this chapter covers empirical attempts in economics
and sociology to develop a test of the dual-economy and/or dual-labor markets.

DEFINING INDUSTRIAL SECTORS EMPIRICALLY

The basic purpose of empirical research on dualism is to differentiate, on the
basis of empirical measures, among a monopoly, a core sector, and a competitive
or peripheral sector. The earlier literature on dualism was descriptive in nature,
focusing on a proper definition of the two sectors as monopoly and competitive,[11] core and periphery,[12] planning and market economies,[13] and concentrated
and unconcentrated.[14] The common description of these sectors was that the
core sector was characterized by oligopolistic or monopolistic firms with high
capitalization, large profits and revenues, high production, and high rates of
unionization, while the periphery sector was characterized by competitive firms
with low capitalization, small profit and size, low productivity, low levels of
technology, and high labor intensity.

In examining the operationalization of the industrial sectors of the U.S. economy, the industry rather than the firm was chosen as the unit of analysis based
on the argument that firms in industries are similar in terms of technologies and

organizational forms and face similar variation in the demands for their products.[15–17]

Quasi-Empirical Attempts at Defining Industrial Sectors

Previous attempts to delineate empirically between the two sectors of the U.S. economy relied on either Averitt's narrative description of the two sectors (as in the case of a study by Bibb and Form[18]) or Bluestone, Murphy, and Stevenson's description of industries[19] (as in a study by Beck, Horan, and Tolbert[20]). A comparison of the classification of industries into peripheral and core sectors appeared in these studies.

Empirical Attempts at Defining Industrial Sectors

Oster's Study

Oster used a factor-analysis technique to provide a test of the theory of the dual economy.[21] He rationalized his use of the factor-analytic technique as follows:

If a core-periphery pattern of stratification is characteristic of the American industrial structure, then from a factor analysis of a broad range of characteristics from a wide spectrum of industries, a "dual economy" factor should emerge. This factor should "load" significantly on those dimensions of industrial variation (e.g., concentration, capital intensity, etc.) discussed in the dual economy literature. Further, the distribution of industry (i.e., factor) scores on this particular factor should reflect (based upon nine predetermined criterion, e.g., bimodality) the proposed duality of core and peripheral industries.[22]

Twenty-four variables are used in Oster's factor analysis based on guidance from the dual-economy literature. They are as follows:

1. Depreciable assets/productive workers for 1965
2. Percentage employment in industry for 1960
3. Median years schooling of females for 1960
4. Median years schooling of males for 1960
5. Percentage black female employment for 1960
6. Percentage white female employment for 1960
7. Average layoffs of 100 workers in 1961, 1965, and 1967
8. Average percentage of total industry receipts accounted for by firms with total assets greater than $100 million in 1958, 1961, and 1965
9. Government purchases/total industry receipts in 1958
10. Government purchases plus exports over total industry for 1958

11. Average after-tax income over total assets for 1953 to 1966

12. Percentage black employment in 1960

13. Percentage female employment in 1960

14. Percentage total minority employment in 1960

15. Percentage industry unionization in 1960

16. Average industry total assets from 1953 to 1966

17. Average industry total receipts for 1953 to 1966

18. 1953 to 1963 value added per worker-hour

19. Capital expenditure per production worker in 1963

20. Four-firm concentration ration in 1963

21. Index of establishment size in 1960

22. 1950–1960 industry employment

23. Percentage self-employment increase in 1960

24. Annual hours per male production worker in 1960[23]

Both variance- and principle-factor techniques were used, yielding three factors: a dual economy factor, a gender factor, and a race factor. The dual-economy factor loaded significantly with the hypothesized signs in all variables, reflecting size and concentration, percentage of industry unionization, depreciable assets over production worker, median years schooling for males and females, and the 10 government-purchase variables. Therefore, Oster's factor analysis for 83 three-digit 1960 census-code industries yielded a core-periphery factor. However, Kaufman, Hodson, and Fligstein criticized Oster's study on the following points:

While Oster presents a number of well-conceived measures of industrial structure there are problems both with the industrial coverage of his data and with his interpretation of the results. Oster does not collect data for the retail, wholesale service, and financial industries. One can question, then, whether or not the dualism which Oster finds represents the economy as a whole. One also wonders what part these excluded industries would play in a more inclusive classification scheme. This inclusion of measures of stability and secularity raises a question of circularity. If one were to attempt to use his results for the testing of hypothesis about these particular labor market outcomes, the analysis would be contaminated by the inclusion of these outcomes as defining characteristics.[24]

Tolbert, Horan, and Beck's Study

Tolbert, Horan, and Beck provide another example of an empirical effort for a measure of economic segmentation.[25] Their effort is drawn from Shepherd's attempts to base the designation of competitive and oligopolistic economic sectors on a set of multiple indicators.[26,27] They grouped the indicators to be used into three categories: (1) measures of the capacity for the oligopoly in an industry, (2) measures of oligopolistic behavior in an industrial product market, and (3) measures of oligopolistic behavior in the industrial labor market. Measures of capacity for oligopoly included a traditional measure of market concentration and several measures of economic scale, including assets, receipts, and number of workers. Measures of oligopolistic behavior in an industrial product market included levels of the advertising expenditures and political contributions and profits. Measures of oligopolistic behavior in the industrial labor market included a measure of the relative size of the bureaucratic workforce and measures of the internal labor-market development in an industry that include unionization, levels of wages, fringe benefits, and job stability in both the short run and the longer run.

A factor analysis on a reduced set of these variables yielded a unidimensional solution. The variables loading in this dimension were found to covary in a manner consistent with dual-economic theory. Factor scores for this section were computed for each industry, with core industries scoring positively and periphery industries scoring negatively. The workers in the two sectors were also found, as expected, to differ significantly in terms of annual earnings, gender, race, years of schooling, and occupational prestige, with the core sector leading the periphery sector. The results were not accepted without various reservations. Hodson and Kaufman raise three important criticisms:

While we think their task is a significant one, serious flaws exist in Tolbert et al.'s theoretical and empirical analysis. Most important, their conceptualization is contaminated by a circularity between the defining characteristics of economic segmentation and outcomes resulting from economic segmentation. Second, their reported finding of one factor solution is incorrect. At least two factors are needed to represent the data adequately. Third, their categorization of factor scores in two sectors is arbitrary. Given the shortcomings, their measure of economic segmentation cannot be used for the analysis of labor market outcome.[28]

Other criticisms were raised by Kaufman, Hodson, and Fligstein as follows:

Even if we were willing to ignore the circularity in the analysis of Tolbert et al., there are still problems concerning the data and methodology. The high degree which they employ, which is not necessarily for many of their indicators, reduces the total variation of industrial differences. Their choice of a cutting point to dichotomize the factor scores is arbitrary since there are four other breaks of comparable magnitude within 1.25 standard deviation of the mean which one could use to define two to six sectors.[29]

Kaufman, Hodson, and Fligstein's Study

Kaufman, Hodson, and Fligstein criticized the preceding two studies because of problems in the coverage of data for reasonably detailed industries and problems in the methodology used.[30] They also hypothesized that the strategy, structure, and technology of firms interact to produce a much more differentiated economy than the dual economy. Using the 10 constructs of concentration, size, capital intensity or labor intensity, foreign involvement, government intervention, profit, conglomerate domination, productivity, unionization, and growth and supporting variables, they obtained a 25-factor solution. For each industry factor, scores were computed for each of 25 factors, which then were used in a hierarchical clustering procedure that generated 15 cluster sectors: (1) oligopoly, (2) core, (3) wholesale, (4) periphery, (5) small-shop, (6) core utilities, (7) finance, (8) periphery utilities, (9) core transport, (10) periphery transport, (11) local monopoly sector, (12) brokers, (13) real estate, (14) ordinance, and (15) tobacco.

ACCOUNTING MODEL OF VALIDATION

All the studies cited above used the industry rather than the firm as the unit of analysis based on the argument that firms in industries are similar in technologies and organizational forms and face similar variations in the demands for their products.[31] In addition, these studies relied on macroeconomic and industry-land variables. This chapter uses the firm as the unit of analysis and financial and accounting variables as the explanatory variables. This implies the existence of fundamental differences in the financial characteristics of the firms from the two sectors of the economy. The suggested hypothesis here is that there are certain dependent variables among the popular financial ratios used in financial analysis and in research that are more similar among firms that occupy the same sector than among firms that occupy different economic sectors. This is modeled as

$$Fics = Fips$$

where

Fics = financial variable in the core sector
Fips = financial variable in the periphery sector

The hypothesis is that Fics will be different from Fips.

RESEARCH METHODOLOGY

Data

The sample contains the total usable population of firms from both the primary, secondary, tertiary, and full-coverage tapes of Compustat for the 20-year period 1968–1988. In addition, three noncontiguous years (1978, 1983, and 1988) were examined. The three years are recent enough to be representative of the current situation and far enough apart to illustrate past conditions. The firms are grouped as core or periphery based on a sectoral classification provided in Exhibit 5.1.

Accounting Characteristics Examined

The variables examined include financial and accounting ratios dealing with capital structure, liquidity, profitability, turnover, price-earnings ratio, and systematic or market risk. They represent the conventional accounting ratios used in regular financial analysis and investment evaluation.

Methods

Three methods were used for the accounting model of validation. The first method was a univariate ratio comparison of firms in the core sector and firms in the periphery sectors over the total sample of firms in the 20-year period 1968–1988.

The second method was similar to the first method except that the univariate ratio analysis was limited to three noncontiguous years: 1978, 1983, and 1988. In addition, because of the usual skewing of these types of data and the resulting departures from normality and accepted practice, the top and bottom 1 percent of results were trimmed to remove extreme outliers and to reduce observed departures from normality.[32]

The third method consisted of deriving a function in 1983 based on the significant ratios found in method two.

RESULTS

Twenty-Year Univariate Analysis

The 20-year univariate analysis consisted of a comparison of the 20-year mean of known accounting variables and ratios between the firms in the core and periphery sectors. The variables used included measures of the size (market value of equity, logarithm of market value of equity, logarithm of total assets, and logarithm of total revenues), measures of financial performance (price-earnings ratio and return on common equity), measures of leverage (long-term debt/total assets), measures of turnover (accounts receivable turnover), and measures of liquidity (sales/working capital and current assets/current liabilities). As shown in Exhibit 5.2 the differences between these variables in the core and periphery sectors were highly significant at levels of confidence below 10 percent.

Univariate Analysis for Three Noncontiguous Years

Some of the variables included in the second univariate analysis were firm size (total assets, market value of equity, and total revenues), leverage (total

Exhibit 5.1
Sectoral Classifications

Industry Group	Sector
Agriculture, forestry, and fisheries	Periphery
Mining	
Metal Mining	Core
Coal Mining	Core
Crude petroleum and natural gas	Core
Nonmetallic mining and quarrying	Core
Construction	Core
Durable Manufacturing	
Lumber and wood products	Periphery
Furniture and fixtures	Periphery
Stone, clay, and glass products	Core
Metal industries	Core
Machinery, except electrical	Core
Electrical machinery, equipment, supplies	Core
Transportation equipment	Core
Professional and photographic equipment	Core
Ordnance	Core
Miscellaneous durable manufacturing	Periphery
Nondurable Manufacturing	
Food and kindred products	Periphery
Tobacco Manufacturers	Periphery
Textile mill products	Periphery
Apparel and other fabricated textiles	Periphery
Paper and allied products	Core
Printing, publishing, and allied industries	Core
Chemical and allied products	Core
Petroleum and coal products	Core
Rubber and miscellaneous plastic products	Core
Leather and leather products	Periphery
Not specified nondurable manufacturing	Periphery
Transportation	
Railroads and railway express service	Core
Street railways and bus lines	Core
Taxicab service	Core
Trucking service	Core
Warehousing and storage	Core
Water transportation	Core
Petroleum and gasoline pipelines	Core
Services incidental to transportation	Core
Communications	
Radio broadcasting and television	Core
Telephone (wire and radio)	Core
Telegraph (wire and radio)	Core

Exhibit 5.1 (Continued)

Industry Group	Sector
Utilities and sanitary services	
Electric light and power	Core
Gas, steam, and supply systems	Core
Electric-gas utilities	Core
Water supply	Core
Sanitation services	Core
Other not specified utilities	Core
Wholesale trade	Core
Retail trade	Periphery
Finance, insurance, and real estate	Core
Business and repair services	Periphery
Personal services	Periphery
Entertainment and recreation services	Periphery
Professional and related services	Core
Public administration	Core

liabilities/market value of common equity), profitability as return on assets (net income before taxes and extraordinary items/total assets), and profitability as return on equity (net income/common equity). Other ratios examined included the following: working-capital ratio, sales/total assets, cash/sales, working capital/sales, debt-service coverage, and price-earnings ratio (definitions of the ratios examined are found in Exhibit 5.3). The following results were obtained.

Firm Size. Firm size was measured as market value of equity, total assets, total revenues, and market value of equity plus book value of debt plus preferred stock. For each of the size measures, and for each of the years examined, the median and mean sizes of the core companies were drastically larger than those of the periphery companies. In all cases, the mean effect of core/periphery distinction is significant at $\alpha = 0.10$ or less.

Rate of Return. Rate of return was measured as either rate of return on assets or rate on common equity for 1978, 1983, and 1988. With one exception, the means of the rate of return measures of the core companies were lower than those of the periphery companies. The exception is for the rate of return on common equity in 1988. However, with no exception, the medians of the rate of return measures of the core companies were lower than that of the periphery companies. With two exceptions, the main effect of core/periphery distinction is significant at $\alpha = 0.10$ less. The exceptions are both rate of return measures in 1988.

Liquidity. Liquidity was measured by the current ratio. For each of the three years, the medians and the means of the currents ratio were higher for the core companies than those of the periphery companies. In all cases, the main effect of the core/periphery distinction is significant at $\alpha = 0.01$.

Exhibit 5.2
Twenty-Year Univariate Analysis

	Core Sector		Periphery Sector			
Variables	Number of Firms	Mean	Number of Firms	Mean	F value	Prob > F
Price-Earnings Ratio	7986	10.99	1100	14.10	2.60	0.09
Accounts Receivable Turnover	7105	47887.90	1079	16.95	6.33	0.0117
Sales/Working Capital	6735	10.47	1061	−13.13	2.96	0.085
Long-Term Debt/ Total Assets	8060	0.20	1118	0.22	8.06	0.0045
Market Value of Equity	8062	642.88	1118	371.59	10.94	0.0009
Logarithm of Market Value of Equity	8058	4.32	1116	4.09	10.94	0.0009
Current Assets/ Current Liabilities	6747	2.79	1065	2.07	5.78	0.0162
Return on Common Equity	8062	−0.01	1112	0.38	4.24	0.0395
Logarithm of Total Assets	8062	5.08	1118	4.59	45.27	0.0001
Logarithm of Total Revenues	8031	4.82	1113	4.98	5.27	0.0218

Exhibit 5.3
Variables and Definitions

DEFINITION	(VARIABLE)	=	(COMPUSTAT DATA ITEMS)
Size			
Market Value of Equity	(MVE)	=	[D24 * D24]
Total Assets	(TA)	=	[D6]
Total Revenue	(TR)	=	[D12]
MVE + Debt + Preferred Debt	(MVEP)	=	[(D24 * D24) + D9 + D10]
Rate of Return			
Return on Assets	(ROA)	=	[D18 + (D15 * (1 −D16/D170)) /(D6 + D7 − D8)]
Return on Common Equity	(ROE)	=	[(D18 − D19) / D60]
Liquidity Current Ratio	(CR)	=	[D4 / D5]
Leverage			
Total Debt/ MV of Equity	(TDMV)	=	[(D9 + D34) / (D24 * D25)]
L.T. Debt / Total Assets	(DLTA)	=	[D9 / D6]
L.T. Debt / Invested Capital	(DLIC)	=	[D9 / D37]
Fixed Charges Coverage Ratio	(FCR)	=	[(D170 + D15) / (D15 + D34 +D19)]
Price Earnings Ratio	(PE)	=	[D24/ D58]
Turnover (Sales)			
Sales Inventory Turnover	(SIT)	=	[D12 / D3]
Sales Receivable Turnover	(SRT)	=	[D12 / D2]
Capital Intensity			
Gross Plant / Sales	(CIS)	=	[D7 / D12]
Depreciable / Total Expenses	(CDS)	=	[D14 / (D12 − D13)]
Market Betas	(BETA)	=	Annual Returns (Market model)

Leverage. For measures of leverage, we used total debt/market value equity, long-term debt/total assets, long-term debt/invested capital, and fixed coverage ratio. For each of the three years examined, and for each of the leverage measures used, the means and the medians of the core companies were lower than those of the periphery companies. With few exceptions, the main effect of the core/periphery distinction was significant at $\alpha = 0.10$ or less. The exceptions are total debt/market value of equity for 1978 and 1988, long-term debt/total assets for 1983, long-term debt/invested capital for 1983, and fixed charge coverage ratio for 1978 and 1983.

Price-Earnings Ratio. Both the means and the medians for the core companies for each of the three years were lower than those for the periphery companies. For each of the turnover measures used, the means and medians of the core companies were greater than those of the periphery companies. The main effect of the core/periphery distinction was significant at $\alpha = 0.10$ or less for both measures and for the three years examined.

Capital Intensity. For measures of capital intensity, we used gross plant and equipment over sales and depreciation over total expenses. For each of the capital intensity measures used, the means and the medians of the companies in the core sector were elastically higher than the companies in the periphery sector. The main effect of the core/periphery distinction is significant at $\alpha = 0.10$ or less for both measures and for the three years examined.

Market Betas. Market betas were generated using annual returns (a minimum of 7 and a maximum of 14 observations were required) based on the market model. Betas were based on annual returns to make them consistent with the other ratios, given the lack of monthly returns data for the smaller firms, especially in earlier periods, and because annual betas are not biased by size as are shorter period betas.[33] Market betas were computed for the entire period for each of the firms in both groups. The means and the medians of the periphery companies were drastically larger than those of the core companies. The main effect was highly significant. The results of all the univariate analyses for the three noncontiguous years are shown in Exhibit 5.4.

Multivariate Analysis

The multivariate analysis was performed on the 1988 data. The statistical methodology adopted is the maximum likelihood logit regression.[34] A logit model of the following general form is illustrated as follows:

$$\text{In} (P\text{csi}/1 - P\text{csi}) = B0 + B1BEi + B2TAi + B3ROEi + B4CRi + B54DLTAi + B6FCRi + B7PEi + B8CISi$$

where

BEi = Systematic risk of firm i
TAi = Total assets of firm i

Exhibit 5.4
Summary of Main Effects, Univariate Analysis

Definition	Variable	CS	MS
Size			
Market Value of Equity	MVE	*	
Total Assets	TA	*	
Total Revenue	TR	*	
MVE + Debt + Preferred Debt	MVEP	*	
Rate of Return			
Return on Assets	ROA		
Return on Common Equity	ROE		
Liquidity			
Current Ratio	CR	*	
Leverage			
Total Debt/MVE	TDMV		*
Long-Term Debt/TA	DLTA		*
LTD/Invested Capital	DLIC		*
Fixed Coverage Ratio	FCR		*
Price Earnings Ratio	PE	*	
Turnover (Sales)			
Sales Inventory Turnover	SIT	*	
Sales Receivable Turnover	SRT	*	
Capital Intensity			
Gross Plant/Sales	CIS	*	
Depreciation/Total Expenses	CDS	*	
Market Betas	Beta	*	

Abbreviation:

CS: Consistently Significant (every year)

MS: Mixed Significant (one or two years)

DI: Dual Class where 0 = core, 1 = periphery

Exhibit 5.5
Logistic Model of Dual-Economy Classes Data for 1988 ($n = 1,423$)

Variable	Coefficient Beta	Standard Error	Chi-Square	Probability
Intercept	(1.2537)	0.3308	14.36	0.0002
BETA	0.1824	0.0719	6.44	0.0112
TA-F5	(0.000023)	0.000005	0.17	0.6803
ROE-F5	(0.46669)	0.7216	0.42	0.5178
CR-F5	(0.5217)	0.1164	20.08	0
DLTA-F5	1.8645	0.49221	14.35	0.0002
FCR-F5	0.0973	0.02735	12.68	0.0004
PE-F5	0.01820	0.00949	3.68	0.0552
CIS-F5	(-1.3282)	0.25167	27.85	0

ROE_i = Rate of return on equity of firm i

CR_i = Current ratio of firm i

$DLTA_i$ = Long-term debt over total assets of firm i

FCR_i = Fixed-charge coverage ratio of firm i

PE_i = Price-earnings ratio of firm i

CIS_i = Capital-intensity ratio of firm i

Exhibit 5.5 presents the results of the logistic model using the complete sample of firms in the core and periphery sectors for 1988. With the exception of total assets and rate of return on equity, all the other variables were significant at $\alpha < 0.05$. They provide an accounting test of the dual economy that allows a distinction between firms and periphery sectors.

CONCLUSION

This chapter investigates whether the distinction between firms in the core and periphery sectors can be made on the basis of accounting variables. Both univariate and multivariate tests were used. The methodology differs from previous studies in economics and sociology by using the firm as the unit of analysis and relying on accounting data rather than industry data. The univariate analysis identified size, turnover, capital intensity, and market beta as delineating factors between firms in the core and periphery sectors. The multivariate logit model also identified a significant accounting test of the dual-economy paradigm based on systematic risk, current ratio, leverage, fixed charge coverage ratio, price-earnings ratio, and capital intensity. These results point to the usefulness of a multivariate accounting test in delineating between firms in the core and periphery sectors and to the need to develop separate prediction models of economic events for both sectors.

NOTES

1. M. Brofenbrenner, "Radical Economics in America: A 1970 Survey," *Journal of Economic Literature* (September, 1970), pp. 749–775.
2. J. H. Boeke, *Economies and Economic Policy of Dual Societies* (Haarlem: Tjeenk Willink, 1983).
3. J. S. Furnivall, *Netherlands and India: A Study of Plural Economy* (New York: Macmillan, 1944).
4. J. S. Furnivall, *Colonial Policy and Practice* (London: Cambridge University Press, 1948).
5. H. M. Baron and B. Hymer, "The Negro Worker in the Chicago Labor Market," in J. Jacobson, ed., *The Negro and the American Labor Movement* (New York: Doubleday, 1968), pp. 232–285.
6. H. M. Wachtel, "The Impact of Labor Market Conditions on Hard-Core Unemployment," *Poverty and Human Resources* (July–August, 1970), pp. 5–13.
7. T. Victoisz and B. Harrison, *The Economic Development of Harlem* (New York: Praeger, 1970).
8. B. Harrison, *Education, Training, and the Urban Ghetto* (Baltimore: Johns Hopkins University Press, 1972).
9. S. Berger and M. J. Piore, *Dualism and Discontinuity in Industrial Societies* (Cambridge: Cambridge University Press, 1980), p. 15.
10. R. Hodson and R. L. Kaufman, "Economic Dualism: A Critical Review," *American Sociological Review* (December, 1982), pp. 727–739.
11. J. O'Connor, *The Fiscal Crisis of the State* (New York: St. Martin's Press, 1973).
12. R. T. Averitt, *The Dual Economy: The Dynamics of American Industry Structure* (New York: W. W. Norton, 1968).
13. J. K. Galbraith, *Economics and the Public Purpose* (Boston: Houghton Mifflin, 1973).
14. B. Bluestone, "The Tripartite Economy: Labor Markets and the Working Poor," *Poverty and Human Resource Abstracts* 5 (1970), pp. 15–35.
15. S. Spilerman, "Careers, Labor Market Structure, and Socioeconomic Achievement," *American Journal of Sociology* 83 (1977), pp. 551–593.
16. C. Tolbert, P. Horan, and E. M. Beck, "The Structure of Economic Segmentation: A Dual Economy Approach," *American Journal of Sociology* 85 (1980), pp. 1095–1116.
17. B. Bluestone, W. Murphy, and M. Stevenson, *Low Wages and the Working Poor* (Ann Arbor: Institute of Labor and Industrial Relations, University of Michigan, 1973).
18. R. Bibb and W. Form, "The Effects of Industrial, Occupational, and Sex Stratification on Wages in Blue-Collar Markets," *Social Forces* 55 (1977), pp. 974–996.
19. Bluestone, Murphy, and Stevenson, *Low Wages and the Working Poor.*
20. E. M. Beck, P. M. Horan, and C. M. Tolbert II, "Stratification in a Dual Economy: A Sectoral Model of Earnings Determination," *American Sociological Review* 43 (1978), pp. 704–720.
21. G. Oster, "A Factor Analytic Test of the Theory of the Dual Economy," *Review of Economics and Statistics* 61 (1979), pp. 33–39.

22. Ibid.

23. Ibid., p. 35.

24. R. L. Kaufman, R. Hodson, and N. D. Fligstein, "Defrocking Dualism: A New Approach to Defining Industrial Sectors," *Social Sciences Research* 10 (1981), p. 60.

25. Tolbert, Horan, and Beck, "The Structure of Economic Segmentation."

26. W. G. Shepherd, *Market Power and Economic Welfare* (New York: Random House, 1970).

27. W. G. Shepherd, *Economics of Industrial Organization* (Englewood Cliffs, NJ: Prentice-Hall, 1979).

28. R. D. Hodson and R. L. Kaufman, "Circulating in the Dual Economy: Comment on Tolbert, Horan, and Beck," *American Journal of Sociology* 86 (1980), p. 882.

29. Kaufman, Hodson, and Fligstein, "Defrocking Dualism," pp. 5–6.

30. Ibid.

31. Spilerman, "Careers, Labor Market Structure and Socioeconomic Achievement."

32. G. Foster, *Financial Statement Analysis* (Englewood Cliffs, NJ: Prentice-Hall, 1986).

33. H. Puneet, S. P. Kothari, and C. Wasley, "The Relation between the Return Interval and Betas: Implication for the Size Effect," *Journal of Financial Economics* 23 (1989), pp. 79–100.

34. The probability of a firm in the core sector is Pcs, while the probability that it will be in the core sector is $1 - $ Pcs. Therefore, the predicted value of the dependent variable is the maximum likelihood estimate of the natural logarithm of the odds that the firm in question is in the core sector.

SUGGESTED READINGS

Averitt, R. T. *The Dual Economy: The Dynamics of American Industry Structure*. New York: W.W. Norton, 1968.

Baran, P. A., and P. M. Sweezy. *Monopoly Capital*. New York: Monthly Review Press, 1966.

Bavishi, B. F., F. Choi, and H. Shawky. "Analysing the Financial Ratio of the World's 1000 Leading Industrial Companies." *Business International* (1981), pp. 135–170.

Beck, E. M., P. N. Horan, and C. M. Tolbert II. "Stratification in a Dual Economy: A Sectoral Model of Earnings Determination." *American Sociological Review* 43 (1978), pp. 704–720.

Bibb, R., and W. Form. "The Effects of Industrial, Occupational, and Sex Stratification on Wages in Blue-Collar Markets." *Social Forces* 55 (1977), pp. 974–996.

Bluestone, B. "The Tripartite Economy: Labor Markets and the Working Poor." *Poverty and the Human Resource Abstracts* 5 (1970), pp. 15–35.

Bluestone, B., W. M. Murphy, and M. Stevenson. *Low Wages and the Working Poor*. Ann Arbor: Institute of Labor and Industrial Relations, University of Michigan, 1973.

Blume, M., and R. Stambaugh. "Biases in Computed Returns: An Implication to the Size Effect." *Journal of Financial Economics* 12 (1983), pp. 387–404.

Bourgeois, J., G. H. Haines, and M. S. Sommers. "Defining an Industry." In D. B. Montgomery and D. R. Wittink, eds., *Market Measurement and Analysis*. Cambridge, MA: Marketing Science Institute, 1980, pp. 120–133.

Bowen, R. M., L. A. Daley, and C. C. Huber. "Evidence on the Existence and Determinants of Inter-Industry Differences in Leverage." *Financial Management* (Winter, 1982), pp. 10–20.

Brown, P., and R. Ball. "Some Preliminary Findings on the Association between the Earnings of a Firm, Its Industry, and the Economy," Empirical Research in Accounting: Selected Studies. *Journal of Accounting Research* (Supplement, 1967), pp. 55–77.

Brown, P., A. W. Kleidon, and T. A. Marsh. "New Evidence on the Nature of Size Related Anomalies in Stock Prices." *Journal of Financial Economics* 12 (1983), pp. 33–56.

Cain, G. C. "The Challenge of Segmented Labor Market Theories to Orthodox Theory: A Survey." *Journal of Economic Literature* 14 (1976), pp. 1215–1257.

Foster, G. *Financial Statement Analysis*. Englewood Cliffs, N.J.: Prentice-Hall, 1986.

Galbraith, J. K. *Economics and the Public Purpose*. Boston: Houghton Mifflin, 1973.

Harrison, B. "The Theory of the Dual Economy." In B. Silverman and M. Yanovitch, eds., *The Worker in "Post Industrial" Capitalism*. New York: Free Press, 1974, pp. 269–282.

Hodson, R. "Labor in the Monopoly, Competitive, and State Sectors of Production." *Politics and Society* 8 (1978), pp. 429–480.

Hodson, R., and R. L. Kaufman. "Economic Dualism: A Critical Review." *American Sociological Review* (December, 1982), pp. 727–739.

Johnston, J. *Economic Methods*, 2nd ed. New York: McGraw-Hill, 1972.

Keim, D. B. "Size Related Anomalies and Stock Return Seasonality: Further Empirical Evidence." *Journal of Financial Economics* 12 (1983), pp. 13–32.

King, B. F. "Market and Industry Factors in Stock Market Price Behavior." *Journal of Business* 39 (1966), pp. 139–190.

Kinney, W. R. "Empirical Accounting Research Design for Ph.D. Students." *The Accounting Review* 61 (1986), pp. 338–350.

O'Connor, James. *The Fiscal Crisis of the State*. New York: St. Martin's Press, 1973.

Oster, G. "A Factor Analytic Test of the Theory of the Dual Economy." *Reviews of Economics and Statistics* 61 (1979), pp. 33–39.

Piore, M. "The Dual Labor Market: Theory and Implications." In *Problems in Political Economy: An Urban Perspective*. Lexington, Mass.: D.C. Heath, 1977, pp. 93–97.

Puneet, H., S. P. Kothari, and C. Wasley. "The Relation between the Return Interval and Betas: Implication for the Size Effect." *Journal of Financial Economics* 23 (1989), pp. 79–100.

Reinganum, M. R. "Misspecification of Capital Asset Pricing." *Journal of Financial Economics* 9 (1981), pp. 19–46.

Spilerman, S. "Careers, Labor Market Structure, and Socioeconomic Achievement." *American Journal of Sociology* 83 (1977), pp. 551–593.

Titman, S., and R. Wessels. "The Determinants of Capital Structure Choice." *Journal of Finance* (March, 1988), pp. 1–20.

Tolbert, C., P. Horan, and E. M. Beck. "The Structure of Economic Segmentation: A Dual Economy Approach." *American Journal of Sociology* 85 (1980), pp. 1095–1116.

Tse, S. "Attributes of Industry, Industry Segment, and Firm-Specific Information in

Security Valuation.'' *Contemporary Accounting Research* 5, no. 2 (Spring, 1988), pp. 592–614.

Watts, R. L., and J. L. Zimmerman. *Positive Accounting Theory*. Englewood Cliffs, N.J.: Prentice-Hall, 1986.

6

The Prediction
of Social Disclosure

INTRODUCTION[1]

In examining the relationship between disclosure, social performance, and economic performance, the empirical literature to date focuses on the potential relationship between (a) social disclosure and social performance, (b) social disclosure an economic performance based on either accounting or marketing variables, and (c) social performance and economic performance. Depending on the type of conceptualization and operationalization of key variables, the results range from strong correlation to no correlation. The diversity of results may be due to the failure to analyze the relationship among social disclosure, social performance, and economic performance within a single conceptual framework.[2-5]

Accordingly, this chapter develops and empirically tests a positive model of the corporate decision to disclose social information in terms of both social performance and economic performance. In short, the model tests the empirical relationship of social disclosure with both social and economic performance. The related literature is then reviewed. The next section identifies the factors influencing the decision to disclosure social information. The variables are then defined before a presentation of the empirical tests. Finally, the summary and conclusion are presented.

RELATED RESEARCH

Three types of empirical studies characterize the research on the social responsibility accounting of firms.[6]

The first type examines the potential relationships between the extensiveness of a firm's social disclosure and its social performance with the hypothesis that the quantity and the quality of social disclosure is positively correlated with its social performance.[7-13] Social disclosure was measured differently, including (a) social disclosure scale derived from Ernst and Ernst,[14] (b) percentage of prose in annual reports, (c) quality of disclosure in annual reports, and (d) quantity of disclosure in annual reports. Similarly, social performance was measured differently, including (a) reputational scales from *Business and Society Review*[15,16] (b) Moskowitz[17] reputational scales, citizenship awards; (c) CEP pollution performance index; and (d) student evaluation of industry reputation. Only two studies controlled for size. The results included no correlation in four studies, negative correlation in one study, and positive correlation in two studies.

The second type of study examines the potential relationships between social performance and economic performance, with the hypothesis that social performance and economic performance can correlated in three ways: positively, negatively, and association between extreme levels.[18-23] The measures of social performance include, in addition to those identified for the first type of studies, a measure based on the existence of social responsibility programs in five different areas.

The economic performance surrogates vary, including (a) measures of stockholder return; (b) measures of rates of return on either equity, assets, sales, or capital; (c) measures of earnings per share; (d) measures of income; and/or (e) measures of price-earning ratios. Three studies controlled for either beta, size, asset age, or asset turnover. The results show partial support for each hypothesis, that is, no correlation, U-shaped correlation, positive correlation, and spurious correlation.

Finally, the third type of study examines potential relationships between social disclosure and economic performance. The hypothesis is that (a) social disclosure reduces investors' information uncertainty and (b) social disclosures are correlated (positively and negatively) with economic performance. The first hypothesis examines the relationship between social disclosure and economic performance based on market variables.[24,25] The second hypothesis examines the relationship between social disclosure and economic performance based on accounting variables.[26] The tested accounting-based economic performance variables include, in addition to those cited for the second type of studies, a measure based on a factor of analysis of 48 accounting ratios. The various market-based economic performance measures include (a) monthly return differences, (b) monthly average residuals, (c) monthly portfolio returns, and (d) standardized abnormal mean adjusted daily returns. Most of these studies control for other variables such as size, beta, year, industry, stock ownership distribution, or industry image. Again, as in the previous two types of studies, the results vary among a continuum from negative correlation to positive correlation and include one case of U-shaped correlation.

This review of these three types of studies points to three major inconsistencies: (a) a lack of theory; (b) diversity of empirical databases examined; and (c) the absence of a single conceptual framework to analyze the relationship between social disclosure, social performance and economic performance. These inconsistencies contribute substantially to the diversity of study results. This chapter attempts to correct these limitations.

FACTORS INFLUENCING THE DECISION TO DISCLOSE SOCIAL INFORMATION

General Rationale

Research on the economic consequences of accounting choice seeks to explain firms' choices of accounting techniques and/or strategies. Using agency theory and other economic factors, these studies draw from analyses by Watts,[27] Jensen,[28] and Watts and Zimmerman.[29] These models attempt to link the choice of accounting techniques to contracting and monitoring costs, and political visibility. In general, it is hypothesized that firms facing higher contracting and monitoring costs are more likely to choose accounting methods that increase reported income, and firms with high political visibility are more likely to choose income-decreasing techniques.[30]

Specific and material expenditures are necessary to achieve social performance goals. The same expenditures reduce net income. While the image-building and public interest concerns may govern the decision to spend for social performance and to disclose social information, more practical considerations may also play a role. In particular, social performance can have a material effect on the current period's reported net income and on key financial variables that are constrained by contractual agreements. Therefore, following the agency framework rationale, given that the decision to disclose social information follows a decrease in reported net income resulting from social performance outlays, this study hypothesizes that firms with lower contracting and monitoring costs, and having high political visibility, are more likely to disclose social information. In addition, given that the outlays for social performance assume adequate resources and therefore good economic performance, the decision to disclose social information is also positively correlated with the economic performance or profitability.

Ceteris paribus, this study hypothesizes that the decision to disclose social information is positively correlated with social performance, economic performance, and political visibility and negatively correlated with contracting and monitoring costs (see Exhibit 6.1). The proxy for contracting and monitoring costs includes leverage. Proxies for political visibility to be examined include size, capital intensity, and systematic risk. The proxy for social performance includes a reputational index that lists companies exhibiting especially good or bad social performance. The detailed rationales for the hypotheses are examined next.

Exhibit 6.1
**Model of the Determinants of the Corporate Decision to Disclose Social
Information**

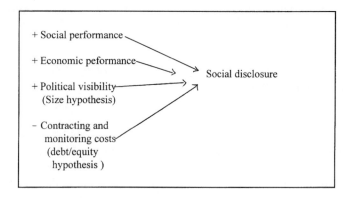

Social Performance

When a firm really engages in socially responsible types of activity involving
the outlay of resources, it is done to create an impression of sensitivity to important nonmarket influences that may be in the long-term interest of the shareholders. Managers, naturally, are eager to reveal this concern to appropriate
interest groups, shareholders, and the public in general. One practical way to
advertise this concern is through some form of social disclosure in the annual
reports. Therefore, the following hypothesis is proposed:

H_{01}: Firms disclose social information in proportion to the perceived social performance
(H_1).

Measuring social performance is difficult, however, because of its link to the
issue of organizational effectiveness: "An organization's social performance is
an indistinguishable component of its effectiveness."[31] Social performance is
adequately defined as the extent to which an organization meets the needs, expectations, and demands of certain external constituencies beyond those directly
linked to the company's products/markets. It is also referred to as participant
observation, ecological model, or external effectiveness.[32–34] Its measurement,
involving the perceptions of all external constituencies in an overall index, is at
best impractical. One approach, however, is to develop *reputational indices*,
listing companies exhibiting good or bad social performance. The one used in
this study is based on a survey conduced by *Business and Society Review* among
business people, in which 45 leading corporations were rated in terms of social
performance.

Financial Variables

The restrictive covenants included in debt agreements are intended to reduce management's ability to create wealth transfers between shareholders and bond-holders.[35,36] Common limitations include limits on financial leverage (long-term debt-to-total assets ratio) and limits on payout rates (dividends to a maximum available unrestricted retained earnings). The decision to disclose social information follows an outlay for social performance, which reduces earnings. Therefore, the following hypothesis is proposed:

H_{02}: Firms that disclose social information are less financially levered (H_2), and have lower ratios of dividends to unrestricted earnings (H_3).

Political Visibility

Politically visible firms are generally criticized by interest groups on the basis of their reported accounting numbers. Such firms can choose accounting techniques and actions that reduce their reported income and alter or reduce their political visibility. Politically visible firms are generally of larger size, have greater capital intensity, and have relatively high systematic market risk (betas). Given that the decision to disclose the social information follows an outlay for social performance that reduces earnings, incentives may exist for politically visible firms to engage in this form of disclosure.

Politically visible firms are also asked to respond to the demands of social activists. Various authors argue that many social disclosures are nothing but public relations gestures meant to ward off grassroots attacks by social activists (Fry and Hock, 1976).

Therefore, based on both arguments the following hypothesis is proposed:

H_{03}: Firms that disclose social information tend to be larger (H_4), have higher capital intensive ratios (H_5), and have higher betas (H_6).

Economic Performance

The relationship between social disclosure, social performance, and economic performance is best expressed by the view that social responsiveness requires from management the same superior skills required to make a firm profitable. As expressed by Alexander and Buchholz, "Socially aware and concerned management will also possess the requisite skills to run a superior company in the traditional sense of financial performance, thus making its firm an attractive investment."[37] Consequently, socially responsive firms in terms of social disclosure and social performance should outperform nonresponsive or less responsive ones in terms of profitability as measured by accounting variables such as a rate of return on investment, and market variables such as a differential stock price return. Therefore, the following hypothesis is proposed:

H_{04}: Firms that disclose social information tend to have greater rates of return (H_7) and greater differential stock price returns (H_8).

If this hypothesis is rejected, it gives more credence to the opposing view that socially responsible firms will be at a competitive disadvantage due to the added expense incurred by such behavior.[38]

VARIABLE DEFINITIONS

As explained earlier, this study proposes a testable model that may explain the decision to disclose social information in terms of variables measuring social performance, monitoring and contracting costs, political visibility, and economic performance. The dependent and independent variables of the model are defined as follows:

1. The decision to disclose social information has been measured in various ways in the empirical studies investigating the relationships between either social disclosure and social performance or social disclosure and economic performance. The most popular and exhaustive measure used is based on a social disclosure scale derived from Ernst and Ernst surveys of social responsibility disclosure by U.S. companies. It is used in this study in the form of the following scale: the number of social responsibility programs. The scale varies from 0 to 13. This scale will be used as the dependent variable expressing the decision to disclose and/or the extent of disclosure of social information.

2. Social performance is measured in several ways in the empirical studies cited in the related literature section. Given the difficulties of measuring social performance as organizational effectiveness, these studies generally rely on a reputational index such as that of 45 leading companies' performance based on a survey conducted by *Business and Society Review* among business people. This study relies on the survey-base reputational scale, which yields a ranking of the firms' degree of social responsibility ranging from outstanding (1) to poor (5).

3. Monitoring and contracting cost variables in this study include leverage and dividends to unrestricted retained earnings. They are measured as follows:

   (a) leverage = total debt/total assets;

   (b) dividends to unrestricted retained earnings = dividends/unrestricted retained earnings.

The variable definitions are compatible with other positive empirical studies to ensure comparability of results.

4. Political visibility proxies in this study include size, capital intensity, and systematic risk. They are measured as follows:

(a) size = log of net sales;

(b) capital-intensive ratio = gross fixed assets/sales;

(c) systematic risk = beta coefficient derived from the market model for the period 1970–1974.

Again, the political visibility variables are compatible with other positive empirical studies ensuring comparability.

5. Economic performance in this study includes rate of return and stock price return. They are measured as follows:

(a) accounting return on assets = net income/total assets;

(b) stock price return = differentiated stock price for five years 1970–1974.

EMPIRICAL TESTS

Model and Data

The various hypotheses and variables are combined into an empirically testable model specified as follows:

$$SOD = \alpha_0 + \alpha_1 SOP + \alpha_2 DR + \alpha_3 BETA + \alpha_4 LEV + \alpha_5 DIVUE$$
$$+ \alpha_6 NITA + \alpha_7 LSAL + \alpha_8 CI + e$$

where

SOD = social disclosure of the firm expressed by the number of social programs disclosed,

SOP = social performance measured as a ranking of corporation by business executives,

DR = stock price differential return,

BETA = systematic market risk,

LEV = total debt/total assets,

DIVUE = dividends/retained earnings,

NITA = net income/total assets,

LSAL = log of net sales, and

CI = capital intensity (gross fixed assets/sales).

Given this specification of the model, the sample includes firms for which information was first available for both SOD (social disclosure) and SOP (social performance). In other words, the companies had to be included in both the Ernst and Ernst social disclosure survey (Ernst and Ernst, 1973) and the survey conducted by *Business and Society Review*, ranking firms' social performance ("Industry Rates Itself," 1972). This procedure results in the sample of 23 corporations shown in Exhibit 6.2.

Exhibit 6.2
Sample of Companies Used in the Study

Company	Industry Code
IBM	3680
General Electric	3600
Ford Motor	3711
General Motors	3711
Mobil Oil	2911
Standard Oil of Indiana	2911
Chrysler	3711
RCA	3651
Westinghouse	3600
Exxon	2911
E.I. Dupont	2800
Shell Oil	2911
Union Carbide	2841
International Telephone and Telegraph	3661
General Telephone and Electric	4811
Gulf Oil	2911
Bethlehem Steel	3558
Goodyear Tire and Rubber	3000
Standard Oil of California	8911
US Steel	2911
LTV	3310
Texaco	2911
Esmark	2010

Empirical Tests of the Model—Regression Results

Based on the model, a regression was run for the year 1973. Exhibit 6.3 contains the overall regression results. The model appears highly significant: (F = 3.158, α = 0.0289), R^2 = 64.347, and $\bar{R}^2$ = 43.79 percent.

The regression coefficients for SOP, BETA, LEV, and LSAL are significant at the 0.10 level or less, and have the expected signs. In other words, the decision to disclose social information is found to be significantly associated with social performance (measured by SOP), financial monitoring and contracting costs (measured by LEV), and political visibility (measured by LSAL and BETA).

Interpretations of the regression results and the individual coefficients are contingent on the aptness of the model and are affected by the presence of multicollinearity. The remainder of this section discusses the results of the tests in each of these areas, a possible problem, and potential remedies.

The tested model appears to be well specified. Results from the various tests and plots suggested by Neter et al.[39] provide evidence that the ordinary least-squares (OLS) linear regression model is appropriate for the analysis. More specifically, statistical tests (Shapiro-Wilks' W statistical test of normality) and plots (including stem and leaf, box, and normal probability graphs) of more

Exhibit 6.3
Regression Results

Variable Definition	Intercept	Social Performance	Return	Market Risk	Leverage	Dividend Payout	Profit-ability	Size	Capital Intensity	Model Significance	
Variable	α_0	SOP	DR	BETA	LEV	DIVUE	NITA	LSAL	CI	F	R^2
Predicted Sign		-	+	+	-	+	+	+	+		
Coefficient	11.475	-0.223	80.009	10.002	-36.42	32.13	-86.13	1.020	-2.25	3.158	64.347
Standardized Estimate	0	-0.4643	0.1828	0.8505	-1.295	0.3911	-0.7480	0.4236	-0.3079		(43.97%)
t-score	1.748	-2.342	0.846	2.763	-2.705	1.396	-1.718	1.997	-1.424		
Significance	0.1023	0.0345[a]	0.4120	0.0153[a]	0.0171[a]	0.1844	0.1078	0.0657[b]	0.1764	0.0289[b]	

[a] significant at $\alpha = 0.05$.

[b] significant at $\alpha = 0.10$.

Exhibit 6.4
Correlation between Variables

				Pairwise				
Variables	SOP	DR	BETA	LEV	DIVUE	NITA	LSAL	CI
SOP	1.000							
DR	0.2248	1.000						
BETA	0.2172	-0.1528	1.000					
LEV	0.1558	-0.1905	0.75469^{a}	1.000				
DIVUE	-0.4284^{b}	-0.1637	-0.5066^{a}	-0.3479^{b}	1.000			
NITA	-0.3558	0.1823	-0.6288^{a}	-0.7710^{a}	0.5273^{a}	1.000		
LSAL	-0.4597^{b}	0.2427	-0.4683	-0.2772	0.4116^{b}	0.4877^{a}	1.000	
CI	0.1780	0.3271	-0.1878	-0.2529	0.2428	0.0962	0.1098	1.000
(Dependent) SOD	-0.5538^{a}	-0.1039	-0.0363	-0.3032	0.2888	0.4167^{b}	0.4334^{b}	-0.19086
Multiple R^2%	22.34	21.68	69.50	82.94	51.08	65.65	13.18	43.07

[a] Significant at $\alpha = 0.01$.

[b] Significant at $\alpha = 0.05$.

R^2, coefficient of multiple determination between variable i and all independent variables.

residuals indicate a linear function and an error term having a constant variance, independence, and a normal distribution.

Exhibit 6.4 results indicate the presence of multicollinearity. There are 10 pairwise correlations of independent variables, which are significant at the $P = 0.05$ level. This can adversely affect the interpretation of regression coefficients. When independent variables provide redundant information relative to the dependent variable, the individual coefficient's significance levels are usually underestimated. In some cases, the sign of the coefficient is reversed versus the zero-order relationship. There is no agreement on what constitutes a high level of multicollinearity.

The method applied by Daley and Vigeland[40] is to calculate the coefficient multiple correlation, R^2, between each variable and all the others. The rule of thumb for serious multicollinearity is a multiple correlation coefficient greater than 80 percent. Exhibit 6.4 shows only one such value, the 82.94 percent for the variable LEV (leverage), which has significant pairwise correlations with both BETA (systematic risk) and NITA (net income/total assets) at 0.75469 and −0.7710, respectively. Thus the presence of these three variables in the model makes the interpretation of each of their regression coefficients potentially misleading. While there is no cure for multiple collinearity, there are several feasible remedies that can help clarify statistical relationships among the model variables.

One approach is to delete variables, thereby directly eliminating the source of the multicollinearity. Exhibit 6.4 reports the zero-order correlations between the dependent variable SOD (number of social programmes disclosed) and each independent variable; the coefficients are significant at the level of $P = 0.05$ for SOP, NITA, and LSAL. Also run are regressions of various combinations of independent variables with SOD. The purpose was to examine the stability of the regression coefficient values as each of the three related variables (LEV, BETA, and NITA) are removed from the model. Only NITA's sign changes, removing LEV creates a positive regression coefficient for NITA. In each case, the overall model's explanatory power is reduced and the model may not be as well specified.

Another approach is to use a different statistical method, such as maximum likelihood (ML)-estimation-based ridge regression or LISREL. Adopting these methods (with their substantial complexities relative to OLS) are not warranted for this analysis because the residuals are normally distributed, so that the ML estimators are identical to those of least-squares regression (Pedhazur, 1982, p. 639).

In summary, the model is well specified and the effects of multicollinearity do not appear serious overall. The fact that some or all independent variables are correlated among themselves does not, in general, inhibit our ability to obtain a good fit nor does it tend to affect inferences about mean responses or predictions of new observations, provided these inferences are made within the region of observations. The major effect of multicollinearity appears to be an unstable estimate of the NITA regression coefficient when LEV is also in the model. This statistical phenomenon may partially explain why previous empirical studies report such varying relationships between social disclosure (SOD) and economic performance (NITA). Otherwise the reported model is well specified and its regressed coefficients stable. Deleting variables, such as LEV, to reduce multicollinearity reduces the model's explanatory power and may lead to specification errors.

Discussion

This chapter proposes a positive model of the decision to disclose social information in terms of social performance, economic performance, financial performance, and political visibility. The results verify the significant importance of (a) social performance as measured by an organizational effectiveness index, (b) financial performance as measured by leverage, and (c) political visibility as measured by size and systematic risk. These results raise fundamental issues and concerns for social responsibility in accounting.

First, the significant and positive association of social disclosure with social performances shows that social improvements by a firm are quickly capitalized by social disclosure in an attempt to create an impression of sensitivity to important nonmarket influences that may be in the long-term interest of the shareholders. It is interesting to note that those studies finding no correlation or negative correlation between social performance and social disclosure rely on either student ratings or on the CEP pollution performance index. Both indices do not, however, measure social performance per se, but rather perceived social performance by individuals who cannot be considered constituents, or pollution control records, which do not represent overall effectiveness. Future research should concentrate on the development of representative measures of overall effectiveness.

Second, the significant and positive association of social disclosure with political visibility, as measured by size and systematic risk, points to the tendency of managers to choose an accounting procedure to reduce reported earnings and political costs. This phenomenon is known as the size hypothesis. It assumes that large firms are more politically sensitive than small firms and face differential incentives in their choice of accounting procedures that lead them to defer reported earnings from current to future periods. In the context of this study, the size hypothesis is verified in the sense that the larger the firm, the more likely it is that the managers authorize outlays for social performance that defer reported earnings from current to future periods. This is consistent with other findings supporting the size hypothesis in the choice of accounting procedures.

Third, the significant negative association of social disclosure with financial leverage points to the tendency of managers with high debt/equity ratios to choose an accounting procedure that reduces reported earnings. This phenomenon is known as the debt/equity hypothesis. It assumes that the larger a firm's debt/equity ratio, the more likely the firm's manager is to select accounting procedures that shift reported earnings from future periods to the current period. In the context of this study, and because of the negative sign of leverage, the size hypothesis is also verified in the sense that the larger the debt/equity ratio of a firm, the more likely it is that a manager is going to authorize outlays for social performance that defer reported earnings from current to future periods. This is consistent with other findings supporting the debt/equity hypothesis in the choice of accounting procedures.

Fourth, the insignificant and negative regression coefficient yet positive pairwise correlation association of economic performance with social disclosure is attributed to the multicollinearity problem encountered in the study. This multicollinearity effect may also explain the observance in other studies of either positive, negative, or no correlation of probability with social disclosure.

Limitations

Various limitations point to the need for more research on the determinants of the decision to disclose social information and replication of this study under new conditions.

First, the choice of the year 1973 was made for two reasons: (a) both social disclosure measures from the Ernst and Ernst publications and social perform-ance measures for the businessmen rankings are available for that period and (b) most studies investigating the issue of the association between social disclo-sure and economic performance relied on the same measures and the same pe-riod, providing us with the opportunity of comparing our results with their findings and showing the superiority of a model of social disclosure that includes as determinants social performance, economic performance, political costs, and financial performance. Needless to say, this study should be replicated to test the model in other periods, using different measures of social disclosure and social performance.

Second, this study relied on a reputational scale as a measure of social per-formance. Studies relying on reputational scales differ in their level of refine-ment and yield conflicting results. In addition, the concept of corporate social performance is best limited to the concept of organizational effectiveness. A measurement of social performance in the context of effectiveness calls for (a) a better identification of the firm's external constituents, (b) a measurement of constituent satisfaction, and (c) the development of an overall index encom-passing these different criteria so that firms can be ranked in terms of their overall social performance.

Third, because of the data constraints on the dependent and independent var-iables, our sample is homogeneous, including companies with a rather high political visibility. Replication of this study using less politically visible com-panies and those that are more service oriented is warranted.

CONCLUSIONS

This study develops and empirically investigates a positive model of the de-cision to disclose social information in terms of social performance, economic performance, financial performance, and political visibility. Based on 1973 data, when measures in all the variables were available, the results suggest that when social performance is measured by business executive rankings, firms that dis-close social information, in terms of the number of categories of social disclo-sure disclosed in the annual report, appear to be (a) those perceived to display social responsiveness, (b) those having higher systematic risk and lower lever-age, and (c) those that are larger in size.

This research relied on the Ernst and Ernst data for a measure of social disclosure and a reputational index for a measure of social performance. More evidence is needed based on other periods, and other countries' measures of social disclosure and social performance before any generalizations can be made.

NOTES

1. This chapter has been adapted with permission of the editor from A. Belkaoui and P. G. Karpik, "Determinants of the Corporate Decision to Disclosure Social Information," *Accounting, Auditing and Accountability Journal* 2, no. 1 (1989), pp. 36–51, first published by MCB University Press.

2. R. J. Aldag and K. M. Bartol, "Empirical Studies of Corporate Social Performance and Policy: A Survey of Problems and Results," in L. E. Preston, ed., *Research in Corporate Social Performance and Policy*, vol. 1 (Greenwich, Conn.: JAI Press, 1978), pp. 165–99.

3. M. Epstein, E. Flamholtz, and J. J. McDonough, "Corporate Social Accounting in the United States of America: State of the Arts and Future Prospects," *Accounting, Organizations and Society* (December, 1976), pp. 23–42.

4. L. E. Preston, "Book Review: Teaching Materials in Business and Society," *California Management Review* (Spring, 1983), pp. 158–73.

5. A. Belkaoui, *Socio-Economic Accounting* (Westport, Conn.: Greenwood Press, 1984).

6. A. A. Ullmann, "Data in Search of a Theory: A Critical Examination of the Relationships among Social Performance, Social Disclosure, and Economic Performance of U.S. Firms," *Academy of Management Review* 10 (1985), pp. 540–557.

7. W. F. Abbott and R. J. Monsen, "On the Measurement of Corporate Social Responsibility: Self-Reported Disclosure as a Method of Measuring Corporate Social Involvement," *Academy of Management Journal* 22 (1979), pp. 501–515.

8. E. H. Bowman and M. Haire, "A Strategic Posture Toward Corporate Social Responsibility," *California Management Review* 18, no. 2 (1975), pp. 49–58.

9. M. Freedman and B. Jaggi, "Pollution Disclosures, Pollution Performance and Economic Performance," *Omega* 10 (1982), pp. 167–176.

10. F. Fry and R. J. Hock, "Who Claims Corporate Responsibility? The Biggest and the Worst," *Business and Society Review/Innovation* 18 (1976), pp. 62–65.

11. R. W. Ingram and K. B. Frazier, "Environmental Performance and Corporate Disclosure," *Journal of Accounting Research* 18 (1980), pp. 614–622.

12. L. E. Preston, "Analyzing Corporate Social Performance: Methods and Results," *Journal of Contemporary Business* 7 (1978), pp. 135–150.

13. J. Wiseman, "An Evaluation of Environmental Disclosures Made in Corporate Annual Reports," *Accounting, Organizations and Society* 7 (1982), pp. 53–63.

14. Ernst and Ernst, *Social Responsibility Disclosure, 1973 Survey* (Cleveland, Ohio: Ernst and Ernst, 1973).

15. "How Business School Students Rate Corporations," *Business and Society Review* 2 (1972), pp. 20–21.

16. "Industry Rates Itself," *Business and Society Review* 1 (1972), pp. 96–99.

17. M. R. Moskowitz, "Choosing Socially Responsible Stocks," *Business and Society Review* 1 (1972), pp. 29–42.

18. G. J. Alexander and R. A. Buchholz, "Corporate Social Responsibility and Stock Market Performance," *Academy of Management Journal* 21 (1978), pp. 479–486.

19. J. H. Bragdon and J. A. T. Marlin, "Is Pollution Profitable?" *Risk Management* 19, no. 4 (1972), pp. 9–18.

20. K. H. Chen and R. W. Metcalf, "The Relationship between Pollution Control Record and Financial Indicators Revisited," *The Accounting Review* 55 (1980), pp. 168–177.

21. P. L. Cochran and R. A. Wood, "Corporate Social Responsibility and Financial Performance," *Academy of Management Journal* 27 (1984), pp. 42–56.

22. H. R. Folger and F. Nutt, "A Note on Social Responsibility and Stock Valuation," *Academy of Management Journal* 18 (1975), pp. 155–160.

23. B. L. Kedia and E. C. Kuntz, "The Contest of Social Performance: An Empirical Study of Texas Banks," in L. E. Preston, ed., *Research in Corporate Social Performance and Policy*, vol. III (Greenwich, Conn: JAI Press, 1981), pp. 133–154.

24. A. Belkaoui, "The Impact of the Disclosure of the Environmental Effects of Organizational Behavior on the Market," *Financial Management* 5, no. 4 (1976), pp. 26–31.

25. B. Jaggi and M. Freedman, "An Analysis of the Impact of Corporate Pollution Disclosures Included in Annual Financial Statements on Investors' Decisions," *Advances in Public Interest Accounting* (forthcoming).

26. R. W. Ingram and K. B. Frazier, "Narrative Disclosures and Annual Reports," *Journal of Business Research* 11 (1983), pp. 49–60.

27. R. Watts, "Corporate Financial Statements: Product of Market and Political Processes," *Australian Journal of Management* (April, 1977), pp. 52–75.

28. M. C. Jensen, "Reflective on the State of Accounting Research and the Regulation of Accounting," *Stanford Lectures in Accounting* (Stanford Calif.: Stanford University, 1976).

29. R. Watts and J. Zimmerman, *Positive Accounting Theory* (Englewood Cliffs, N.J.: Prentice-Hall, 1986).

30. R. Holthausen and R. Leftwich, "The Economic Consequences of Accounting Choice: Implications of Costly Contracting and Monitoring," *Journal of Accounting and Economics* 5 (1983), pp. 75–117.

31. R. Strand, "A Systems Paradigm of Organizational Adaptations to the Social Environment," *Academy of Management Review* 8 (1983), p. 90.

32. M. A. Keeley, "Social Justice Approach to Organizational Evaluation," *Administrative Quality* 23 (1978), pp. 272–92.

33. R. H. Kilman and R. P. Herden, "Towards a Systematic Methodology for Evaluating the Impact of Interviews on Organizational Effectiveness," *Academy of Management Review* 1, no. 3 (1976), pp. 87–88.

34. R. H. Miles, *Macro-Organizational Behavior* (Glenview, Ill.: Scott, Foresman, 1980).

35. M. C. Jensen and W. Meckling, "Theory of the Firm: Managerial Behavior, Agency Costs and Ownership Structure," *Journal of Financial Economics* 3 (1976), pp. 305–360.

36. C. Smith and J. Warner, "Financial Contracting: An Analysis of Bond Covenants," *Journal of Financial Economics* 7 (1979), pp. 117–162.

37. Alexander and Buchholz, "Corporate Social Responsibility and Stock Market Performance," p. 479.

38. S. C. Vance, "Are Socially Responsible Corporations Good Investment Risks?" *Management Review* 64, no. 8 (1975), pp. 19–24.

39. N. Neter, W. Wasserman, and M. H. Kutner, *Applied Linear Statistical Models*, 2nd ed. (Homewood, Ill.: Richard D. Irwin, 1985).

40. L. A. Daley and R. L. Vigeland, "The Effects of Debt Covenants and Political Costs on the Choice of Accounting Methods: The Case of Accounting for R&D Costs," *Journal of Accounting and Economics* (December, 1983), pp. 195–212.

SUGGESTED READINGS

Abbott, W. F., and R. J. Monsen. "On the Measurement of Corporate Social Responsibility: Self-Reported Disclosure as a Method of Measuring Corporate Social Involvement." *Academy of Management Journal* 22 (1979), pp. 501–515.

Aldag, R. J., and K. M. Bartol. "Empirical Studies of Corporate Social Performance and Policy: A Survey of Problems and Results." In L. E. Preston (ed.), *Research in Corporate Social Performance and Policy*, Vol. 1. Greenwich, Conn.: JAI Press, 1978, pp. 165–199.

Alexander, G. J., and R. A. Buchholz. "Corporate Social Responsibility and Stock Market Performance." *Academy of Management Journal* 21 (1978), pp. 479–486.

Anderson, J. C., and A. W. Frankle. "Voluntary Social Reporting: An Iso-Beta Portfolio Analysis." *The Accounting Review* 55 (1980), pp. 468–479.

Belkaoui, A. "The Impact of the Disclosure of the Environmental Effects of Organizational Behavior on the Market." *Financial Management* 5, no. 4 (1976), pp. 26–31.

Belkaoui, A. *Socio-Economic Accounting*. Westport, Conn.: Greenwood Press, 1984.

Bowen, R., E. Noreen, and J. Lacey. "Determinants of the Corporate Decision to Capitalize Interest." *Journal of Accounting and Economics* 3 (1981), pp. 151–179.

Bowman, E. H. "Strategy, Annual Reports, and Alchemy." *California Management Review* 20, no. 3 (1978), pp. 64–71.

Bowman, E. H., and M. Haire. "A Strategic Posture Toward Corporate Social Responsibility." *California Management Review* 18, no. 2 (1975), pp. 49–58.

Bragdon, J. H., and J. A. T Marlin. "Is Pollution Profitable?" *Risk Management* 19, no. 4 (1972), pp. 9–18.

Chen, K. H., and R. W. Metcalf. "The Relationship between Pollution Control Record and Financial Indicators Revisited." *The Accounting Review* 55 (1980), pp. 168–177.

Cochran, P. L., and R. A. Wood. "Corporate Social Responsibility and Financial Performance." *Academy of Management Journal* 27 (1989), pp. 42–56.

Cowen, S. S., L. B. Ferreri, and L. D. Parker. "The Impact of Corporate Characteristics on Social Responsibility Disclosure: A Typology and Frequency-Based Analysis." *Accounting, Organizations and Society* (March, 1987), pp. 111–122.

Daley, L. A., and R. L. Vigeland. "The Effects of Debt Covenants and Political Costs on the Choice of Accounting Methods: The Case of Accounting for R&D Costs." *Journal of Accounting and Economics* (December, 1983), pp. 195–212.

Deakin, E. B. "An Analysis of Differences between Non-Major Oil Firms Using Successful Efforts and Full Cost Methods." *The Accounting Review* (October, 1979), pp. 722–734.

Dhaliwal, D. "The Effect of Firm's Capital Structure on the Choice of Accounting Network." *The Accounting Review* 50 (1980), pp. 78–84.

Dhaliwal, D., G. Salamon, and E. Smith. "The Effect of Owner versus Management Control on the Choice of Accounting Methods." *Journal of Accounting and Economics* 4 (July 1982), pp. 41–53.

Epstein, M., E. Flamnoltz, and J. J. McDonough. "Corporate Social Accounting in the United States of America: State of the Arts and Future Prospects." *Accounting Organizations and Society* (October 1976), pp. 23–42.

Ernst and Ernst. *Social Responsibility Disclosure, 1973 Survey.* Cleveland, Ohio: Ernst and Ernst, 1973.

Fogler, H. R., and F. Nutt. "A Note on Social Responsibility and Stock Valuation." *Academy of Management Journal* 18 (1975), pp. 155–160.

Freedman, M., and B. Jaggi. "Pollution Disclosures, Pollution Performance and Economic Performance." *Omega* 10 (1982), pp. 167–176.

Fry, F., and R. J. Hock. "Who Claims Corporate Responsibility? The Biggest and the Worst." *Business and Society Review/Innovation* 18 (1976), pp. 62–65.

Gray, R., D. Owen, and K. Maunders. "Corporate Social Reporting: Emerging Trends in Accountability and the Social Contract." *Accounting, Auditing and Accountability* 1, no. 1 (1988), pp. 6–20.

Hagerman, R., and M. Zmijewski. "Some Economic Determinants of Accounting Policy." *Journal of Accounting and Economics* 1 (1979), pp. 142–161.

Holthausen, R., and R. Leftwich. "The Economic Consequences of Accounting Choice: Implications of Costly Contracting and Monitoring." *Journal of Accounting and Economics* 5 (1983), pp. 75–117.

"How Business School Students Rate Corporations." *Business and Society Review* 2 (1972), pp. 20–21.

"Industry Rates Itself." *Business and Society Review* 1 (1972), pp. 96–99.

Ingram, R. W. "An Investigation of the Information Content of (Certain) Social Responsibility Disclosures." *Journal of Accounting Research* 18 (1980), pp. 614–622.

Ingram, R. W., and K. B. Frazier. "Environmental Performance and Corporate Disclosure." *Journal of Accounting Research* 18 (1980), pp. 614–622.

Ingram, R. W., and K. B. Frazier. "Narrative Disclosures and Annual Reports." *Journal of Business Research* 11 (1983), pp. 49–60.

Jaggi, B., and M. Freedman. "An Analysis of the Impact of Corporate Pollution Disclosures Included in Annual Financial Statements on Investors' Decisions." *Advances in Public Interest Accounting* (forthcoming).

Jensen, M. C. "Reflections on the State of Accounting Research and the Regulation of Accounting." *In Stanford Lectures in Accounting.* Stanford, Calif.: Stanford University, 1976.

Jensen, M. C., and W. Meckling. "Theory of the Firm: Managerial Behavior, Agency Costs and Ownership Structure." *Journal of Financial Economics* 3 (1976), pp. 305–360.

Judge, G. G., et al. *The Theory and Practice of Econometrics.* New York: Wiley, 1980.

Kedia, B. L., and E. C. Kuntz. "The Contest of Social Performance: An Empirical Study of Texas Banks." In L. E. Preston, ed., *Research in Corporate Social Performance and Policy,* vol. III. Greenwich, Conn.: JAI Press, 1981, pp. 135–154.

Keely, M. A. "Social Justice Approach to Organizational Evaluation." *Administrative Quality* 23 (1978), pp. 272–292.

Kilman, R. H., and R. P. Herden. "Towards a Systematic Methodology for Evaluating the Impact of Interviews on Organizational Effectiveness." *Academy of Management Review* 1, no. 3 (1976), pp. 87–88.

Lilien, S., and V. Pastena. "Determinants of Intramethod Choice in the Oil and Gas Industry." *Journal of Accounting and Economics* (December, 1982), pp. 145–170.

Miles, R. H. *Macro-Organizational Behavior.* Glenview, Ill.: Scott, Foresman, 1980.

Moskowitz, M. R. "Choosing Socially Responsible Stocks." *Business and Society Review* 1 (1972), pp. 29–42.

Neter, N., W. Wasserman, and M. H. Kutner. *Applied Linear Statistical Models,* 2nd ed. Homewood, Ill.: Richard D. Irwin, 1985.

Parket, L. R., and H. Eibirt. "Socially Responsible: The Underlying Factors." *Business Horizons* 18, no. 4 (1975), pp. 5–10.

Pedhauzer, E. J. *Multiple Regression in Behavioral Research,* 2nd ed. New York: Holt, Rinehart and Winston, 1982.

Preston, L. E. "Analyzing Corporate Social Performance: Methods and Results." *Journal of Contemporary Business* 7 (1978), pp. 135–150.

Preston, L. E. "Book Review: Teaching Materials in Business Society." *California Management Review* (Spring, 1983), pp. 158–173.

Shane, P. B., and B. H. Spicer. "Market Response to Environmental Information Produced Outside the Firm." *The Accounting Review* 58 (1983), pp. 521–538.

Smith, C., and J. Warner. "Financial Contracting: An Analysis of Bond Covenants." *Journal of Financial Economics* 7 (1979), pp. 117–162.

Spicer, B. H. "Investors, Corporate Social Performance and Information Disclosure: An Empirical Study." *The Accounting Review* 53 (1978), pp. 94–111.

Spicer, B. H. "Market Risk, Accounting Data and Companies' Pollution Control Records." *Journal of Business Finance and Accounting* 5 (1978), pp. 67–83.

Strand, R. "A Systems Paradigm of Organizational Adaptations to the Social Environment." *Academy of Management Review* 8 (1983), p. 90.

Trotman, K. T., and G. W. Bradley. "Association between Social Responsibility Disclosure and Characteristics of Companies." *Accounting, Organizations and Society* (December, 1981), pp. 355–362.

Ullmann, A. A. "Data in Search of a Theory: A Critical Examination of the Relationship among Social Performance, Social Disclosure, and Economic Performance of U.S. Firms." *Academy of Management Review* 10 (1985), pp. 540–557.

Vance, S. C. "Are Socially Responsible Corporations Good Investment Risks?" *Management Review* 64, no. 8 (1975), pp. 19–24.

Watts, R. "Corporate Financial Statements: Product of Market and Political Processes." *Australian Journal of Management* (April, 1977), pp. 52–75.

Watts, R., and J. Zimmerman. *Positive Accounting Theory.* Englewood Cliffs, N.J.: Prentice-Hall, 1986.

Watts, R., and J. Zimmerman. "Towards a Positive Theory of the Determination of Accounting Standards." *The Accounting Review* 53 (1978), pp. 112–134.

Wiseman, J. "An Evaluation of Environmental Disclosures Made in Corporate Annual Reports." *Accounting, Organizations and Society* 7 (1982), pp. 53–63.

Zmijewski, M. E., and R. L. Hagerman. "An Income Strategy Approach to the Positive Theory of Accounting Standard Setting/Choice." *Journal of Accounting and Economics* 3 (1981), pp. 129–149.

7

The Prediction of Takeovers

INTRODUCTION[1]

A large number of mergers and acquisitions took place during the period from 1960 to 1968. In Canada, for example, two out of three industrial companies listed on the Toronto Stock Exchange completed at least one business combination over this period. This study attempts to identify the financial characteristics of the companies that become the object of a takeover. The term "takeover" will be used in its broadest sense: an acquisition of one enterprise by another where the corporate identity of the acquired firm disappears. The above definition makes the distinction between buyer and seller on the basis of the identity of the surviving firm. Consequently, this study considers companies subject to both voluntary and involuntary mergers.

RELATED RESEARCH

The prominence of takeovers has led to several studies in recent years. Marris' study of managerial capitalism showed that the companies acquired are those that are undervalued by the market.[2] Similarly, Gort[3] supported a related hypothesis that the level of takeover activity varies with the degree of share undervaluation in the market. This type of analysis relies heavily on a meaningful share price valuation model. More explicitly, the parameters measuring the relationship between the market prices of shares and relevant factors should be reasonably constant. Bomford[4] found that the market will sometimes attach differing weights to those factors. Similarly, Tzoannos and Samuels[5], in experimenting with a number of valuation models, found that the variables, whether explaining earning yield or dividend yield, were not significant. Thus the type of analysis based only on share valuation might lack external validity.

Because of the difficulties of appraising the "true" value of share, most of the other studies have attempted to identify the financial characteristics of the acquired firms. Accordingly, Chambers[6] examined the undervaluation of net assets as a result of conservative accounting policies. The undervaluation of net assets was seen as a key factor for predicting takeovers. These findings were later contested by Taussig and Hayes[7] on the basis of the absence of a control group in Chambers' study. They rejected the hypothesis of a statistically significant relationship between understated asset values and the possibility of a takeover. Their results were based on an investigation of 50 subject and 50 control companies in the United States. Both Chambers' and Taussig and Hayes' studies are, however, univariate in nature in the sense that they considered only involuntary mergers. The first limitation with regard to the univariate nature of the analysis was corrected by Vance.[8] He developed a "raider's index" composed of four financial ratios, which he applied to 21 companies subject to a bid. Seventeen out of the 21 companies scored above the "criterion" value on most of the financial ratios. The second limitation was also corrected by Monroe and Simkowitz,[9] Singh,[10] and Stevens.[11] They studied companies acquired through voluntary mergers by examining financial characteristics such as liquidity, profitability, capital structure, and the like. However, their results were restricted to U.S. corporations.

The present work differs from previous studies in the following respects: (1) both univariate and multivariate analyses of financial ratios are conducted and (2) information decomposition measures are used.

MULTIVARIATE MODEL

Problem and Database

This study attempts to distinguish among a sample of companies those that will be *subject* to a takeover on the basis of an examination of the financial ratios of acquired firms. Similar models have been devised for the prediction of a different economic event, namely, bankruptcy. Beaver[12] used the dichotomous classification test to determine the error rate a potential predictor would experience if he classified firms on the basis of their financial ratios as failed or not failed. Altman used discriminant analysis to rank firms on the basis of a weighted combination of five ratios. Both methods showed some predictive ability. This study will first use the dichotomous test on the ratios of the firms and then, using discriminant analysis, will search for a combination of the same ratios, which best predict takeover.

Twenty-five companies were randomly selected from a population of firms that were the subject of takeovers in the years 1960 to 1968. The choice and the number of these companies were restricted by the availability of accounting information. The data were taken from the annual reports of the companies for each of the five years preceding the takeover. A control group of companies

Exhibit 7.1
List of Financial Ratios Tested

	CLASS	RATIO
I.	Non-Liquid-Asset Group	Cash-Flow/Net Worth Cash-Flow/Total Assets Net Income/ Net Worth Net Income/Net Assets Long-Term Debt + Preferred Stock/ Total Assets
II.	Liquid Asset to Total Asset Group	Current Assets/ Total Assets Cash/Total Assets Working Capital/Total Assets Quick Assets/Total Assets
III.	Liquid Asset to Current Debt Group	Current Assets/Current Liabilities Quick Assets/Current Liabilities Cash/Current Liabilities
IV.	Liquid Asset Turnover Group	Current Assets/Sales Quick Assets/Sales Working Capital/Sales Cash Sales

was then selected from the Financial Post list. These companies came from the same industries as the experimental companies and were within a range of 25 percent of the assets of the experimental companies. The matching by size was motivated by the fact that acquired firms, in general, tend to be smaller than their buyers. Firms in the control group were still in existence in 1973.

For each of the 50 companies (25 experimental and 25 control) the annual reports were examined for the five years prior to the takeover date. Because of the sizable number of ratios found to be good indicators in the accounting and financial literature, a list of 16 potential predictor ratios was compiled for examination as shown in Exhibit 7.1. These ratios were chosen on the basis of

1. their popularity in the literature; they represent the "traditional" categories in ratio analysis: balance sheet ratios (liquidity and solvency), income statement ratios (profit margin), and mixed ratios (capital turnover);
2. their possible relevance to the takeover phenomenon;
3. their distinction between liquid and nonliquid ratios; and
4. their appearance in the literature as indicators of the ability of a firm to avoid takeovers.

Mergers have been described as consummated to "avoid bankruptcy (for the acquired firm), to capitalize upon managerial inefficiencies, to gain from valu-

ation discrepancies, to achieve portfolio diversification, and for synergistic purposes and many other reasons."[13] Similarly, it is often "supposed in the
economic literature that the companies taken over are the inefficient companies,
the less profitable; and the acquiring companies are the more efficient, the more
profitable."[14] Thus, it may logically be assumed that most of the chosen ratios
in this study will indicate a low value to predict takeovers. In other words, a
company may be acquired because it has lower than average profitability, liquidity, and asset turnover. An opposite prediction rule is used for the "long-
term debt + preferred stock divided by total assets." This expectation conforms
to the "theory that the victim companies have already used their borrowing
possibilities and are not, therefore, being purchased because they will allow the
purchasing company access to new loan funds."[15]

Results of the Dichotomous Classification Test

One index of predictive ability frequently used is the dichotomous classification test. The procedure is as follows:

1. the entire sample of experimental and control firms is divided into two equal subsam-
   ples;
2. an optimal "cutoff" ratio, which gives the smallest number of misclassifications in
   one subsample, is selected;
3. the obtained "cutoff" ratio is used to classify the firms in the second subsample;
4. the number of firms misclassified is then counted.

The same procedure is applied to the second subsample. The number of misclassifications obtained by the use of each of the optimal cutoff ratios in each
of the five years is used to compute the percentage error rate of classification.
The results obtained by the dichotomous test are summarized in Exhibit 7.2.
The percentage error rate has a predictive ability in the sense that the lower the
error, the greater the predictive power.

First, a review of the error percentage results shows a superior performance
of the nonliquid-asset ratios. With one single exception, the "net income over
the net worth" and the "cash flow over net worth" ratios have a lower percentage error than all the 14 remaining liquid and nonliquid ratios. The exception
is the performance of the "working capital over total assets" ratio in the second
year prior to takeover.

This superiority in the predictive power of the nonliquid ratios is more striking
in the short term, particularly in years 1, 2, and 3, than in the long term. One
could interpret this result in two stages. First, the nonliquid ratios involved and
the "working capital over total assets" ratio indicate the degree of corporate vulnerability to a takeover attempt. They convey the attractive characteristics of the
company in terms of earnings, debt, and liquidity positions. Second, the short-

Exhibit 7.2
Percentage Error for 16 Ratios on Dichotomous Classification Test

Ratio	Years Before Takeover				
	1	2	3	4	5
Non-Liquid-Asset Group					
Cash-Flow/Net Worth	26	24	24	24	30
Cash-Flow/Total Assets	40	38	48	46	50
Net Income/Net Worth	24	28	28	32	30
Net Income/Total Assets	38	34	40	48	50
L.T. Debt – Preferred Stock/ Total Assets	42	42	32	34	38
Liquid Asset to Total Asset Group					
Current Assets/Total Assets	48	38	38	34	38
Cash/Total Assets	48	44	42	42	36
Working Capital/Total Assets	34	20	42	32	52
Quick Assets/Total Assets	42	32	40	36	28
Liquid Asset to Current Debt Group					
Current Assets/Current Liabilities	44	52	40	50	50
Quick Assets/Current Liabilities	34	50	36	34	44
Cash/Current Liabilities	44	48	42	48	46
Liquid Asset Turnover Group					
Current Assets/Sales	44	42	32	32	40
Quick Assets/Sales	34	36	40	42	48
Working Capital/Sales	50	46	44	54	44
Cash/Sales	40	50	58	50	48

term and hence present attractiveness or vulnerability of the companies is of major interest to the acquired. The necessity of surprise required from the takeover bidder may have led to a greater emphasis on short-term appraisals. Hence an improvement in the cash flow or profit position of a firm in the second or third year may have led to a greater probability of a takeover bid.

The second major result pertains to the differences of prediction among the liquid-asset ratios. The "working capital over total assets" ratio predicted relatively better than the other liquid ratios, one, two, three, and four years before takeover; better than 10 in the first and the second year, better than five in the third year; and better than nine in the fourth year. It had a superior predictive ability to both the current ratio and the asset test ratio in years 1, 2, and 4. The cash ratio had a low predictive performance. An improvement in predictive ability existed when cash was replaced by quick assets for most of the nonliquid ratios. However, the improvement decreased slightly when current assets were introduced.

This second major result pertaining to the differences in predictive ability of the liquid ratios does not seem to conform to the literature's point of view in one case. Working capital performed better than most ratios suggested as good measures. The quick asset ratio performed better than cash and current asset ratios, which does not conform to the literature. One might be tempted, following Beaver's reasoning, to conclude in this context that "popularity is self-defeating" for certain ratios and not for others. Such an explanation would not be satisfying. Therefore, a comparison of the means of 10 financial items was made in order to gain more insight into the differences in predictive ability of liquid ratios. The results are shown in Exhibit 7.3. With respect to the means of working capital, current assets and receivables for both experimental and control firms, acquired firms have higher and hence favorable differences for the third, fourth, and fifth years. This result vanishes in the case of the means of the quick assets where the differences for the same years become favorable to the firms in the control group. The changes in the differences from negative to positive are due to high inventory amounts kept by the experimental firms, which were included in both the computation of working capital and current assets and excluded in the computation of quick assets. Quick assets are those items that can easily be converted into cash.

It is *because of the exclusion of inventory* that quick asset ratios are better predictors than cash and current assets.

With regard to the superiority of the working capital assets over asset ratios, the comparison of the means shows that the acquired firms have higher current debt for years 3, 4, and 5. The "net working capital over total assets" ratio conveys these differences between acquired and control firms, and enables both the liquidity and size characteristics to be explicitly considered.

In general, it may be stated that the acquired companies had better records than the control companies in years 3, 4, and 5, and worse records in years 1 and 2 for total assets, receivables, sales, current assets, working capital, and current debt. However, the control companies definitely had better records than the acquired companies in all years for quick assets, cash flow, net income, and inventory.

Although the results of the classification test provided a certain degree of accuracy, the following section will be based on the results of a discriminant analysis. It is hoped that the second methodology will improve on the 20 percent error in misclassification obtained by the "working capital over total assets" ratio in the second year prior to takeover.

Results of the Discriminant Analysis

The purpose of discriminant analysis is to classify an observation into one of several a priori groupings on the basis of a profile of its characteristics. In our context, we hope to determine a linear combination of financial ratios that best discriminates between the acquired and control groups. Stevens (1973) dealt

Exhibit 7.3
Comparison on Means of 13 Financial Items

Item a	Years Before Takeover				
	1	2	3	4	5
Total Assets					
C	33,790	33,160	18,508	16,285	15,680
E	21,925	20,602	19,000	11,700	16,560
Diff	11,865	9,558	(492)	(1,415)	(880)
Receivables					
C	3,610	3,600	2,208	2,146	2,218
E	3,224	3,260	3,518	2,693	2,493
Diff	476	340	(1,310)	(547)	(275)
Quick Assets					
C	5,028	5,594	3,732	3,304	3,914
E	3,354	3,090	3,576	2,664	2,364
Diff	1,674	2,504	156	640	1,550
Sales					
C	54,180	51,962	16,012	14,554	13,680
E	27,609	26,008	24,922	22,154	19,517
Diff	26,571	25,954	(8,910)	(7,600)	(5,837)
Cash Flow					
C	4,090	3,880	2,224	1,940	2,030
E	2,000	1,560	1,964	1,900	1,760
Diff	2,090	2,320	260	40	270
Net Income					
C	3,550	3,320	1,570	1,310	1,500
E	1,800	1,205	1,215	1,222	1,316
Diff	1,750	115	355	88	284
Inventory					
C	8,602	7,680	5,530	4,920	4,630
E	3,710	6,280	4,100	3,720	3,080
Diff	4,892	1,400	1,430	1,200	1,550
Current Assets					
C	14,600	15,800	6,660	6,230	6,140
E	10,765	10,290	10,270	9,075	9,490
Diff	3,835	5,590	(3,610)	(2,845)	(3,350)

Exhibit 7.3 (continued)

Item a	Years Before Takeover				
	1	2	3	4	5
Working Capital					
C	7,500	7,730	4,220	3,500	2,750
E	4,900	5,220	5,785	5,140	4,790
Diff	2,600	2,510	(1,565)	(1,640)	(2,040)
Current Debt					
C	6,960	6,670	2,830	3,630	3,650
E	5,800	5,300	4,880	4,675	3,920
Diff	1,160	1,370	(2,050)	(1,045)	(330)

Item E denotes firms belonging to the experimental group; C denotes those belonging to the control
group. The mean values are expressed in thousands of dollars.

with the multicollinearity of variables by subjecting his data to a factor analysis
and reducing the original 20 ratios to six factors. These six factors were interpreted to represent (1) leverage, (2) profitability, (3) activity, (4) liquidity, (5)
dividend policy, and (6) price earnings. However, similar to Elam (1975) the
purpose of this study is to develop the set of ratios with optimal predictive
power and to analyze the predictive power of both liquid and nonliquid ratios.
The 16 ratios used in the dichotomous classification test were input to the BMD
04M discriminant analysis program for each of the five years prior to takeover
for the firms in both groups. The output for every year was in the form of a
vector of weights $(V_1, V_2, \ldots, V_{16})$ such that the summation or discriminant
score $(Z = V_1X_1 + V_2X_2 + \ldots + V_{16}X_{16})$ for every year maximized the distinction between the acquired and control firms. These coefficients of discriminant function V_I for each of the five years are shown in Exhibit 7.4.

To measure the significance of each discriminant function the Mahalanobias
D^2 was used; this measure is the distance between two multivariate normal
populations. Under random sampling with sizes n_1 and n_2, respectively, from
group 1 and group 2, and under the hypothesis that $\mu_1 = \mu_2$ or that the means
of the ratio vectors for each group are equal, the statistic

$$F = \frac{n_1 - n_2 - p - 1}{p} \times \frac{n_1n_2}{(n_1 + n_2)(n_1 + n_2 - 2)} D^2$$

is distributed as $F(P, n_1 + n_2 - p - 1)$. This F ratio is used to determine the
probability of a significant difference between the scores of acquired and control
firms. An examination of the F values in Exhibit 7.4 shows that they were
significant at $\alpha = 0.05$ in the third, fourth, and fifth years and insignificant at

Exhibit 7.4
Coefficients of Discriminant Functions and Significance Tests

Ratios	Year 1	Year 2	Year 3	Year 4	Year 5
Cash Flow/Net Worth	-0.05699	-0.04873	-0.07209	-0.12516	-0.10842
Cash Flow/Total Assets	0.06193	0.00819	0.15693	0.33359	0.23390
Net Income/Net Worth	0.05251	0.03903	0.03587	0.08908	0.07953
Net Income/Total Assets	-0.03333	-0.19860	-0.08349	-0.17424	-0.13008
LT Debt + Preferred/Total Assets	-0.00317	-0.01890	0.11576	-0.01842	-0.02801
Current Assets/Total Assets	-0.03280	-0.00583	-0.05502	0.16184	0.07621
Cash/Total Assets	0.11758	0.15185	0.12712	0.15114	-0.23027
Working Capital/Total Assets	-0.02427	-0.05758	0.02146	-0.30738	-0.18708
Quick Assets/Total Assets	0.04061	0.05671	-0.15501	-0.21040	-0.03840
Current Assets/Ct Liabilities	0.00286	0.00824	-0.00323	0.00628	0.00566
Quick Assets/Ct Liabilities	-0.01080	-0.01202	0.03049	0.01923	-0.00831
Cash/Current Liabilities	0.00431	0.00470	-0.01461	-0.01725	0.03342
Current Assets/Sales	-0.00255	-0.01728	0.02637	-0.00153	-0.00639
Quick Assets/Sales	-0.00102	-0.00031	-0.04474	-0.00409	-0.01536
Working Capital/Sales	0.00458	0.01253	-0.01134	0.00326	0.02200
Cash/Sales	-0.00941	-0.01057	-0.04834	0.00726	-0.05233
Mahalabonias D Square	2.21319	2.64546	3.84375	3.57160	3.85773
F (16,33)	1.18872	1.42090	2.06451	1.91834	2.07202
Significant at	0.25	<0.10	0.05	<0.05	0.05

this level in years 1 and 2. This result is consistent with that of the classification test in the sense that it is possible to correctly identify a potential takeover as far as three or four years beforehand. The major difference stems from the high confidence level presented in year 5.

Misclassification errors of either type can occur. An acquired firm can be incorrectly classified as nonacquired or a nonacquired firm may be classified as acquired. It is assumed in this study that both types of errors are equally costly. In other words, from the user's point of view, the classification of a firm that will be acquired in a nonacquired group may be as costly as the classification of a firm that will not be acquired as a potential takeover target. If the cost of both types of errors were known, the discriminant model could be adjusted toward the minimization of total cost.

To extend the model for more general application, it would be appropriate to select a "cutoff" point for every year, to attain the smallest number of misclassifications. The procedure, used in Altman's (1968) study and adopted here, consists of defining two values of $Z:Z_2$, above which is defined the nonacquired sector; and Z_2, below which is defined the acquired sector. The area between the two Z scores is defined as the "zone of ignorance because of the susceptibility to error classification." The next step would be to look for the value of Z^* or the cutoff point that would minimize the number of misclassifications for

Exhibit 7.5
Zones of Ignorance and Critical Z Score

Year	Zones of Ignorance		Cutoff Point Z*	Misclassification rate
	Above Z_1	Under Z_2		
Year 1	-0.10998	0.08565	-0.02051	28%
Year 2	-0.14146	0.02957	-0.02365	20%
Year 3	-0.13668	0.08098	-0.00243	16%
Year 4	-0.14245	0.07651	-0.00921	22%
Year 5	-0.16617	0.04876	-0.02543	20%

every year. The zones of ignorance and the cutoff point for every year are shown in Exhibit 7.5. Given these cutoff points, the rates of misclassification are, respectively, 28, 20, 16, 22, and 20 percent for years 1, 2, 3, 4, and 5.

It can be concluded, on the basis of the initial firms included in our study, that the discriminant analysis model reduces the misclassification rate to 16 percent in year 3 from the 20 percent obtained by the "working capital over total assets" ratio in year 2 using the dichotomous test. However, this approach, based on the choice of an optimal cutoff discriminant score, fails to take the relative score into account. Most of the classification errors will tend to occur close to the cutoff value of the score.

Belkaoui[16] considered classification according to probabilities of group membership. Assuming the vectors of the scores follow a p-variate normal distribution and that the variance-covariance matrix of the group included matches the population variance-covariance matrix, it is possible to "assign a probability of group membership based on the multivariate extension of the univariate Z test as follows":

$$d' \; \Sigma^{-1} \; d_p^{X2}$$

where

d' = the row vectors of deviation scores,

d = the column vectors of deviation scores,

Σ = the population variance-covariance matrix, and

p = the degrees of freedom of the chi-square distribution and equals the number of elements in the deviation score vector.

The results of classifying both experimental and control firms in the above manner are shown in Exhibit 7.6. The results in Exhibit 7.6 show that the misclassification errors are almost equivalent to those obtained by the method

Exhibit 7.6
Classification Errors for Firms Used in Deriving the Discriminant

FUNCTIONS

Incorrectly Classified as	Probability	Total
1st year before takeover		
not acquired	.56 .62 .80 .50 .75 .70	6
acquired	.60 .65 .75 .96 .80 .85 .62 .75 .64	9
2nd year before takeover		
not acquired	.52 .70 .56 .75 .70	5
acquired	.65 .87 .79 .92 .57 .63	6
3rd year before takeover		
not acquired	.59 .75 .69 .72 .69	5
acquired	.82 .86 .73 .63	4
4th year before takeover		
not acquired	.52 .54 .65 .73 .85	5
acquired	.85 .86 .90 .53 .52 .54	6
5th year before takeover		
not acquired	.64 .62 .96 .80 .56 .72	6
acquired	.73 .54 .90 .92 .57	5

of the optimal cutoff score. They averaged 30, 22, 18, 22, and 22 percent for the first, second, third, fourth, and fifth years, respectively.

At this stage, the model is basically explanatory. To assess the predictive nature of the discriminant analysis model, a second sample of companies was chosen including 11 Canadian acquired companies and 11 equivalent control companies. Using financial ratios similar to those of the initial sample, the discriminant coefficients obtained in Exhibit 7.4 were applied toward the computation of a discriminant score for the new companies for each of the five years before takeover. A comparison of the obtained scores with the cutoff point Z shows 30, 24, 15, 24, and 25 percent for years 1, 2, 3, 4, and 5, respectively. The results are surprising in that the new sample's results are very similar to those of the initial sample. A noticeable improvement took place in year 3. The results on both the initial and secondary sample determined the overall effectiveness of the discriminant model for a longer period of time prior to takeover. Two explanations seem possible: either the long-term financial position as conveyed by the accounting data is more indicative of a possible takeover, or the changes in the reliability of the model from year to year have little or no meaning.

Conclusions in the Multivariate Model

This section has attempted to assess the predictive ability of certain liquid and nonliquid financial ratios in the case of a takeover. The use of the dichotomous test showed the superiority of the nonliquid ratios in predicting takeovers. Among the liquid ratios the surprising result was the superiority of "working capital over total assets." In general, the ratios were better predictors two of three years before takeover. In order to improve on a 20 percent misclassification rate, the same set of financial ratios was combined in a discriminant analysis approach to the problem of a corporate takeover prediction. The results verified the superiority of the second or the third year prediction. A decision rule based on a determination of a cutoff point for the discriminant score improved the misclassification rate to 16 percent from the 20 percent given by the dichotomous test. At this stage the model was basically self-explanatory. When new companies from a second sample were classified, the predictive ability of the model improved to a 15 percent misclassification rate.

The decision to limit the choice of companies to those with low asset size was due to the high incidence in Canada of takeovers in that particular group. This does not imply that large companies are never undervalued or inefficient.

In addition, it must be realized that the results are based on a relatively small population of acquired firms from both the initial and secondary sample. Furthermore, the inclusion of nonfinancial characteristics would add to the external validity of the model.

Similarly, a cross-sectional analysis was used over all industries. Given the interindustry differences, a control by industry, with a sufficient number of experimental companies in each, may correct for any specific factors creating major changes in the economic environment and in takeover activity in certain years. Because of the limited number of industries and companies involved, the decision in this study was to pool the ratios over all industries. Accordingly, the results may be best interpreted as most to the prediction of takeover of small firms.

THE ENTROPY LAW, INFORMATIONAL DECOMPOSITION MEASURES, AND CORPORATE TAKEOVER

Information theory is concerned with the problem of measuring changes in knowledge.[17] Theil applied information theory and the related entropy concept to develop a set of measures for financial statements analysis.[18] Lev reported a test in which these informational decomposition measures were found to be associated with the event of corporate bankruptcy.[19] His results indicated that the measures discriminate between failing and nonfailing firms at least as far as five years before failure. Different economic events could be associated with the informational decomposition measures. This study will report a test in which the informational measures were found to be fairly associated with the event of

Exhibit 7.7
Summary of Informational Concepts

	A Single Event (Information)	A Set of Events (Expected) (Information)
Definite (Certain) Message	$-\log p$	$-\Sigma\ p_i\ \log\ p_i$
Nondefinite Message	$\log \dfrac{q}{p}$	$\Sigma\ q_i\ \log\ \dfrac{q_i}{p_i}$

corporate takeover. The event of takeover is defined as including all acquisitions of one enterprise by another where the corporate identity of the one taken over disappears and only the other remains. The order of discussion is as follows. First, the basic information theory concepts are described and these are then applied to compute the informational decomposition measures. Then the companies and the event of takeover are presented. Lastly, the summary of the results and their discussion are pursued.

The Expected Information of a Message

The set of informational decomposition measures to be used in this study are derived as a result of the application of the entropy concept to the aggregation problem of financial statements items. These information concepts are summarized in Exhibit 7.7 and will be briefly elaborated here.

The function generally used to compute the amount of information conveyed by a message is $h(p) = \log 1/p = -\log p$ where p is the probability of occurrence of an event Σ.[20] This function declines from infinity with $p = 0$ to zero when $p = 1$. It suggests that the amount of information conveyed by a definite message specifying that event Σ has occurred is a decreasing function of the event probability prior to the arrival of the message. Consequently, the information amount can be computed only if the message states that Σ has occurred. In case the message states the Σ will not occur, the amount of information will be then expressed by $h(1-p)$. Before the arrival of the message, the value of information will be either $h(p)$ or $h(1-p)$; accordingly the expected informational content of a forthcoming message or entropy is

$$H = p\ h(p) - (1-p)\ h(1-p),$$

or

$$H = -p \log p - (1-p) \log (1-p)$$

The above formula can be extended to a situation of a complete set of n mutually exclusive events with probabilities $p_1, \ldots, p_n$. The expected information or entropy of the resulting message is

$$H = \sum_{I=1}^{n} p_i \, h(p_i) = -\sum_{I=1}^{n} p_i \log p_i$$

The above expression could be used as a measure of uncertainty. As stated by Lev:

Uncertainty and information are closely related; the former exists before the arrival of the message: the larger the uncertainty, the larger on the average the amount of information conveyed by the message.[21]

The nature of the message could also be nondefinite in the sense that the message no longer states with certainty that event Σ took place. A nondefinite message might state that the odds in favor of Σ have changed with the resulting situation that probability p is replaced by probability q. In such a case, the amount of information is $h(p)$ before the arrival of the message and $h(q)$ after the arrival. Accordingly the informational content of a nondefinite message is equal to the difference, or

$$h(p) - h(q) = \log p - \log q = \log \frac{q}{p}$$

Again the above formula could be extended to the case of a set of n mutually exclusive events $\Sigma_1, \ldots, \Sigma_n$ with probabilities of occurrences, respectively, $p_1, \ldots, p_n$. A nondefinite message will transform the original set of probabilities $p_1, \ldots, p_n$ to $q_1, \ldots, q_n$. One event Σ_i has to occur with an informational amount of $\log (q_i/p_i)$. Similarly the final probability of E_i occurring and hence of $\log (q_i/p_i)$ will both be q_i. So the expected informational content of the resulting message will be

$$I = \sum_{I=1}^{n} q_i \log \frac{q_i}{p_i}$$

The above expression is important; when applied to consecutive financial statements it will enable the development of some informational decomposition measures that will be used in this study. These are mainly the asset information measure, the liabilities information measure, and the balance sheet information measure.

The Information Decomposition Measures

The information measures express the degree of stability over time in financial statement decomposition. Thus balance sheets and income statements could be seen as numerical decomposition of certain total sums: total assets and total liabilities. For instance, with the asset size, dividing the individual assets by their total assets leads to a set of non-negative functions that sums to one. These fractions are equivalent to the probability statements p and q mentioned earlier.[22] So, given two consecutive financial statements, the formula for the expected information will provide the asset information measures (AIM):

$$\text{AIM} = \sum_{i=1}^{n} q_i \log_2 \frac{q_i}{p_i}$$

In this study, the items on the asset side are aggregated under current assets and fixed assets categories. So the asset information measure is expressed as

$$\text{AIM} = \sum_{i=1}^{2} q_i \log_2 \frac{q_i}{p_i}$$

where q_1 and q_2 are the fractions of current assets and fixed assets, each divided by total assets, and p_1 and p_2 are the corresponding factors of an earlier balance sheet.

Similarly, considering the liabilities side of the balance sheet, the liabilities information measure (LIM) is developed as follows:

$$\text{LIM} = \sum_{i=1}^{3} q_i \log_2 \frac{q_i}{p_i}$$

where q_1, q_2, and q_3 are the fractions of current liabilities, long-term liabilities, and equity, each respectively divided by the balance sheet's total, and p_1, p_2, and p_3 are the corresponding fractions of an earlier balance sheet.

The third measure used in this study is the balance sheet information measure (BIM). It includes both assets and liabilities and is expressed as

$$\text{BIM} = \sum_{i=1}^{2} \sum_{i=1}^{2} q_{ij} \log_2 \frac{q_{ij}}{p_{ij}}$$

where

q_{11} = fraction of current assets divided by twice the balance sheet total

q_{12} = fraction of fixed assets divided by twice the balance sheet total

q_{21} = fraction of current liabilities divided by twice the balance sheet total

q_{22} = fraction of long-term liabilities (including equity) divided by twice the balance sheet total

Here p_{11} to p_{22} are the corresponding fractions of an earlier balance sheet.

The three informational decomposition measures portray the behavior of their individual components expressed as a fraction of total assets over the time spanned by two balance sheets.

The informational analysis takes a proportional development of assets or liabilities items as a norm and indicates the degree to which the actual development of the items deviates from a proportional one.[23]

Whether or not the above determined measures could be supported in accounting research depends on the specific purpose in mind. In this case, they can be viewed as a measure of the extent of decomposability of some set of data.[24] Every decomposable datum, including the financial statements, has an entropy. The informational decomposition measures are then both entropies and financial statement measures. As entropies they measure the extent of the decomposition of the data and the extent of uncertainty (stability of financial items).[25] As financial statement measures, one might wonder about their usefulness for financial statement users. The accounting literature has related usefulness to the facilitation of decision making. This point has been noted in *A Statement of Basic Accounting Theory*:

The Committee defines accounting as the process of identifying, measuring, and communicating economic information to permit informed judgements and decisions by users of the information.[26]

Decision making requires a knowledge of the decision models of potential users of accounting data. However, the lack of knowledge about the decision models led the accountants to evaluate alternative accounting measures in terms of their predictive ability because it requires a lower level of specificity regarding the decision model. Beaver et al. noted that "The predictive ability of accounting data can be explored without waiting for the further specification of the decision models."[27] Consequently the usefulness of the informational decomposition measures can be studied in terms of their predictive ability.

Because prediction is an inherent part of the decision process, knowledge of the predictive ability of the informational decomposition measures is a necessary condition for their use as a decision-making criterion. The predictive ability criterion has already been applied in several different contexts.[28]

Problem and Database

The predictive ability of the informational decomposition measures can be studied by associating them with a business event. The takeover event is considered in this study for two reasons. First, it is relevant to the present-day economic situation. In Canada, for example, two out of three of the industrial companies listed on the Toronto Stock Exchange completed at least one business combination over the period 1960–1968.[29] Second, it has been advanced that switches in accounting methods or the adoption of the other policies that normalize accounting ratios may improve the market price and make the takeover more costly to the bidder.[30]

Consequently, one a priori argument may be that the companies taken over might have resorted to more changes in accounting policies prior to the takeover than would a control group of companies. In our context, given that the informational decomposition measures indicate the stability of financial items over time, the argument would be that the informational decomposition measures of companies taken over would be superior to those of a control group of companies.

Our null hypothesis will then be that there are no differences between the informational decomposition measures of the taken-over companies and the control group.

The hypothesis will be tested for each informational decomposition measure. It could be stated as:

$$H_0 = M_t = M_c \text{ against } H_1 = M_T > M_C$$

where M stands for the mean of the informational decomposition measure, T stands for the companies taken over, and C stands for the companies in the control group.

Twenty-five Canadian companies that were the subject of the takeovers in the years 1960–1968 were selected and constitute the experimental group (Exhibit 7.8). The number of the companies was restricted by the availability of accounting information. The data were collected for each of the five years preceding the takeover. A control group was selected. The companies included came from the same industries as the acquired firms of the experimental group. They were chosen within a range of $\pm$ 25 percent of sales and assets of the experimental companies. Firms in the control group were still in existence in 1973 (Exhibit 7.8).

Summary of Results

Each information measure was computed for consecutive and nonconsecutive years. The computation for the consecutive years (5 and 4, 4 and 3, 3 and 2, 2 and 1, prior to takeover) resulted in four measures for each firm. Each information measure for a firm in the experimental group was then compared with

Exhibit 7.8
List of Companies Included in the Study

	Experimental Companies	Control Companies
1	Blue Bonnets Raceway	Yonkers Raceway
2	Standard Structural Steel	Niagara Structural Steel
3	Norbeau Mines	Pamour Porcupine Mines
4	Lamontagne	Coporate Food
5	Barnat Mines	Little Long Lac Gold Mines
6	Dominion Steel and Coal Mines	Dominion Foundries & Steel
7	Canadian Western Natural Gas	Canadian Deli Oil
8	Codville Distributors	Canadian Food Products
9	Freiman, A.J.	Dupuis Freres
10	McAllister Towing	Nanaim Towing
11	National Hees Industries	National Food Management
12	Cummings Property	Great Plains Development
13	Cunningham Drug Stores	National Drugs and Chemicals Can.
14	Hunter Douglas	Canadian Vickers
15	Mill City Petroleum	National Pertroleum Corp.
16	Endako Mines	Matagami Lake Mines
17	New Continental Oil Company	North Canadian Oils
18	Permo Gas and Oil	Canadian Export Gas and Oil
19	Highland Bell	Madsen Red Lake Gold Mines
20	Leitch Gold Mines	Lake Shore Mines
21	Macassa Gold Mines	New Calumet Mines
22	Lafarge Canada	Le Tourneau Inc.
23	Salada Foods	Canadian Salt Co.
24	S.K.D. Manufacturing	Teledyne Canada
25	Avnor Gold Mines	Canadian Merril

the corresponding measure for the equivalent firm in the control group. For instance, the balance sheet information measure of a firm in the experimental group for years 5 and 4 is compared with the balance sheet information measure of an equivalent control firm for years 5 and 4. This resulted in four individual comparisons for each pair of firms, and thus 100 comparisons for the whole sample. Averaging the four measures for each firm gave one comparison per firm and 25 comparisons for each of the three information measures tested. The results of these comparisons are listed in Exhibit 7.9 for the asset information measure, in Exhibit 7.10 for the liabilities information measure, and in Exhibit 7.11 for the balance sheet information measure.

The paired comparisons in the above-mentioned exhibits show that the information measures for the firms taken over are larger than for the firms in the control group (68 percent for the balance sheet information, 64 percent for the liabilities information measure, and 64 percent for the asset information measure). This result is even more accentuated for the asset information measure when the consecutive measures for each firm are averaged, 77 percent. These findings illustrate the predictive or discriminating ability of the information measures with respect to the takeover event. The information measures have a

Exhibit 7.9
Comparison of Assets Information Measures for Firms in the Sample

	Total Number of Comparisons	Number of Cases in which $I_t > I_n$	Average Information over all samples		t Value Computed
			takeover	control	
Consecutive	100	64%	0.037	0.029	
Firm's average	25	77%			
2 and 1	25	60%	0.071	0.060	2.35
3 and 2	25	64%	0.010	0.016	2.55
4 and 3	25	68%	0.012	0.015	3.80
5 and 4	25	64%	0.038	0.025	3.75
Non-Consecutive Years	75	66%	0.046	0.039	
Firm's	25	72%			
3 and 1	25	72%	0.102	0.038	3.65
4 and 2	25	64%	0.018	0.015	3.05
5 and 3	25	64%	0.065	0.006	2.95

discriminating ability in the sense that the larger the measure the less stable are the financial statements items. The firms might have a tendency to resort to changes in accounting techniques and changes in assets and liabilities to prevent takeovers. Consequently the firms in the experimental group will have larger information measures as an indication of the instability of their financial items.

Another result is the superior discriminant ability of the balance sheet information measure (68 percent for individual comparisons and 64 percent for firm's averages). This superiority is possibly due to inclusion in the measure of all the changes that take place on the asset side and the liability side simultaneously. In general, the liabilities information measure was larger and had a better discrimination power than the asset information measure. The difference between both measures was 0.056 versus 0.037 for the experimental group. The liabilities are less stable than assets and this difference in even larger for firms taken over. It might be due to the attempt by the firms in the control group to resort to

Exhibit 7.10
Comparison of Liability Information Measures for Firms in the Sample

	Total Number of Comparisons	Number of Cases in which $I_t > I_n$	Average Information over all samples		t Value Computed
			takeover	control	
Consecutive	100	64%	0.054	0.034	
Firm's average over 5 years	25	64%			
2 and 1	25	52%	0.036	0.016	2.01
3 and 2	25	72%	0.023	0.019	2.65
4 and 3	25	72%	0.051	0.014	2.55
5 and 4	25	60%	0.107	0.087	4.01
Non-Consecutive	75	72%	0.128	0.114	
Firm's average	25	68%			
3 and 1	25	72%	0.075	0.067	4.70
4 and 2	25	72%	0.095	0.070	4.15
5 and 3	25	72%	0.215	0.206	5.01

reorganization and consolidation of their debts and equities. Another noticeable result shown in the Exhibits 7.9–7.11 concerns the comparisons obtained from the information measures computed from nonconsecutive years. A noticeable difference is that the average information measures are larger for the nonconsecutive years than for the consecutive years.

To further test the significance of the above results, a performance indicator was computed as the difference between the experimental firm information measure and the control firm information measure for each of the consecutive and the nonconsecutive years. The difference indicator was defined as

$$D = I_e - I_c.$$

For each information measure and each consecutive or nonconsecutive year, there are 25 D's. The distribution has a mean M_d and a standard deviation.[31]

$$S_D = \sqrt{\frac{n_1 S^2_1 - n_2 S^a_e}{n_1 - n_2 - 2}} \times \sqrt{\frac{n_1 - n_2}{n_1 n_2}}$$

where D_1 and S_1 represent, respectively, the number of observations and standard deviation in group 1, with n_2 and s_2 representing those of group 2. Our hypothesis was that if two groups are completely identical in terms of financial stability their mean information measures will be equal. So, the observed difference M_d is tested to determine if it is statistically different from zero.

The t distribution is used for inferring about the difference between the two means:

$$t = \frac{M_d}{S_d}$$

Where

$$S_{-d} = S_d/\sqrt{N}$$

An examination of Exhibits 7.9–7.11 shows that relatively none of the t coefficients was statistically significant at alpha error equals 0.05. So H_1 is accepted. It mainly states that the information decomposition measures of the companies taken over are generally larger than those of an identical control group of companies. The evidence is then in support of the information decomposition data as a measure of information provided by accounting data in annual reports. Its discriminating power for the economic event of takeover could be added to its other uses in a variety of contexts.[32] Within the limits of our sample size, we can point to a clear direction of the predictive ability of the information decompositions measures in the context of a takeover. It could be suggested that the informational decomposition measures be added to accounting-ratios-based predictive models to test the improvements in the validity of these models.[33] One might even infer that they would be more powerful than accounting ratios given their dynamic nature and their disaggregation properties. However, the possibility of bias due to imperfect matching should be kept in mind when interpreting the results.

Conclusions on the Information Decomposition Measures

By looking at balance sheets and income statements as numerical decompositions of certain total sums, total assets, or total liabilities, information decomposition measures could be derived for a study of differences between companies of the same industry. In this study, three information measures—the balance sheet information measures, the liabilities information measures, and the asset information measures—were computed from the balance sheets of a sample of 25 acquired firms and 25 equivalent companies. An examination of the results of the comparisons of these information measures for both consecutive years and nonconsecutive years illustrated the discriminating power of the measures. The discriminating power was explained by the fact that the measures indicating

Exhibit 7.11
Comparison of Balance Sheet Information for Firms in the Sample

	Total Number of Comparisons	Number of Cases in which $I_t > I_n$	Average Information over all samples		t Value Computed
			takeover	control	
Consecutive	100	68%	0.025	0.021	
Firm's average over 5 years	25	64%			
2 and 1	25	68%	0.035	0.025	
3 and 2	25	64%	0.024	0.016	3.01
4 and 3	25	68%	0.018	0.027	5.23
5 and 4	25	72%	0.023	0.018	6.01
Non-Consecutive	75	62%	0.047	0.052	3.02
Firm's average	25	64%			
3 and 1	25	56%	0.074	0.065	5.01
4 and 2	25	60%	0.021	0.051	3.21
5 and 3	25	72%	0.048	0.040	4.80

the stability of financial statement item of firms taken over will tend to be less stable (and hence have larger information measures) than those of equivalent firms in a control group.

Although limited to one sample, the results point to the usefulness of the entropy concept in financial analysis and suggest more opportunities for future research.

NOTES

1. Portions of this chapter have been adapted with the permission of the editor from Ahmed Belkaoui, "Financial Ratios as Predictors of Takeovers," *Journal of Business Finance and Accounting* 5, no. 1 (1978), pp. 93–107, and Ahmed Belkaoui, "The Entropy Law, Information Decomposition Measures and Corporate Takeover," *Journal of Business Finance and Accounting* 3, no. 3 (1976), pp. 41–52.

2. R. Marris, *The Economic Theory of Managerial Capitalism* (New York: Macmillan, 1964).

3. Michael Gort, "An Economic Disturbance Theory of Mergers," *Quarterly Journal of Economics* (November, 1969), pp. 624–643.

4. M. D. Bomford, "Changes in the Evaluation of Equities," *The Investment Analyst* (December, 1968), pp. 215–218.

5. J. Tzoannos and J. M. Samuels, "Mergers and Takeovers: The Financial Characteristics of Companies Involved," *Journal of Business Finance* (December, 1972), pp. 5–12.

6. R. J. Chambers, "Finance Information and the Securities Market," *Abacus* (September, 1965), pp. 4–30.

7. Russell A. Taussig and Samuel L. Hayes III, "Cash Takeovers and Accounting Valuation," *Accounting Review* (January, 1968), pp. 68–72.

8. J. Vance, "Is Your Company a Takeover Target?" *Harvard Business Review* (May–June, 1969), pp. 93–102.

9. Robert J. Monroe and Michael A. Simkowitz, "Investment Characteristics of Conglomerate Targets: A Discriminant Analysis," *Southern Journal of Business* (November, 1971), pp. 115–123.

10. Ajit Singh, "Takeovers, Economic Natural Selection, and the Theory of the Firm: Evidence from the Post-War United Kingdom Experience," *The Economic Journal* (September, 1975), pp. 497–515.

11. Donald L. Stevens, "Financial Characteristics of Merged Firms: A Multivariate Analysis," *Journal of Financial and Quantitative Analysis* (March, 1973), pp. 149–158.

12. William H. Beaver, "Financial Ratios as Predictors of Failure," *Empirical Research in Accounting: Selected Studies, Journal of Accounting Research* (Supplement, 1966), pp. 71–111.

13. Stevens, "Financial Characteristics of Merged Firms: A Multivariate Analysis," pp. 149–158.

14. Taussig and Hayes, "Cash Takeovers and Accounting Valuation," pp. 68–72.

15. Ibid.

16. Belkaoui, "The Entropy Law, Information Decomposition Measures and Corporate Takeover," pp. 41–52.

17. S. Kullback, *Information Theory and Statistics* (New York: John Wiley and Sons, 1959), p. 7.

18. Henri Theil, "On the Use of Information Theory Concepts in the Analysis of Financial Statements," *Management Science* XV, no. 9 (May, 1969), pp. 459–480.

19. Baruch Lev, *Accounting and Information Theory* (Evanston, Ill.: American Accounting Association, 1969), pp. 18–34.

20. C. E. Shannon, "A Mathematical Theory of Communication," *Bell System Technical Journal* XXVII (1948), pp. 379–423.

21. Lev, "Accounting and Information Theory," p. 7.

22. These are probabilities in the sense that if we asked what is the chance that one specific dollar taken from a company's assets falls under current assets, the answer would be the fraction current assets/total assets.

23. Lev, "Accounting and Information Theory," p. 21.

24. Nicholas Georgescu-Roegen, *The Entropy Law and the Economic Process* (Cambridge, Mass.: Harvard University Press, 1971).

25. It should be mentioned that this point of view has been rejected by Abdel-Khalik. He tried to find an association between the entropy measure and decisions made by business loan officers of commercial banks in 36 states. He basically rejected the rele-

vance of the entropy measure with the respect to the loan-granting decision. See A. Rashad Abdel-Khalik, "The Entropy Law, Accounting Data, and Relevance to Decision Making," *The Accounting Review* (April, 1974), pp. 271–283.

26. American Accounting Association, *A Statement of Basic Accounting Theory* (Sarasota, Fla.: American Accounting Association, 1966), p. 1.

27. William H. Beaver, John W. Kennelly, and William M. Voss, "Predictive Ability as a Criterion for the Evaluation of Accounting Data," *The Accounting Review* (October, 1968), p. 679.

28. Phillip Brown, "The Predictive Abilities of Alternative Income Concepts," presented to the Conference for Study of Security Prices, Graduate School of Business (Chicago: University of Chicago, November, 1966); David Green, Jr., and Joel Segall, "The Predictive Power of First-Quarter Earnings Reports: A Replication," in *Empirical Research in Accounting: Selected Studies*, 1966, Institute of Professional Accounting, Graduate School of Business (Chicago: University of Chicago, 1967), pp. 21–36; James Horrigan, "The Determination of Long Term Credit Standing with Financial Ratios," *Empirical Research in Accounting: Selected Studies*, 1966, Institute of Professional Accounting, Graduate School of Business (Chicago: University of Chicago, 1967), pp. 44–61; Beaver, "Financial Ratios as Predictors of Failure," pp. 71–102.

29. Samuel A. Martin, Stanley N. Laiken, and Douglas F. Haslam, *Business Combination in the 60's: A Canadian Profile*, The Canadian Institute of Chartered Accountants and the School of Business Administration (London: University of Western Ontario, 1969).

30. Bertrand Horwitz and Allan Young, "An Empirical Study of Accounting Policy and Tender Offers," *Journal of Accounting Research* (Spring, 1972), pp. 77–107.

31. The computation of the formula for estimating the standard error of the difference between independent sample means is illustrated in most statistics books. See Lincoln L. Chao, *Statistics: Methods and Analysis*, 2nd ed. (New York: McGraw-Hill, 1974), p. 269.

32. Philip J. Owen, "The Applicability of Information Theory Measure to Group Discussion Research," Unpublished Master's Thesis, Department of Speech (Champaign: University of Illinois, 1965); Paul E. Green, "Uncertainty, Information and Marketing Decisions," in R. Cox, W. Alderson, and S. J. Shapiro, eds., *A Theory of Marketing* (Homewood, Ill.: Irwin, 1964), pp. 333–343; D. Hirsch and B. Lev, "Sales Stabilization through Export Diversification," *The Review of Economics and Statistics* LIII, no. 3 (August, 1971), pp. 7–27.

33. Vance, "Is Your Company a Takeover Target?" p. 93.

SUGGESTED READINGS

Altman, Edward I. "Financial Ratios, Discriminant Analysis, and the Prediction of Corporate Bankruptcy." *Journal of Finance* (September, 1968), pp. 589–609.

American Accounting Association. *A Statement of Basic Accounting Theory*. Sarasota, Fla.: American Accounting Association, 1966, p. 1.

Beaver, William H. "Alternative Financial Ratios as Predictors of Failure." *Accounting Review* (January, 1968), pp. 113–122.

————. "Financial Ratios as Predictors of Failure." *Empirical Research in Accounting:*

Selected Studies, Journal of Accounting Research (Supplement, 1966), pp. 71–111.

Beaver, William H., John W. Kennelly, and William M. Voss. "Predictive Ability as a Criterion for the Evaluation of Accounting Data." *The Accounting Review* (October, 1968), p. 679.

Bomford, M. D. "Changes in the Evaluation of Equities." *The Investment Analyst* (December, 1968).

Chambers, R. J. "Finance Information and the Securities Market." *Abacus* (September, 1965), pp. 4–30.

Deakin, Edward R. "A Discriminant Analysis of Predictors of Business Failure." *Journal of Accounting Research* (Spring, 1972), pp. 167–179.

Dixon, W. J., ed. *Biomedical Computer Programs.* Berkeley: University of California Press, 1971.

Elam, Rick. "The Effect of Lease Data on the Predictive Ability of Financial Ratios." *Accounting Review* (January, 1975), pp. 25–43.

Georgescu-Roegen, Nicholas. *The Entropy Law and the Economic Process.* Cambridge, Mass.: Harvard University Press, 1971.

Gort, Michael. "An Economic Disturbance Theory of Mergers." *Quarterly Journal of Economics* (November, 1969), pp. 624–643.

Horwitz, Bertrand, and Allan Young. "An Empirical Study of Accounting Policy and Tender Offers." *Journal of Accounting Research* (Spring, 1972), pp. 77–107.

Kullback, S. *Information Theory and Statistics.* New York: John Wiley and Sons, 1959, p. 7.

Lev, Baruch. *Accounting and Information Theory.* Evanston, Ill.: American Accounting Association, 1969, pp. 18–34.

Marris, R. *The Economic Theory of Managerial Capitalism.* New York: Macmillan, 1964.

Martin, Samuel A., Stanley N. Laiken, and Douglas F. Haslam. *Business Combination in the 60's: A Canadian Profile.* The Canadian Institute of Chartered Accountants and the School of Business Administration. London: University of Western Ontario, 1969.

Monroe, Robert J., and Michael A. Simkowitz. "Investment Characteristics of Conglomerate Targets: A Discriminant Analysis." *Southern Journal of Business* (November, 1971).

Shannon, C. E. "A Mathematical Theory of Communication." *Bell System Technical Journal* XXVII (1948), pp. 379–423.

Singh, Ajit. "Takeovers, Economic Natural Selection, and the Theory of the Firm: Evidence from the Post-War United Kingdom Experience." *The Economic Journal* (September, 1975), pp. 497–515.

Stevens, Donald L. "Financial Characteristics of Merged Firms: A Multivariate Analysis." *Journal of Financial and Quantitative Analysis* (March, 1973), pp. 149–158.

Tatsuoka, Maurice M. *Multivariate Analysis.* New York: John Wiley & Sons, 1971.

Taussig, Russell A., and Samuel L. Hayes III. "Cash Takeovers and Accounting Valuation." *Accounting Review* (January, 1968), pp. 68–72.

Theil, Henri. "On the Use of Information Theory Concepts in the Analysis of Financial Statement." *Management Science*, XV, no. 9 (May, 1969), pp. 459–480.

Tzoannos, J., and J. M. Samuels. "Mergers and Takeovers: The Financial Characteristics of Companies Involved." *Journal of Business Finance* (1972), pp. 5–16.

Vance, J. "Is Your Company a Takeover Target?" *Harvard Business Review* (May–June, 1969), pp. 93–102.

Winer, B. J. *Statistical Principles in Experimental Design.* New York: McGraw-Hill, 1962.

8

The Prediction and Explanation of CEO Compensation

INTRODUCTION

CEO compensation is another important economic variable in need of explanation and prediction. This chapter provides three models of prediction of CEO compensation.[1] The first model deals with the effects of personal attributes and performance on the level of CEO compensation. The second model deals with the determinants of executive tenure in large U.S. firms. Finally, the third model deals with the impact of CEO experience, nature of deviation from the analysts' forecasts, and accounting and market measures of performance.

EFFECTS OF PERSONAL ATTRIBUTES AND PERFORMANCE ON THE LEVEL OF CEO COMPENSATION

The purpose of this section is to expand on the nature of the evidence on the determinants of the level of compensation to CEOs of American industrial corporations. Most research to date has focused on testing the relative importance of measures of firm performance as determinants of executive salaries, in general, and those of CEOs, in particular. This study proposes that the personal attributes of CEOs may have an important role in the determination of CEO compensation either through direct or interaction effects. Drawing on unique data on the personal attributes of CEOs from a sample of *Fortune* 500 firms, the study addresses the question, how do the personal attributes of CEOs affect the determinants of CEO compensation?

Determinants of the Level of CEO Compensation

The model in this section builds and expands on previous analyses of executive compensation that focus on the relative importance of different measures of performance.[2-8] Three main avenues characterize our model:

First, various studies estimated the determinants of executive incomes, with an emphasis on firm size. Size effects were consistently found.[9-11] In addition, Kostiuk[12] found the relationship between executive income and firm size to be relatively stable over time and in different countries.

Building on these findings, this section includes both sales as a measure of firm size and income as a measure of profitability as independent variables in the CEO compensation valuation model. The relationship between CEO compensation and firm size is expected to be positive based on the rationale that bigger firms tend to pay more because the CEO oversees substantial resources, rather than because of the firms' ability to pay more or because of their number of hierarchical pay levels. The relationship between CEO compensation and profitability is also expected to be positive, based on the rationale that firms may attempt to improve gauging of CEOs' marginal product of paying for delivered performance.[13]

Second, recent theoretical work by Rosen[14] found the supposed conflict between size and profitability to be misplaced, given that differences in executive ability may partially explain the presence of substantial firm size differentials. We posit that CEOs are paid in part on the basis of their personal attributes. This is congruent with a human capital argument that for many types of jobs, the marginal product of a person is in part estimated to be his or her human capital, for example, his or her investments in education and experience.[15,16]

Accordingly we posit that the level of CEO compensation will be a function of the age, the number of years as a CEO, and tenure. We expect the relationship between CEO compensation, on one hand, and age and tenure in the organization to be negative, based on the idea that younger and "imported" CEOs will require a pay level determined by market factors, while older and "home-grown" CEOs will require a pay level that is the result of performance-linked increases to base salary. We expect, moreover, the years as a CEO in the firm to be positively related to CEO compensation based on the argument that the better the profitability of the firm, the larger a CEO he or she will be and the higher the performance-based compensation.

Third, while the direct effects of CEO age, number of years as a CEO, and tenure are important, their interactions can be also an important determinant of CEO compensation level. To our knowledge, this is the first study investigating the interaction effects of personal attributes. We posit that the interaction between the tenure, on one hand, and CEO age and years as a CEO, on the other hand, to be positive based on the argument that the number of years in the organization acts as a salient factor to the importance of age and experience as a CEO. We expect, however, the interaction between age and number of years as a CEO to be negative based on the argument that younger CEOs can still command a higher market-based salary than the internally determined salary of older CEOs. The final model is expressed as follows;

$$\log Y = à_0 + à_1A + à_2T + à_3Y + à_4AT + à_5AY + à_6TY + à_7P + à_8S + E$$

where

Y = CEO Compensation

A = Age of the CEO

Y = Number of years as the CEO

T = Tenure

AY, AT, and TY = Interaction between A, Y, and T

P = Profitability of the firm

S = Size of the firm

E = Residual term

The Data

Dependent Variables

Cash compensation for the year 1987 (i.e., salary plus annual bonus) is used as a measure of executive compensation. As discussions of the issues involved in various compensation studies indicate, salary plus bonus is almost a significant position of total compensation (salary plus bonus, long-term bonuses, perquisites, pensions, and grants or stock options). In addition, evidence shows that the total salary plus bonus represents between 80 percent and 90 percent of total compensation.[17-19] Finally, Jensen and Murphy[20] also provide evidence that indicates that the slope coefficient relating salary plus bonus to changes in performance is not statistically different from the slope coefficient that relates total compensation to changes in performance.

Independent Variables

The independent variables included firm performance, firm size, CEO age, years as a CEO, and CEO tenure. They deserve explanation:

a. Firm performance was measured as either profit or profit over total assets for the year 1987.

b. Firm size was measured by total sales for the year 1987.

Exhibit 8.1
1987 Summary Statistics

Variable	Mean	Standard Deviation	Minimum	Maximum
1. CEO Compensation (1,000)	852.269	369.15	178.000	3,445.0
2. Sales (1,000)	5,247.341	10,587.41	464.900	101,781.9
3. Assets (1,000)	4,802.744	10,043.30	226.000	87,421.9
4. Age	56.884	5.75	42.000	74.0
5. Tenure	26.537	11.36	10.000	53.0
6. Years as a CEO	9.103	7.92	0.080	43.0
7. Profit	276.609	670.79	−4,407.000	5,258.0

Source: Janice Monti-Belkaoui and Ahmed Riahi-Belkaoui, ''Effects of Personal Attributes and Performance in the Level of CEO Compensation: Direct and Interaction Effects,'' *Managerial Finance* 19, no. 2 (1993), p. 10. Reprinted with permission of the editor.

Sample

To ensure the greatest sample of firms for which data will be available for all the variables, the initial sample chosen was the *Fortune* 500 industrial corporations. The next task was to collect the needed information from the Compustat tape, the proxy statements, the 1988 *Business Week* compensation survey and other sources.

The final sample included 216 companies from 28 different industries. Exhibit 8.1 lists the summary statistics for the sample. As found in previous studies by Roberts[21] and Lewellen[22] these executives have been employed for a great part of their careers by their current firm. The demographic profile of our sample is almost similar to the one used by Kostiuk (1990) with an average age of 57, a mean tenure of 26, and mean years as a CEO of 9.

Results

The logarithms of executive compensation, profit, and sales were used in the analysis. These variables, before transformation, were skewed to the right. If the distribution of the variables is skewed to normalize it a logarithmic transformation is necessary. Exhibit 8.2 gives the results of the regression analysis using either profit or profit over assets as measures of performance. Various interesting results emerge:

Exhibit 8.2
1987 Cross Section Estimates[1]

Dependent Variable: log (Salary+Bonus)		
Intercept	5.5036 (8.781)*	3.7989 (6.653)*
Age : A	-0.00319 (0.283)	0.0011 (0.11)
Tenure: T	-0.03951 (1.641)***	-0.041 (1.862)***
Years as a CEO: Y	0.0675 (2.037)**	0.0597 (2.026)**
AT	0.000597 (2.388)**	0.00063 (2.587)**
AY	-0.0010 (1.612)***	-0.00099 (1.758)***
TY	0.00011 (0.307)	0.0001 (0.300)
log (Profit)	0.1656 (4.363)*	——
Profit/Assets	——	0.4423 (8.730)*
log (Sales)	0.0695 (1.708)***	0.3376 (13.603)*
R^2 adjusted	35.40%	48.53%
F	14.904*	26.345*

(1) Absolute Value of t - statistic in parentheses
*Significant at α =0.01 **Significant at α =0.05 ***Significant at α =0.10

Source: Janice Monti-Belkaoui and Ahmed Riahi-Belkaoui, "Effects of Personal Attributes and
   Performance in the Level of CEO Compensation: Direct and Interaction Effects," *Managerial
   Finance* 19, no. 2 (1993), p. 11. Reprinted with permission of the editor.

1. The model is highly significant and explains an adequate amount of variables.

2. A nonsurprising result is the irrelevancy of age, a phenomenon also observed by
   Kostiuk.

3. The direct effects of the other personal attributes are significant and the signs are as
   predicted. Tenure is negatively related to CEO compensation, while years as a CEO
   is positively related.

4. Of the interaction effect, the surprising result is the irrelevancy of the tenure and years
   as a CEO interaction. The other interactions are significant and the signs are as predicted. The age-tenure interaction is positively related to CEO compensation, while
   the age-years as a CEO is negatively related.

5. As expected the performance and size factors are significant and positively related to
   CEO compensation.

Discussion

Personal attributes significantly affect a CEO's pay in two ways: directly and in tandem. The direct effects of personal attributes were present in the case of tenure and years as a CEO. Basically, executives with less tenure in the firm and more years as a CEO are paid more than those with high tenure and fewer years as a CEO. Experience rather than tenure appears to be a more important factor in the determination of CEO compensation.

The interaction effects of personal attributes were present in the case of the age-tenure interaction and the age-years as a CEO interaction. First, older executives with high tenure are paid more. While tenure by itself is not rewarding, when associated with age it leads to better pay. The passage of time worked with loyalty to the same firm, in other words, the survival factor, led to better pay.

Second, older executives with more years as a CEO are paid less than younger CEOs with fewer years as a CEO. While years as a CEO by itself is rewarding, when associated with age it leads to lower pay. There is definitely a salary compression phenomenon as well as a market factor favoring younger CEOs.

DETERMINANTS OF EXECUTIVE TENURE IN LARGE U.S. FIRMS

The purpose of this section is to expand on the nature of the evidence on the determinants of executive tenure of the CEOs of large American industrial corporations. Salancik and Pfeffer[23] related executive tenure to both ownership and performance. Performance measures were found to be related to the tenure of chief executives, depending on the concentration of stock ownership. Basically, tenure was unrelated to performance for owner-managed firms, positively related to profit margins in externally controlled firms, and positively related to stock market returns in management-controlled firms.

This study proposes a different way of expressing performance and ownership structure, and adds diversification strategy and CEO compensation level as important variables affecting executive tenure. Drawing on unique data on CEOs from a sample of *Fortune* 500 firms, the study addresses the question of how performance, compensation level, diversification strategy, and ownership structure affect the tenure of CEOs in large U.S. firms.

Determinants of Executive Tenure

The research model is illustrated in Exhibit 8.3. Each line represents a specific research hypothesis. Related diversification, unrelated diversification, and stock concentration are shown to be negatively related to executive tenure. Management stockholding, performance, and compensation levels are shown to be positively related to executive tenure.

Exhibit 8.3
Research Model

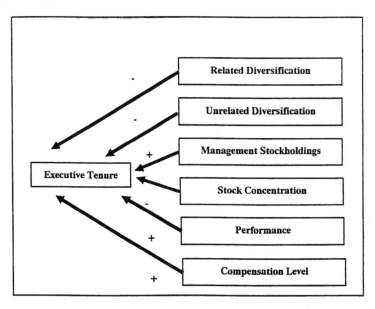

Source: Ellen Pavlik and Ahmed Riahi-Belkaoui, "Determinants of Executive Tenure in Large U.S. Firms," *Managerial Finance* 19, no. 2 (1993), p. 13. Reprinted with the permission of the editor.

Executive Tenure and Diversification Strategy

The strategic management literature differentiates between two types of diversification strategies: related and unrelated. Firms adopting a related strategy diversify predominantly within their industries, while those adopting an unrelated strategy diversify predominantly across industries. To realize the benefits associated with pursuing either of the two strategies within an M-form (multidivisional) firm structure, control requirements that fit the strategies are required. These controls involve determination of the degrees of decentralization of decisions to divisions, decomposition between divisions, and accountability for divisional profits.

As these controls need to be updated, revised, and adapted to new environmental characteristics, the situation calls for the use of different managerial styles to effect changes. Different executives may be needed to adopt different controls as the firms increase their diversification programs. The argument is that when an organization diversifies its activities according to a related or unrelated strategy, different executives are needed to adopt and adapt new control mechanisms that fit these strategies, and replacement of managers might be expected. From the above reasoning the first hypothesis is derived:

Hypothesis 1: Diversification strategy affects executive tenure. Tenure will be negatively related to the level of related and unrelated diversification.

Ownership Structure and Executive Tenure

Ownership represents a source of power that can affect executive tenure. Various studies have examined the impact of ownership structure on executive tenure.[24] Our study differentiates between managers' and stockholders' interests, and views the firm as an imperfect and unstable risk-sharing arrangement between managers, employees, and shareholders that is in flux rather than in equilibrium.[25] The distinction between managers' and stockholders' interests is based on the following premises made in the literature on managerial discretion: While stockholders are wealth maximizers requiring a maximization of efficiency, managers have a tendency to maximize a personal utility function that has remuneration, power, security, and status as major arguments, requiring a maximization of firm size and diversity. The impact of ownership structure on executive tenure is assumed to differ depending on whether ownership structure is expressed by stock concentration or management stockholding.

First, according to the entrenchment hypothesis, market value and profitability of a firm do not increase with management ownership. Demsetz[26] and Fama and Jensen[27] have pointed out the offsetting costs associated with higher management stockholding. If managers hold a large enough proportion of the common stock, they will opt for non-value-maximizing behavior and behavior that would increase their tenure with the firm.

Second, with concentrated ownership, stockholders are better able to both coordinate action and demand information that will allow them to overcome any information asymmetries[28] and influence management's decisions and responsibility toward value-maximization, and strategies that are in the stockholders' interests. The power given to them by stock concentration puts owners in more instances to oppose management's policies, even in the case of good performance. Accordingly,

Hypothesis 2: There will be a positive relationship between management stockholding and executive tenure.

Hypothesis 3: There will be a negative relationship between stock concentration and executive tenure.

Performance and Executive Tenure

Common sense dictates that a poor firm performance will cause a manager to be replaced. Evidence, in fact, supports a positive association between performance and executive tenure. This includes findings that (a) chief executives are more likely to quit after a four-year or more decline in profits;[29] (b) executive tenure was negatively related to financial risk;[30] (c) baseball managers are likely to be dismissed with declining team performance;[31] (d) academic department heads are likely to quit in times that are difficult in terms of resource acquisition;

(e) hospital administrators have lower tenure when there is great competition for funding and staff; and (f) tenure is related positively to profit margins for externally controlled firms, and to stock market rates of return for management controlled firms. Accordingly:

Hypothesis 4: There will be a positive relationship between firm performance and executive tenure.

Executive Tenure and Level of Compensation

It is customary to use the level of executive salary as the appropriate dependent variable in the empirical estimation of the determinants of executive compensation. The rationale is that the level of executive salary is the most important reason for seeking employment with the firm and it should be set commensurate with the firm performance. There are, of course, transaction costs to the firm of hiring a new executive and to the departing executive upon leaving the firm. Consequently, these transaction costs define a bargaining range within which the executive salary may vary without creating an incentive for the firm to let an executive go and without motivating the executive to leave.[32] If the level of salary is below this range, or if a competing firm offers a level of salary beyond this range, an executive may be tempted to leave. Therefore executive tenure is a positive function of the level of compensation.

Hypothesis 5: There will be a positive relationship between executive tenure and the level of executive compensation. The higher the level of executive compensation, the longer the tenure.

Methods

Model and Measurement of Variables

The five hypotheses state that executive tenure is negatively related and unrelated to diversification and stock concentration, and positively related to firm performance, management stockholding, and level of compensation. The linear regression model used follows:

$$Et_i = à_1 + à_2 RTD_i + à_3 UTD_i + à_4 MSH_i + à_5 STC_i + à_6 PERF_i + à_7 COMP_i + \mu_i$$

where

Et_i = Executive tenure

RTD_i = Related diversification

UTD_i = Unrelated diversification

MSH_i = Management stockholding

STC_i = Stock concentration
$PERF_i$ = Firm performance
$COMP_i$ = Level of compensation
μ_i = Residual term

The variables were measured as follows:

1. The dependent variable of executive tenure was measured as the number of years as CEO up to 1987.
2. The product-count method was used to determine the extent of related and unrelated diversification. The extent of unrelated diversification was measured by the number of two-digit Standard Industrial Classification (SIC) industries outside the primary two-digit industry in which the firm was active during 1987. The extent of related diversification was measured by the number if five-digit SIC industries within the main two-digit industry in which the firm was active during 1987. Dunn and Bradstreet's *Reference Book of Corporate Management* was used to collect the data.
3. Ownership structure was measured by both management stockholding and stock concentration. The data were collected from 1988 proxy statements. Stock concentration was computed as the share of ownership by outside stockholders owning more than 5 percent of the common voting stock in 1987. Management stockholding were measured by the percentage of common voting stock held by officers and directors in 1987.
4. Firm performance was measured by the 1987 profit deflated by the 1987 level of executive compensation.

Sample

To ensure a large sample size with readily available data, the initial sample chosen was the *Fortune* 500 industrial corporations; the information needed was gathered from both the Compustat tape and the 1988 *Business Week* survey of executive compensation. The final sample for which information on all variables was available included 196 companies from 28 different industries.

Results and Discussion

Exhibit 8.4 presents the results of the regression model that relates executive tenure in large U.S. corporations and related diversification, unrelated diversification, management stockholding, stock concentration, firm performance, and level of compensation for the year 1987. As predicted in the five hypotheses, executive tenure in large U.S. corporations is negatively related to unrelated and related diversification, and to stock concentration, and positively related to management stockholding, firm performance, and the level of compensation.

It appears as if tenure with a firm depends on the manager's actions, which include (a) holding enough voting power via the acquisition of enough stock, (b) ensuring an adequate firm performance through a judicious allocation of resources and value maximization behavior, and (c) negotiating an adequate

Exhibit 8.4
1987 Cross Section Estimates[1]

Dependent Variables: Executive Tenure		
Intercept	-22.301	(-2.336)**
Related Diversification	-1.326	(-3.137)*
Unrelated Diversification	-1.348	(-2.704)*
Management Stockholdings	0.146	(3.143)*
Stock Concentration	-0.0617	(-2.076)**
Profit/Compensation	2.539	(2.041)**
Compensation	5.111	(3.555)*

[1] Value of T statistic in parentheses
*significant at $\alpha=0.01$ **Significant at $\alpha=0.05$

Source: Ellen Pavlik and Ahmed Riahi-Belkaoui, "Determinants of Executive Tenure in Large U.S. Firms," *Managerial Finance* 19, no. 2 (1993), p. 17. Reprinted with the permission of the editor.

level of executive compensation within a broad acceptable range. Furthermore, it seems that tenure is also affected by the actions of others, namely, the shareholders who can (a) hold enough voting rights through acquisition of stock and (b) call for policies of diversification that demand the constant upgrading of control mechanisms and consequently the turnover of executives.

Executives' tenure appears to be a complex phenomena that depends on a host of important environmental factors. Other factors that have not been included in this study need to be investigated. Future research should also investigate the relationship examined here for other contracts and time periods.

Influence of Other Variables

The purpose of this section is to expand the nature of evidence on the determinants of compensation for CEOs of American industrial corporations. Most research to date has focused on measures of performance as determinants of executive salaries in general, and CEOs in particular. This study proposes such measures of performance are not the sole determinants of compensation. It is held that personal characteristics of CEOs, as well as measures of organizational effectiveness, may have important roles in the determination of CEO compensation. More explicitly, this study posits that CEO experience—as one salient measure of the personal characteristics of CEOs—and the nature of the financial analysts' forecast of earnings per share—as one salient measure of organizational effectiveness—are important determinants of CEO compensation. In what follows, the theoretical framework, the methods used, the empirical results, and a discussion of the findings are presented.

Exhibit 8.5
A Model of the Determinants of CEO Compensation

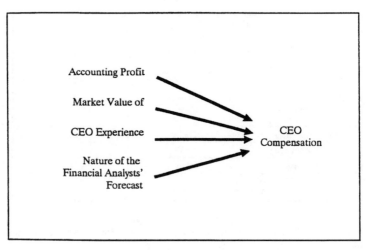

Source: Ahmed Riahi-Belkaoui and Ron D. Picur, "An Analysis of the Use of Accounting Market
Measures of Performance, CEO Experience and Nature of the Deviations from the Analysts'
Forecasts in CEO Compensation Contracts," *Managerial Finance* 19, no. 2 (1993), p. 21.
Reprinted with the permission of the editor.

Theoretical Framework

Exhibit 8.5 illustrates the model. Each line represents a research hypothesis.
The CEO experience, the nature of the deviation from the analysts' forecasts,
and both the accounting and market measures of performance are shown as
directly influencing executive compensation. The main hypotheses are presented
below.

CEO Experience and Executive Compensation

Most studies dealing with the determinants of executive compensation rely
on the traditional marginal productivity approach to wage determination. That
approach considers performance as the principal determinant of compensation.
With one exception, little attention has been directed to the broader determinants
of executive compensation, such as the personal characteristics of the individual
executives.[33] In contrast, this study assumes that CEO experience in terms of
the number of years as CEO in the firm can be identified as an explicit determinant in two alternative views of wage determination. These two views include
the screening hypothesis.[34–37] and the job competition hypothesis.[38]

The *screening hypothesis* suggests that in a world of imperfect information,
such personal characteristics as the number of years as CEO (i.e., CEO experience) are indicators of qualities conducive to successful performance. Thus, a
compensation board is likely to take that variable into account in setting exec-

utive compensations, since it will be perceived as an indicator of future performance.

The *job competition hypothesis* favors the heavy investment in employee training for a specific job and for the particular conditions of the firm.[39] CEO experience is considered favorable because training costs incurred by the firm prepare the executive for a future productive post. It is therefore a good indicator of future performance.

The hypothesis suggests that CEO experience provides an assessment of future performance and will be related to executive compensation.

Hypothesis 1: There will be a positive relationship between CEO experience and compensation.

Firm Performance and Executive Compensation

There is ample evidence indicating a positive relationship between firm profitability and executive compensation. Those studies demonstrate that executive compensation committees of the board of directors—in their search for incentive arrangements that will encourage management to act in the shareholders' interests—set compensation on the basis of financial performance measures, which are themselves related to shareholders' wealth.

One such performance measure is the accounting profit of the firm. However, various arguments suggest inclusion of a market measure of performance, in addition to the accounting measure. First, using the results of Holstrom[40] and others, which suggest that relative weight placed on a measure in a compensation contract is an increasing function of its "signal-to-noise" ratio with respect to the agent's functions, Lambert and Larcker[41] examined whether the relative use of security market and accounting measures of performance in executive compensation is related to the amount of "consistent noise" inherent in two signals and the "sensitivity" of these two signals to managerial actions. Their results were consistent with the hypothesis that firms place relatively more weight on market performance (and less weight on accounting performance) in compensation contracts for situations in which, (i) the variance of the accounting measure is high relative to the variance of the market measure of performance, (ii) the firm is experiencing high growth rates in assets and sales, and (iii) the value of the manager's personal holdings of his firm's stock is low.

Second, much of the previous empirical research[42] relied on an annual stock return as a measure of performance. Such a measure impounds changes in a firm's financial condition associated with both current and anticipated actions and events. In addition, unlike accounting measures used to evaluate executives, market-based performance measures are not subject to a moral hazard. While these arguments are commonly accepted, Antle and Smith[43] present two reasons why accounting measures can be used in addition to (or instead of) the market measures of performance. First, stock prices impound information relevant for valuing the firm, but do not necessarily impound all information relevant for

evaluating the performance of the firm's management.[44] Second, it is easier for
the executive to hedge the risk from a contract based on stock returns than one
based on accounting variables.

Moreover, one widely held position is that stockholders' welfare—in the form
of increases in stock prices or dividends paid, rather than profitability—should
dictate executive pay.[45,46] However, concern about the effect of paying out dividends on reinvestments and research and development (R & D) projects, and
the sensitivity of stock prices to other external events, has led various compensation consultants to discourage use of market-based performance as the primary
basis for establishing CEO pay.[47–49] These arguments suggest that while market
measures of performance may not always dominate accounting-based variables,
they are still likely candidates for consideration in the compensation plans linking pay to financial performance measures. Thus,

Hypothesis 2: There is a positive relationship between accounting and market measures
of financial performance and executive compensation.

Executive Compensation and Nature of the Analysts' Forecasts

Outside groups (i.e., shareholders, executives from other firms, watchdog
groups, financial analysts, etc.) monitor performance of managers of a given
firm. Such groups then organize their relationship with that firm (i.e., investing
in, purchasing from, forecasting, etc) in terms of their perception of the effectiveness of the managerial ability of the firm. This perception, known as organizational effectiveness, has also been termed participant satisfaction, the ecological model, or the external effectiveness domain.[50–53] The ecological model of
organizational effectiveness suggests a multiconstituent view of effectiveness.[54]
It treats organizations as systems generating differential assessments of effectiveness by different constituencies. The approach, following suggestions by
Scott[55] and Ullman,[56] consists of (a) choosing one constituency, (b) measuring
the members' satisfaction using different measures, and (c) combining the results
of each measure to develop an overall index so that firms can be ranked by
overall organizational effectiveness. Such a measure of overall effectiveness will
create pressure on the compensation-setting board, because it represents the perception of an important outside group regarding managers' overall performance.
Recognizing the impact of this outside group decision on the firm's survival,
the compensation-setting board will use the measures of overall effectiveness in
the setting of the level of executive compensation.

Financial analysts are seen as an outside group esteemed for the superiority
of their effectiveness measure. The evidence from recent empirical tests comparing the accuracy of financial analysts' forecasts of firm earnings to the accuracy of predictions from univariate time-series forecasting models indicates a
clear superiority of the financial analysts' forecasts. In addition, the financial
analysts' forecasts were found to be a better surrogate for market expectations[57]
and firm size.[58]

Given the superiority of the analyst's forecast of earnings, the compensation board will view the nature of the analyst's forecast—expressed as either a percentage increase or decrease from the actual earnings per share—as a measure of overall effectiveness. The board will then utilize it for the setting of the level of executive compensation. Thus,

Hypothesis 3: There will be a positive relationship between the nature of the analyst's forecast of earnings and executive compensation for a given year.

Measurement of Variables

A. Executive Compensation Data: Cash compensation (i.e., salary plus annual bonus) is used as the measure of executive compensation. As indicated in discussions of the issues involved in valuing various forms of compensation, salary plus bonus is almost always a significant portion of total compensation (i.e., salary plus bonus, long-term bonuses, prerequisites, pensions, and grants of stock options). In addition, evidence shows that salary plus bonus represents between 80 and 90 percent of total compensation. Finally, evidence exists that suggests that the slope coefficient relating salary plus bonus to changes in performance is not statistically different from the slope coefficient that relates total compensation to changes in performance.

B. CEO Experience: CEO experience is defined as the number of years the person has been a CEO in the firm.

C. Nature of the Financial Analyst's Forecast of Earnings (NFAFE): NFAFE is measured as the difference between the analyst's estimate of the earnings per share of the forthcoming year and the actual earnings per share, divided by the actual earnings per share. Because various analyst forecasts are available in the marketplace, the premise adopted is that the compensation board will be looking for a measure of consensus estimate, when setting executive compensation, rather than relying on one particular individual financial analyst's forecast.

D. Firm Performance: The firm performance is defined by two measures: (1) the *accounting measure* is the net profit of the firm, and (2) the *market measure* is the end of the year market value of the firm.

Sample

The main sample of firms was primarily obtained from the 1988 *Business Week* compensation survey. That survey includes CEO profits and compensation for the 1,000 largest corporations in the United States, ranked by market value. Of interest to this study that survey included 1987 data on cash compensation and bonus, and number of years as CEO. Accordingly, this study focuses on 1987 data.

Because a consensus of 1987 analysts' forecasts was sought, it was derived from the consensus estimates compiled by the *Institutional Brokers Estimate (IBES)* and reprinted in the 1987 *Business Week's Investment Outlook Scoreboard*. Each *IBES* forecast is a consensus of as many as 60 analysts. It follows that the nature of the analysts' forecasts was computed as the difference between the 1987 *IBES* forecast of earnings per share and the actual 1986 earnings per share, divided by the actual 1986 earnings per share. The actual 1986 earnings per share, as well as the 1987 accounting profit, was obtained from Compustat.

To be encompassed in our sample, a firm had to be (1) included in the 1988 *Business Week* compensation survey, (2) the subject of an *IBES* consensus estimate, and (3) included in Compustat. The final sample consisted of 247 firms in 22 industries.

Empirical Tests

Model

The various hypotheses and variables are combined into an empirically testable model specified as follows:

$$\text{CEOC}_i = a_{0I} + a_{1i}\text{PRFT}_i + a_{2i}\text{MVF}_i + a_{3i}\text{CEOE}_i + a_{4i}\text{NFAFE}_i + e_i$$

where

CEOC_i = CEO 1987 salary and bonus

PRFT_i = 1987 net profit

MVF_i = 1987 market value of the firm

CEOE_i = CEO experience in terms of number of years as CEO of the firm

NFAFE_i = 1987 IBES Estimate of EPS − 1987 Actual EPS/1986 Actual EPS

e_i = Error term

a_1, a_2, a_3, a_4 = Coefficients for the PRFT, MVF, CEOE, and NFAFE

I = firm.

Empirical Tests of the Model

Based on the model, a regression was run for the year 1987. Exhibit 8.6 contains the overall regression results. The model appears highly significant ($F = 14.205$, $X = 0.0001$; R^2 = adjusted = 17.68 percent).

The regression coefficients for PRFT, MVF, CEOE, and NFAFE are significant at the 0.10 level or less and have the expected signs. In other words, the CEO salary and bonus is found to be significantly associated with accounting profit (PRFT), the market value of the firm (MVF), the CEO experience (CEOE), and the nature of the analyst's forecast of the future earnings per share.

Interpretations of the regression results and the individual coefficients are contingent on the aptness of the model and are affected by the presence of multicollinearity. The remainder of this section discusses such issues.

Exhibit 8.7 results indicate the presence of some multicollinearity. There are two pairwise correlations of independent variables that are significant at the $P = 0.10$ level. This may adversely affect the interpretation of regression coefficients. However, there is no agreement on what constitutes a high level of

Exhibit 8.6
Regression Results

Variable Definition	Intercept	Net Profit	Market Value	CEO Experience	Nature of Analyst's Forecast	Model Significance
Variable		PRFT	MVF	CEOE	NFAFE	F A²
Coefficient	748.059	0.1910	0.00878	5.437	55.510	14.205 17.68%
Standardized Estimates	0	0.8018	0.1406	0.1002	0.0841	
t-Score	15.52[a]	3.194[a]	1.634[b]	1.711[b]	1.647[b]	

[a]Significant at $\alpha = 0.05$.
[b]Significant at $\alpha = 0.10$.
Source: Ahmed Riahi-Belkaoui and Ron D. Picur, "An Analysis of the Use of Accounting Market Measures of Performance, CEO Experience and Nature of the Deviations from the Analysts' Forecasts in CEO Compensation Contracts," *Managerial Finance* 19, no. 2 (1993), p. 26. Reprinted with the permission of the editor.

multicollinearity. The method calculates the coefficient of multiple correlations R^2 between each variable and all the others. The rule of thumb for serious multicollinearity is a multiple correlation coefficient greater than 80 percent. Exhibit 8.7 shows no such value. Thus, it can be concluded that serious multicollinearity is not present.

The next issue relates to the functional form of the model's relationship between compensation and the independent variables. Linearity has been assumed, although there are some theoretical results available on the basic property of contracts. For example, the condition under which contracts are increasing[59–61] is convexly or bang-bang.[62] Therefore given the lack of theoretical support for the linear contracts, the decision was to consider the sensitivity of the results to potential model misspecifications. Two tests were used. The first test consists of plotting the residuals for each observation against the corresponding PRFT, MVF, CEOE, and NFAFE. No systematic patterns consistent with the nonlinear contracts were apparent for the sample. The second test was to compute a Spearman rank correlation test between the dependent variable of compensation and each of the independent variables. The results in each test were significant, indicating a close match of compensation with each of the independent variables.

Discussion of Findings

This study proposed a positive model of the CEO compensation as being a function of accounting and market measures of performance, CEO experience,

Exhibit 8.7
Correlation Results

Variable	CEOC	MVF	PRFT	NFAFE	CEOE
CEOC	1.000 0.00				
MVF	-0.135 (0.0355)	1.000 (0.000)			
PRFT	-0.1070 (0.0903)	0.7899 (0.0001)	1.000 (0.000)		
NFAFE	0.0705 (0.2595)	0.0727 (0.2548)	0.0537 (0.7639)	1.000 (0.000)	
CEOE	0.0549 (0.3503)	0.3712 (0.0001)	0.9064 (0.0001)	0.1182 (0.0635)	1.000 (0.000)
R^2	0.5205	0.5350	0.6333	0.0042	0.1758

Source: Ahmed Riahi-Belkaoui and Ron D. Picur, "An Analysis of the Use of Accounting Market Measures of Performance, CEO Experience and Nature of the Deviations from the Analysts' Forecasts in CEO Compensation Contracts," *Managerial Finance* 19, no. 2 (1993), p. 27. Reprinted with the permission of the editor.

and the nature of the financial analyst forecasts of earnings. The results are significant for each of the independent variables examined based on the 1987 sample. For that year and for the companies included, CEOs are compensated as if their performance is evaluated relative to the accounting profit, the market value of the firm, their experience as a CEO, and the nature of the analyst forecasts of earnings per share.

The significance of CEO experience as a determinant of executive compensation verifies the underlying premises of both the screening hypothesis and the job competition hypothesis—that is, that CEO experience is a good indicator of future performance.

The significance of both the accounting profit and the market value of the firm as determinants of CEO compensation (1) adds to the existing evidence that compensation plans approved by boards of directors are generally linked to performance measures and (2) point to the importance of both accounting and market measures of performance in the compensation decision.

The significance of the nature of the analyst forecasts suggests that compensation boards take into account external indicators as measures of overall effectiveness in their compensation-setting decision. The financial analyst estimates of future earnings per share act as measures of overall effectiveness expressed by an important outside group.

This study has implications for the determinants of CEO compensation. It points to the importance of both internal and external indicators of performance, as well as personal characteristics of the CEO, in the determination of CEO compensation. It raises the need to examine other external indicators and other personal characteristics of CEOs as potential determinants of compensation.

NOTES

1. This chapter has been partially adapted with permission of the editor from the following three articles: Janice Monti-Belkaoui and Ahmed Riahi-Belkaoui, "Effects of Personal Attributes and Performance in the Level of CEO Compensation: Direct and Interaction Effects," *Managerial Finance* 19, no. 2 (1993), pp. 3–11; Ellen Pavlik and Ahmed Riahi-Belkaoui, "Determinants of Executive Tenure in Large U.S. Firms," *Managerial Finance* 19, no. 2 (1993), pp. 12–19; Ahmed Riahi-Belkaoui and Ron D. Picur, "An Analysis of the Use of Accounting Market Measures of Performance, CEO Experience and Nature of the Deviation from the Analysts' Forecasts in CEO Compensation Contracts," *Managerial Finance* 19, no. 2 (1993), pp. 20–32.

2. R. T. Mason, "Executive Motivations, Earnings and Consequent Equity Performance," *Journal of Political Economy* (December, 1971), pp. 1278–1292.

3. R. Antle and A. Smith, "Measuring Executive Compensation: Methods and an Application," *Journal of Accounting Research* (Spring, 1985), pp. 296–337.

4. D. Ciscel and T. Carroll, "The Determinants of Executive Salaries: An Econometrics Survey," *Review of Economics and Statistics* (February, 1980), pp. 7–13.

5. A. Coughlin and R. Schmidt, "Executive Compensation, Management Turnover, and Firm Performance: An Empirical Investigation," *Journal of Accounting and Economics* (April, 1985), p. 66.

6. R. A. Lambert and D. F. Larcker, "An Analysis of the Use of Accounting and Market Measures of Performance in Executive Compensation Contracts," *Studies in Stewardship Uses of Accounting Information*, Supplement to the *Journal of Accounting Research* 25 (1987), pp. 85–129.

7. J. McGuire, J. Chiu, and A. Elbing, "Executive Incomes, Sales and Profits," *Journal of Political Economy* (September, 1962), pp. 753–761.

8. W. Lewellen and B. Huntsman, "Managerial Pay and Corporate Performance," *American Economic Review* (September, 1970), pp. 710–720.

9. Wesley Mellow, "Employer Size and Wages," *Review of Economics and Statistics* 69 (1982), pp. 495–501.

10. M. E. Personick and C. B. Barsky, "White-Collar Pay Levels Linked to Corporate Work Force and Size," *Monthly Labor Review* 105 (1982), pp. 115–130.

11. Walter Oi, "Heterogeneous Firms and the Organization of Production," *Economic Inquiry* 21 (1983), pp. 147–171.

12. Peter F. Kostiuk, "Firm Size and Executive Compensation," *The Journal of Human Resources* 25 (1990), pp. 90–105.

13. S. Finkelstein and D. Hambrick, "Chief Executive Compensation: A Study of the Intersection of Markets and Political Processes," *Strategic Management Journal* 10 (April, 1989), pp. 121–134; S. Finkelstein, and D. Hambrick, "Chief Executive Compensation: A Synthesis and Reconciliation," *Strategic Management Journal* 9 (1988), pp. 543–558.

14. Sherwin Rosen, "Authority, Control and the Distribution of Earnings," *Bell Journal of Economics* 13 (1982), pp. 311–323.

15. Gary S. Becker, *Human Capital* (New York: Columbia University Press for National Bureau of Economic Research, 1964).

16. Jacob Mincer, "The Distribution of Labor Incomes: A Survey with Special Ref-

erence to the Human Capital Approach,'' *Journal of Economic Literature* 8 (1970), pp. 1–26.

17. G. Benston, ''The Self-Serving Hypothesis: Some Evidence,'' *Journal of Accounting and Economics* (April, 1985), pp. 67–84.

18. Booz, Allen and Hamilton, *Executive Pay in the Eighties: Major Exposures Ahead* (New York: Booz, Allen and Hamilton, 1988).

19. Hay Associates, ''Fifth Annual Hay Report on Executive Compensation,'' *Wharton Magazine* (April, 1985), pp. 85–107.

20. M. Jensen and F. Murphy, ''Are Executive Compensation Contracts Structured Properly?'' Working Paper (Rochester, N.Y.: University of Rochester, 1987).

21. David Roberts, ''A General Theory of Executive Compensation based on Statistically Tested Propositions,'' *Quarterly Journal of Economics* 70 (1956), pp. 270–294.

22. W. G. Lewellen, *Executive Compensation in Large Industrial Corporations* (New York: National Bureau of Economic Research, 1968).

23. G. R. Salancik and J. Pfeffer, ''Effects of Ownership and Performance on Executive Tenure in U.S. Corporations,'' *Academy of Management Journal* 23, no. 4 (1980), pp. 653–664.

24. J. Pfeffer and G. R. Salancik, ''Organizational Context and the Characteristics and Tenure of Hospital Administrators,'' *Academy of Management Journal* 20 (1977), pp. 74–88.

25. J. C. Coffee, ''Shareholders versus Managers: The Strain in the Corporate Web,'' in J. C. Coffee et al., *Knights, Raiders and Targets: The Impact of the Hostile Takeover* (New York: Oxford University Press, 1988).

26. H. Demsetz, ''The Structure of Ownership and the Theory of the Firm,'' *Journal of Law and Economics* 26 (1983), pp. 375–390.

27. E. F. Fama and M. C. Jensen, ''Agency Problems and Residual Claims,'' *Journal of Law and Economics* 20 (1983), pp. 327–345.

28. A. A. Berle and G. C. Means, *The Modern Corporation* (New York: Macmillan, 1932).

29. W. A. McEachern, *Managerial Control and Performance* (Lexington, Mass.: Lexington Books, 1975).

30. J. Pfeffer and H. Leblebici, ''Executive Recruitment and the Development of Interfirm Organizations,'' *Administrative Science Quarterly* 18 (1973), pp. 449–461.

31. O. Grusky, ''Managerial Succession and Organizational Effectiveness,'' *American Journal of Sociology* 67 (1961), pp. 263–269.

32. R. T. Mason, ''Executive Motivation, Earnings and Consequent Equity Performance,'' *Journal of Political Economy* 75, no. 6 (November–December, 1971), pp. 1278–1292.

33. T. D. Hogan and L. R. McPheters, ''Executive Compensation: Performance Versus Personal Characteristics,'' *Southern Economic Journal* 46 (1980), pp. 1060–1068.

34. K. Arrow, ''Higher Education as a Filter,'' *Journal of Public Economics* (December, 1973), pp. 193–216.

35. J. E. Stiglitz, ''The Theory of 'Screening,' Education, and the Distribution of Income,'' *American Economic Review* (1975), pp. 283–305.

36. P. J. Taubman and T. Wales, ''Higher Education, Mental Ability, and Screening,'' *Journal of Political Economy* (January–February, 1973), pp. 28–55.

37. K. Wolpin, ''Education and Screening,'' *American Economic Review* (December, 1977), pp. 949–958.

38. L. C. Thurow, *Generalizing Inequality* (New York: Basic Books, 1975).

39. Becker, *Human Capital*.

40. B. Holstrom, "Moral Hazard and Observability," *Bell Journal of Economics* (November, 1979), pp. 74–91.

41. Lambert and Larcker, "An Analysis of the Use of Compensation Contracts," pp. 85–129.

42. R. Antle and A. Smith, "Measuring Executive Compensation: Methods and an Application," *Journal of Accounting Research* (Spring, 1985), pp. 296–237.

43. R. Antle and A. Smith, "An Empirical Investigation into Relative Performance Evaluation of Corporate Executives," *Journal of Accounting Research* (Spring, 1986), pp. 1–39.

44. F. Gjesdal, "Accounting for Stewardship," *Journal of Accounting Research* (Spring, 1981), pp. 208–231.

45. C. Z. Poster, "Executive Compensation: Taking Long-Term Incentives Out of the Corporate Tower," *Compensation Review* 17, no. 2 (1985), pp. 30–31.

46. A. Rappaport, "Executive Incentives Versus Corporate Growth," *Harvard Business Review* 56, no. 4 (1978), pp. 81–88.

47. C. C. Bickford, "Long-Term Incentives for Management, Part 6: Performance Attainment Plans," *Compensation Review* 12, no. 3 (1981), pp. 14–29.

48. B. Ellig, "Incentive Plans: Over the Long Term," *Compensation Review* 16, no. 3 (1984), pp. 39–54.

49. J. T. Rich and J. A. Larrson, "Why Some Long-Term Incentives Fail," *Compensation Review* 16, no. 1 (1984) pp. 26–37.

50. M. S. Keely, "Social Justice Approach to Organizational Evaluation," *Administrative Science Quarterly* 23 (1978), pp. 272–292.

51. R. H. Kilman, and R. P. Herden, "Towards a Systematic Methodology for Evaluating the Impact of Interventions on Organizational Effectiveness," *Academy of Management Review* 1, no. 3 (1976), pp. 87–98.

52. T. Connolly, Edward J. Conlon, and Stuart Jay Deutsh, "Organizational Effectiveness: A Multiple-Constituency Approach," *Academy of Management Review* 5, no. 2 (1980), pp. 43–66.

53. J. L. Price, "The Study of Organizational Effectiveness," *Sociological Quarterly* 13 (1972), pp. 3–15.

54. R. H. Miles, *Macro-Organizational Behavior* (Glenview, Ill.: Scott, Foresman, 1980).

55. W. R. Scott, *Organizations: Rational, Natural and Operational Systems* (Englewood Cliffs, N.J.: Prentice-Hall, 1981).

56. A. A. Ullman, "Data in Search of a Theory: A Critical Examination of the Relationship among Social Performance, Social Disclosure and Economic Performance of U.S. Firms," *The Academy of Management Review* (July, 1985), pp. 540–547.

57. L. Brown, P. Griffin, R. Hagerman, and M. H. Zmijewske, "An Evaluation of Alternate Proxies for the Market's Assessment of Unexpected Earnings," *Journal of Accounting and Economics* (Fall, 1987), pp. 137–147.

58. L. D. Brown, F. D. Richardson, and S. J. Schwages, "An Information Interpretation of Financial Analyst Superiority in Forecasting Earnings," *Journal of Accounting Research* (Spring, 1987) pp. 49–67.

59. J. Mirrless, "The Optimal Structure of Incentives and Authority within an Organization," *Bell Journal of Economics* (Spring, 1976), pp. 105–71.

60. S. Grossman and O. Hart, "An Analysis of the Principal-Agent Problem," *Econometrica* (January, 1983), pp. 7–46.

61. P. Milgrom, "Good News and Bad News: Representation Theorems and Applications," *Bell Journal of Economics* (Autumn, 1981), pp. 380–391.

62. M. Harris and A. Raviv, "Optimal Incentive Contracts with Imperfect Information," *Journal of Economic Theory* (1979), pp. 231–259.

SUGGESTED READINGS

Antle, R., and A. Smith. "An Empirical Investigation into Relative Performance Evaluation of Corporate Executives." *Journal of Accounting Research* (Spring, 1986), pp. 1–39.

Antle, R., and A. Smith. "Measuring Executive Compensation: Methods and an Application." *Journal of Accounting Research* (Spring, 1985), pp. 296–337.

Arrow, K. "Higher Education as a Filter." *Journal of Public Economics* (December, 1973), pp. 193–216.

Becker, G. *Human Capital*. New York: Columbia University Press for National Bureau of Economic Research, 1964.

Benston, G. "The Self-Serving Hypothesis: Some Evidence." *Journal of Accounting and Economics* (April, 1985), pp. 67–84.

Berle, A. A., and G. C. Means. *The Modern Corporation* New York: Macmillan, 1932.

Bickford, C. C. "Long-Term Incentives for Management, Part 6: Performance Attainment Plans." *Compensation Review* 12, no. 3 (1981), pp. 14–29.

Booz, Allen and Hamilton. *Executive Pay in the Eighties: Major Exposures Ahead*. New York: Booz, Allen and Hamilton, 1988.

Brown, L., P. Griffin, R. Hagerman, and M. Zmijewske. "An Evaluation of Alternate Proxies for the Market's Assessment of Unexpected Earnings." *Journal of Accounting and Economics* 9 (1987), pp. 159–193.

Brown, L. D., F. D. Richardson, and S. J. Schwages. "An Information Interpretation of Financial Analyst Superiority in Forecasting Earnings." *Journal of Accounting Research* 25 (1987), pp. 49–67.

Ciscel, D., and T. Carroll. "The Determinants of Executive Salaries: An Econometric Survey." *Review of Economics and Statistics* (February, 1980), pp. 7–13.

Coffee, J. C. "Shareholders versus Managers: The Strain in the Corporate Web." In J. C. Coffee et al., *Knights, Raiders and Targets: The Impact of the Hostile Takeover*. New York: Oxford University Press, 1988.

Connolly, T., Edward J. Conlon, and Stuart Jay Deutsh. "Organizational Effectiveness: A Multiple-Constituency Approach." *Academy of Management Review* 5, no. 2 (1980), pp. 43–66.

Coughlin, A., and R. Schmidt. "Executive Compensation, Management Turnover, and Firm Performance: An Empirical Investigation." *Journal of Accounting and Economics* (April, 1985), pp. 43–66.

Demsetz, H. "The Structure of Ownership and the Theory of the Firm." *Journal of Law and Economics* (December, 1983), pp. 375–390.

Ellig, B. "Incentive Plans: Over the Long Term." *Compensation Review* 16, no. 3 (1984), pp. 39–54.

Fama, E. F., and M. C. Jensen. "Agency Problems and Residual Claims." *Journal of Law and Economics* 20 (1983), pp. 327–345.

Finkelstein, S., and D. Hambrick. "Chief Executive Compensation: A Study of the Intersection of Markets and Political Processes." *Strategic Management Journal* 10 (April, 1989), pp. 121–134.

Gjesdal, F. "Accounting for Stewardship." *Journal of Accounting Research* (Spring, 1981), pp. 208–231.

Grossman, S., and O. Hart. "An Analysis of the Principal–Agent Problem." *Econometrica* (January, 1983), pp. 7–46.

Grusky, O. "Managerial Succession and Organizational Effectiveness." *American Journal of Sociology* 67 (1961), pp. 263–269.

Harris, M., and A. Raviv. "Optimal Incentive Contracts with Imperfect Information." *Journal of Economic Theory* (1979), pp. 231–259.

Hay Associates. "Fifth Annual Hay Report on Executive Compensation." *Wharton Magazine* (April, 1985), pp. 85–107.

Hogan, T. D., and L. R. McPheters. "Executive Compensation: Performance Versus Personal Characteristics." *Southern Economic Journal* 46 (1980), pp. 1060–1068.

Holstrom, B. "Moral Hazard and Observability." *Bell Journal of Economics* (November, 1979), pp. 74–91.

Jensen, M., and F. Murphy. "Are Executive Compensation Contracts Structured Properly?" Working Paper. Rochester, N.Y.: University of Rochester, 1987.

Keely, M. A. "Social Justice Approach to Organizational Evaluation." *Administrative Science Quarterly* 23 (1978), pp. 272–292.

Kilman, R. H., and R. P. Herden. "Towards a Systematic Methodology for Evaluating the Impact of Interventions on Organizational Effectiveness." *Academy of Management Review* 1, no. 3 (1976), pp. 87–98.

Kostiuk, Peter F. "Firm Size and Executive Compensation." *The Journal of Human Resources* 25 (1990), pp. 90–105.

Lambert, R. A., and D. F. Larcker. "An Analysis of the Use of Accounting and Market Measures of Performance in Executive Compensation Contracts." *Studies in Stewardship Uses of Accounting Information*, Supplement to the *Journal of Accounting Research* 25 (1987), pp. 85–129.

Lewellen, W. G. *Executive Compensation in Large Industrial Corporations*. New York: National Bureau of Economic Research, 1968.

Lewellen, W., and B. Huntsman. "Managerial Pay and Corporate Performance." *American Economic Review* (September, 1970), pp. 710–720.

Masson, R. T. "Executive Motivations, Earnings and Consequent Equity Performance." *Journal of Political Economy* (December, 1971), pp. 1278–1292.

McEachern W. A. *Managerial Control and Performance*. Lexington, Mass.: Lexington Books, 1975.

McGuire, J., J. Chiu, and A. Elbing. "Executive Incomes, Sales and Profits." *Journal of Political Economy* (September, 1962), pp. 753–761.

Mellow, Wesley. "Employer Size and Wages." *Review of Economics and Statistics* 69 (1987), pp. 495–501.

Miles, R. H. *Macro-Organizational Behavior*. Glenview, Ill.: Scott, Foresman, 1980.

Milgram, P. "Good News and Bad News: Representation Theorems and Application." *Bell Journal of Economics* (Autumn, 1981), pp. 380–391.

Mincer, Jacob. "The Distribution of Labor Incomes: A Survey with Special Reference to the Human Capital Approach." *Journal of Economic Literature* 8 (1970), pp. 1–26.

Mirrless, J. "The Optimal Structure of Incentives and Authority within an Organization."
    Bell Journal of Economics (Spring, 1976), pp. 105–171.

Oi, Walter. "Heterogeneous Firms and the Organization of Production." *Economic Inquiry* 21 (1983), pp. 147–171.

Personick, M. E., and C. B. Barsky. "White-Collar Pay Levels Linked to Corporate Work Force and Size." *Monthly Labor Review* 105 (1982), pp. 115–130.

Pfeffer, J., and H. Leblebici. "Executive Recruitment and the Development of Interfirm Organizations." *Administrative Science Quarterly* 18 (1973), pp. 449–461.

Pfeffer, J., and G. R. Salancik. "Organizational Context and the Characteristics and Tenure of Hospital Administrators." *Academy of Management Journal* 20 (1977), pp. 74–88.

Poster, C. Z. "Executive Compensation: Taking Long-Term Incentives Out of the Corporate Tower." *Compensation Review* 17, no. 2 (1985), pp. 30–31.

Price, J. L. "The Study of Organizational Effectiveness." *Sociological Quarterly* 13 (1972), pp. 3–15.

Rappaport, A. "Executive Incentives Versus Corporate Growth." *Harvard Business Review* 56, no. 4 (1978), pp. 81–88.

Rich, J. T., and J. A. Larrson. "Why Some Long-Term Incentives Fail." *Compensation Review* 16, no. 1 (1984), pp. 26–37.

Roberts, David. "A General Theory of Executive Compensation Based on Statistically Tested Propositions." *Quarterly Journal of Economics* 70 (1956), pp. 270–294.

Rosen, Sherwin. "Authority, Control and the Distribution of Earnings." *Bell Journal of Economics* 13 (1982), pp. 311–323.

Salancik, G. R., and J. Pfeffer. "Effects of Ownership and Performance on Executive Tenure in U.S. Corporations." *Academy of Management Journal* 23, no. 4 (1980), pp. 653–664.

Scott, W. R. *Organizations: Rational, Natural and Operational Systems.* Englewood Cliffs, N.J.: Prentice-Hall, 1981.

Stiglitz, J. E. "The Theory of 'Screening,' Education, and the Distribution of Income." *American Economic Review* (June, 1975), pp. 283–305.

Taubman, P. J., and T. Wales. "Higher Education, Mental Ability, and Screening." *Journal of Political Economy* (January–February, 1973), pp. 28–55.

Thurow, L. C. *Generalizing Inequality.* New York: Basic Books, 1975.

Ullman, A. A. "Data in Search of a Theory: A Critical Examination of the Relationship among Social Performance, Social Disclosure and Economic Performance of U.S. Firms." *The Academy of Management Review* (July, 1985), pp. 540–547.

Wolpin, K. "Education and Screening." *American Economic Review* (December, 1977), pp. 949–958.

9

The Prediction of
Corporate Performance

INTRODUCTION[1]

The separation of ownership and control in the large corporation causes owners' motivations to differ from those of managers.[2] The debate on the importance of stock ownership led to argument in one school of thought that the distribution of ownership has important implications for corporate efficiency and strategic development,[3] while in another, argument was for the irrelevancy of the distribution of ownership.[4]

Empirical examination of the issue led to conflicting results that were attributed to data problems when attempting to construct meaningful measures of the distribution of stock ownership[5] and performance.[6] Here, we suggest that the effects of ownership structure on performance are best examined in the context of structural differences between firms, and develop and test a model that describes the influence of ownership structure and diversification strategy on performance.

THEORETICAL FRAMEWORK

Morck, Schleifer, and Vishny[7] (hereafter MSV) estimated the cross-sectional relationship between stock ownership by the board of directors and corporate performance in 1980 for a sample of 249 *Fortune* 500 firms. Two measures of corporate performance were used: Tobin's Q and the ratio of net cash flows to the replacement cost of capital stock. Unlike Demsetz and Lehn[8] (hereafter DL), MSV relax the assumption of a linear relation between performance and stock ownership, and instead propose a nonmonotonic relationship. They test for different average performance (i.e., regression-model intercept) for each of the

Exhibit 9.1
Research Model

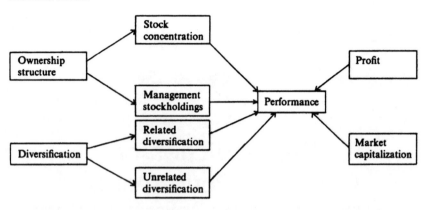

Source: Ahmed Belkaoui and Ellen Pavlik, ''The Effects of Ownership Structure and Diversification
Strategy on Performance,'' *Managerial and Decision Economics* 13 (1992), p. 344. Copyright
John Wiley & Sons Limited. Reproduced with permission.

following categories of board holdings: (1) less than 0.2 percent, (2) between
0.2 percent and 5 percent, (3) between 5 percent and 20 percent, and (4) greater
than 20 percent. They find evidence of a nonmonotonic relationship. Tobin's Q
increases, then declines, and finally rises slightly as ownership by the board of
directors rises.

This chapter expands on MSV along the following three lines. First, MSV
restricted ownership structure to board ownership as the level of equity ownership of the board of directors. We propose two different measures of ownership structure: namely, stock concentration and management stockholdings.
Second, MSV had one independent variable: ownership structure. We propose
as additional independent variable: diversification as measured by related and
unrelated diversification. Third, MSV used Tobin's Q as a performance measure.
We examine the impact of profit and market capitalization as performance measures.

The model, which is illustrated in Exhibit 9.1, indicates that ownership structure, as expressed by the degree of stock concentration and management stockholdings, and diversification, as expressed by the degree of related and unrelated
diversification, influence performance as measured by either profit or market
capitalization.

Ownership Structure and Performance

Our study differentiates between managers' and stockholders' interests, and
views the firm as an imperfect and unstable risk-sharing arrangement between
managers, employees, and shareholders that is in flux rather than in equilibrium.[9]

The distinction is based on the premises made in the literature on managerial discretion that while stockholders are wealth maximizers requiring a maximization of efficiency, managers have a tendency to maximize personal utility functions that have remuneration, power, security, and status as major factors, requiring a maximization of firm size and diversity. The impact of ownership structure on performance is assumed to differ depending on whether ownership structure is expressed by stock concentration or management stockholdings.

Management Stockholdings and Performance

Building on Berle and Means'[10] thesis on the deterioration in managerial efficiency associated with the separation of ownership and control characterizing the modern corporation, various theorists have examined the effects of such conflicts of interests on firm performance, and the disciplinary forces that may reduce managers' private returns (e.g., shirking and consumption of perquisites), that is, the market for corporate control,[11] the managerial labor market,[12] incentive contracts,[13] and debt.[14] The empirical evidence of the relationship between firm performance and corporate ownership structure is mixed. Two competing hypotheses characterize this relationship: namely, the convergence-of-interest hypothesis and the entrenchment hypothesis.

According to the convergence-of-interest hypothesis, market value and profitability increase with management ownership. Berle and Means[15] argued that the dispersion of shareholders' ownership allows managers holding little equity in the firm to forego value (wealth) maximization and use corporate assets to benefit themselves rather than the shareholders. Jensen and Meckling[16] argued instead that the costs of deviation from value maximization decline as the manager's stake in the firm rises, since managers are less likely to squander corporate wealth when they bear a larger share of the costs.

According to the entrenchment hypothesis, market value and profitability do not increase with management ownership. Demsetz[17] and Fama and Jensen[18] have pointed out the offsetting costs associated with higher management stockholdings. If managers have a small stockholding, they will work toward value maximization as a result of factors including market discipline, the product market,[19] and the market for corporate control.[20] If managers hold a large enough proportion of a firm's stock to have the voting power that guarantees their jobs, they may opt for non-value-maximizing behavior.

What the two hypotheses imply in conjunction with the empirical findings of MSV is that performance will be positively related to lower ranges of management ownership and negatively related to higher ranges of management ownership: in other words, a nonmonotonic relationship is implied.

H_1: There will be a positive (negative) relationship between a firm's performance and management stockholdings held at a lower (higher) range.

Stock Concentration and Performance

Shareholders are generally assumed to be value maximizers who view managers' responsibility to be the maximization of efficiency. With concentrated ownership, stockholders are better able to both coordinate action and demand information that will allow them to overcome any information asymmetries, and influence management's decisions and responsibility toward value maximization and strategies that are in the stockholders' interest. Therefore, performance will be negatively related to lower ranges of stock concentration and positively related to higher ranges of stock concentration.

H_2: There will be negative (positive) relationship between a firm's performance and stock concentration at a lower (higher) range.

Diversification and Performance

Empirical results on the M-form hypothesis differentiated between the impact of related diversification and unrelated diversification on performance.[21] In the case of unrelated diversification, managers are thought to trade efficiency for an increase in firm size and decreased operating risks. Empirical evidence shows that unrelated diversification is associated with lower economic returns[22] and lower risk[23] rather than related diversification. In contrast, both theory and empirical results indicate an association of related diversification with superior economic performance.[24]

H_3: There will be a positive relation between, on the one hand, performance and, on the other, related and unrelated diversification. The relationship will be lower for unrelated diversification as compared to related diversification.

Ownership Structure, Diversification, and Performance

The three hypotheses, H_1, H_2, and H_3, state that performance, as measured by profit or market capitalization, is associated with ownership structure as expressed by the degrees of stock concentration and management stockholdings and diversification as expressed by the degrees of related and unrelated diversification. Following the different results obtained by MSV and DL, both piecewise linear regression and strictly linear regression models will be tested.

The piecewise linear regression model allowing for two changes in the slope coefficient of stock concentration and management stockholdings is as follows:

$$PERF_i = \alpha_1 + \alpha_2 RTD_i + \alpha_3 UTD_i + \alpha_4 STC1_i$$
$$+ \alpha_5 STC2_i + \alpha_6 STC3_i + \alpha_7 MSH1_i$$
$$+ \alpha_8 MSH2_i + \alpha_9 MSH3_i + u_i$$

where

$PERF_i$ = Performance of the firm as measured by profit or market capitalization, measured in millions of dollars

RTD_i = Related diversification

UTD_i = Unrelated diversification

STC_i = Stock concentration defined as follows:

if $STC_i < 5.00$, then $STC1_i = STC_i$

if $STC_i \geq 5.00$, then $STC1_i = 5.00$

if $STC_i < 5.00$, then $STC2_i = 0$

if $(5 \leq STC_i < 25$, then $STC2_i = STC_i - 5.00$

if $STC_i \geq 25$, then $STC2_i = 20.00$

if $STC_i < 25$, then $STC3_i = 0$

if $STC_i \geq 25$, then $STC3_i = STC_i - 25$

MSH_i = Management stockholdings defined as follows:

if $MSH_i < 5.00$, then $MSH1_i = MSH1_i$

if $MSH_i \geq 5.00$, then $MSH1_i = 5.00$

if $MSH_i < 5.00$ then $MSH2_i = 0$

if $5 \leq MSH_i < 25$, then $MSH2_i = MSH_i - 5.00$

if $MSH_i \geq 25$, then $MSH2_i = 20.00$

if $MSH_i < 25$, then $MSH3_i = 0$

if $MSH_i \geq 25$, then $MSH3_i = MSH_i - 25$.

The first stage of this analysis starts with turning points of 5 percent and 25 percent for both STC_i and MSH_i. Basically, 5 percent stockholding requires filings on substantial holdings, and 20 to 30 percent stockholding is considered a deterrent against takeover.

METHODS

Dependent Variable

The dependent variable expressing performance of a firm was chosen as either the logarithm of net profit or market capitalization. Market capitalization was computed as the product of the number of shares outstanding and the year-end price per common share. Both variables are highly skewed to the right, given their dependence on firm size. The skewness was 2.80591 for profit and 5.1672 for market capitalization. The Kolomogorov D statistic was $D = 0.29003$ (Prob. $> D < 0.01$) for profit and $D = 0.2996$ (Prob. $> D < 0.01$) for market capitalization. If the distribution of the dependent variable is skewed to the right, using a logarithmic transformation helps to normalize it.

Ownership Structure

The data were collected from 1988 proxy statements. Stock concentration was computed as the share of ownership by outside stockholders owning more than 5 percent of the common voting stock in 1987. Management stockholdings were measured by the percentage of common voting stock it held in 1987.

Diversification

The product-count method was used to determine the extent of related and unrelated diversification. The extent of unrelated diversification was measured by the number of two-digit SIC industries outside the primary two-digit industry in which a firm was active during 1987. The extent of related diversification was measured by the number of four-digit SIC industries within its main two-digit industry in which a firm was active during 1987. Dunn and Bradstreet's *Reference Book of Corporate Management* was used to collect the data.

Sample

To ensure a large sample size with readily available data, the initial sample chosen was the *Fortune* 500 industrial corporations; the information needed was gathered from the Compustat tape, proxy statements, and other sources. The final sample for which all the information was available included 228 companies from 28 different industries. Exhibits 9.2 and 9.3 present relevant statistics on ownership structure and performance for the sample firms.

RESULTS

Exhibit 9.4 reports the piecewise linear regression results of profit and market capitalization on ownership structure and diversification strategy. For comparison purposes the results are presented both with and without the control variable of total assets.

First, as suggested by hypothesis 1, the relationship between performance as measured by profit and market capitalization and management stockholdings is negative at a low range of management stockholdings (0–5 percent), positive at a higher range (5–25 percent), and negative at levels superior to 25 percent. Basically, for each 1 percent increase in ownership between 0 and 5 percent, profit and market capitalization decline, respectively, by an average of 0.0014 and 0.0016. For each 1 percent increase in ownership between 5 and 25 percent, profit and market capitalization increase by 0.00029 and 0.00026. As ownership rises beyond 25 percent, both profit and market capitalization decline, respectively, by 0.0000093 and 0.000034. These results are consistent with both the convergence-of-interests and entrenchment hypotheses. At levels lower than 5 percent, and in accordance with the Berle and Means' thesis, the dispersion of

Exhibit 9.2
Mean Values of Profit and Market Capitalization for 228 *Fortune* **500 Firms in**
1987 Grouped by Level of Management Stockholdings (*MSH***)**

MSH (%)	Number of firms	Mean profit	Standard error of mean profit	Mean market capitalization	Standard error of mean market capitalization
0–5	154	405.5	879.5	5635.4	8749.2
5–10	29	120.3	133.9	1692.0	1425.9
10–15	16	134.7	167.2	2220.4	2649.6
15–20	7	133.3	91.0	1461.9	773.8
20–25	8	38.3	105.2	1520.0	1215.8
25–30	5	611.7	619.6	8909.8	7904.1
30–35	2	149.0	117.5	2542.3	2246.3
35–40	2	−0.3	70.4	1838.3	255.4
40–45	1	155.2	n/a	2424.5	n/a
45–50	2	154.0	41.5	1745.7	489.9
50–55	0	n/a	n/a	n/a	n/a
55–60	0	n/a	n/a	n/a	n/a
60–65	1	89.6	n/a	1500.3	n/a
65–70	0	n/a	n/a	n/a	n/a
70–75	0	n/a	n/a	n/a	n/a
75–80	0	n/a	n/a	n/a	n/a
80–85	1	186.7	n/a	2443.0	n/a

Source: Ahmed Belkaoui and Ellen Pavlik, ''The Effects of Ownership Structure and Diversification Strategy on Performance,'' *Managerial and Decision Economics* 13 (1992), p. 346. Copyright John Wiley & Sons Limited. Reproduced with permission.

shareholders' ownership allows managers holding little equity to forego value maximization. As managers' stake in the firm increases beyond 5 percent, and in accordance with the convergence-of-interests hypothesis, managers focus more on value maximization. Finally, as their stake in the firm grows very large, beyond 25 percent, and in accordance with the entrenchment hypothesis, managers have enough voting power, tenure, and job guarantee to opt for non-value-maximizing behavior.

Second, as suggested by hypothesis 2, the relationship between stock concentration and performance, as measured by profit and market capitalization, is negative at the low range of stock concentration (0–25 percent) and positive at the high range of stock concentration (above 25 percent). Basically, for each 1 percent increase in stock concentration between 0 and 5 percent, profit and market capitalization decline, respectively, by 0.00083 and 0.00060. As shareholders' ownership rises beyond 5 percent, profit and market capitalization continue to decline, respectively, by 0.00010 and 0.00026. As ownership rises beyond 25 percent, both profit and market capitalization rise, respectively, by 0.00002 and 0.000069. These results are consistent with the agency theory view that with a large concentration of stock, stockholders are in better position to coordinate action, demand information symmetry, and influence management's actions more toward value maximization.

Exhibit 9.3
Mean Values of Profit and Market Capitalization for 228 *Fortune* 500 Firms in 1987 Grouped by Level of Stock Concentration (*STC*)

STC (%)	Number of firms	Mean profit	Standard error of mean profit	Mean market capitalization	Standard error of mean market capitalization
0–5	97	506.7	895.0	6531.9	10164.3
5–10	48	359.3	587.8	4463.6	5550.6
10–15	15	−176.4	1138.3	2474.2	2697.8
15–20	16	143.8	146.7	2012.1	2497.5
20–25	8	112.2	201.9	2008.8	3193.1
25–30	14	110.3	106.0	1539.5	1518.5
30–35	6	107.8	201.5	1102.9	877.4
35–40	6	80.6	131.2	1643.2	1737.3
40–45	3	41.2	88.6	1577.8	589.2
45–50	4	432.2	460.1	7442.7	6098.8
50–55	2	58.0	12.1	1276.6	306.3
55–60	2	151.5	95.8	2106.0	1550.4
60–65	1	8.4	n/a	491.1	n/a
65–70	0	n/a	n/a	n/a	n/a
70–75	0	n/a	n/a	n/a	n/a
75–80	1	157.7	n/a	2689.0	n/a
80–85	3	425.1	566.3	7113.6	5151.3
85–90	2	39.6	20.5	480.2	20.1

Source: Ahmed Belkaoui and Ellen Pavlik, "The Effects of Ownership Structure and Diversification Strategy on Performance," *Managerial and Decision Economics* 13 (1992), p. 347. Copyright John Wiley & Sons Limited. Reproduced with permission.

Third, as suggested by hypothesis 3, both profit and market capitalization are found to be positively related and unrelated diversification. The positive relationship is higher with related as opposed to unrelated diversification, when assets are used as a control variable. These results show that both profit levels and the market performance of related diversifiers are higher than those of the unrelated diversifiers.

Fourth, the choice of turning points may be arbitrary. As seen in Exhibit 9.5, various alternate specifications of turning points are chosen. The results conform to those in Exhibit 9.4. Basically,

1. Profit and market capitalization are positively related to related and unrelated diversification, with the impact of related higher than unrelated diversification;

2. Profit and market capitalization are negatively related to ownership structure for low and very high ranges of management stockholdings, but positively related to ownership structure for a moderate range of management stockholdings; and

3. Profit and market capitalization are negatively related to ownership structure for low to moderate levels of stock concentration and positively related to ownership structure for very high levels of stock concentration.

Exhibit 9.4
Piecewise Linear Ordinary-Least-Squares Regression of 1987 Profit and Market Capitalization on Ownership Structure and Diversification Strategy for 228 *Fortune* 500 Firms

	Profit	Profit	Market capitalization	Market capitalization
		Dependent variable		
Intercept	5.3839	4.8023	8.274	7.7582
Total assets	—	0.00006	—	0.00053
	—	(0.000005)[b]	—	(0.0000051)[b]
RTD	0.1445	0.1534	0.1019	0.1104
	(0.0582)[b]	(0.0473)[b]	(0.0499)[c]	0.0407)[b]
UTD	0.1843	0.1120	0.1234	0.05749
	(0.0665)[b]	(0.0545)[c]	(0.056)[c]	(0.0266)[c]
MSH1	−2.8216	−0.1473	−0.2906	−0.1698
	(0.0504)[b]	(0.0430)[b]	(0.0438)[b]	(0.0375)[b]
MSH2	0.0561	0.0296	0.0475	0.0263
	(0.0177)[b]	(0.0146)[c]	(0.0146)[b]	(0.0121)[c]
MSH3	−0.0123	−0.00093	−0.00533	−0.00343
	(0.0050)[b]	(0.00033)[c]	(0.0024)[c]	(0.0019)[d]
STC1	−0.0851	−0.0838	−0.0602	−0.0602
	(0.0386)[c]	(0.0314)[b]	(0.0337)[d]	(0.02756)[c]
STC2	−0.0237	−0.0107	−0.0365	−0.0265
	(0.01424)[d]	(0.004)[b]	(0.0122)[c]	(0.01000)[d]
STC3	0.00005	0.00224	0.00798	0.00692
	(0.00003)[d]	(0.00134)[d]	(0.0044)[c]	(0.0038)[b]
F	9.667[b]	24.875[b]	13.670[b]	30.608[b]
R^2	0.2720	0.5208	0.3087	0.5582

[a] Numbers in parentheses are standard errors computed according to White (1980).
[b] Significant at 99% confidence level.
[c] Significant at 95% confidence level.
[d] Significant at 90% confidence level.

Source: Ahmed Belkaoui and Ellen Pavlik, ''The Effects of Ownership Structure and Diversification Strategy on Performance,'' *Managerial and Decision Economics* 13 (1992), p. 347. Copyright John Wiley & Sons Limited. Reproduced with permission.

These results verify the initial results found for the turning points of 5 and 25 percent.

Finally, following DL, we estimate a linear relationship between performance, on the one hand, and ownership structure and diversification, on the other. The results using profit and market capitalization as dependent variables are shown in Exhibit 9.6 and reflect a negative relationship between the two types of ownership structure and the two types of performance, as well as a consistently insignificant estimated coefficient on management stockholdings, which may be attributed to the failure of linear specification to capture the important nonmonotonic nature of the relationships.

Exhibit 9.5

Alternative Piecewise Linear Specification of 1987 Profit and Market Capitalization on Ownership Structure and Diversification (Assets [A] Is a Control Variable)

Panel A: The dependent variable is the 1987 profit

A1: *The turning points are 2.5% and 25% for both MSH_i and STC_i*

$P = 5.15 + 0.00005^a\ A + 0.157^a\ RTD + 0.115^b\ UTD - 0.428^a\ MSH1 + 0.024^b\ MSH2 - 0.00107^c\ MSH3$
$- 0.13^b\ STC1 - 0.014^c\ STC2 + 0.002^c\ STC3$

$F = 26.521,\ R^2 = 0.5368$

A2: *The turning points are 7.5% and 25% for both MSH_i and STC_i*

$P = 4.61 + 0.00005^a\ A + 0.183^a\ RTD + 0.168^a\ UTD - 0.116^a\ MSH1 + 0.049^a\ MSH2 - 0.007^c\ MSH3$
$- 0.08^a\ STC1 - 0.006^c\ STC2 + 0.004^c\ STC3$

$F = 20.815,\ R^2 = 0.5425$

A3: *The turning points are 5% and 15% for both MSH_i and STC_i*

$P = 4.80 + 0.00006^a\ A + 0.149^a\ RTD + 0.114^b\ UTD - 0.14^a\ MSH1 + 0.077^c\ MSH2 - 0.0061^c\ MSH3$
$- 0.069^b\ STC1 - 0.029^c\ STC2 + 0.0011^c\ STC3$

$F = 24.92,\ R^2 = 0.5213$

A4: *The turning points are 5% and 20% for both MSH_i and STC_i*

$P = 4.80 + 0.00006^a\ A + 0.151^a\ RTD + 0.112^b\ UTD - 0.145^a\ MSH1 + 0.031^c\ MSH2 - 0.003^c\ MSH3$
$- 0.078^b\ STC1 - 0.016^c\ STC2 + 0.0015^c\ STC3$

$F = 24.831,\ R^2 = 0.5203$

A5: *The turning points are 5% and 30% for both MSH_i and STC_i*

$P = 4.79 + 0.00006^a\ A + 0.154^c\ RTD + 0.111^b\ UTD - 0.145^a\ MSH1 + 0.026^b\ MSH2 - 0.003^c\ MSH3$
$- 0.08^a\ STC1 - 0.008^c\ STC2 + 0.0026^c\ STC3$

$F = 24.853,\ R = 0.5206$

Panel B: The dependent variable is the 1987 market capitalization

B1: *The turning points are 2.5% and 25% for both MSH_i and STC_i*

$MC = 8.06 + 0.00005^a\ A + 0.115^a\ RTD + 0.059^c\ UTD - 0.42^a\ MSH1 + 0.01^c\ MSH2 - 0.006^c\ MSH3$
$- 0.075^c\ STC1 - 0.030^a\ STC2 + 0.005^c\ STC3$

$F = 31.77,\ R^2 = 0.5674$

B2: *The turning points are 7.5% and 25% for both MSH_i and STC_i*

$MC = 7.56 + 0.00005^a\ A + 0.129^a\ RTD + 0.116^b\ UTD - 0.119^a\ MSH1 + 0.039^b\ MSH2 - 0.001^c\ MSH3$
$- 0.063^a\ STC1 - 0.021^c\ STC2 + 0.011^c\ STC3$

$F = 24.495,\ R^2 = 0.5645$

B3: *The turning points are 5% and 15% for both MSH_i and STC_i*

$MC = 7.74 + 0.00005^a\ A + 0.11^a\ RTD + 0.06^c\ UTD - 0.16^a\ MSH1 + 0.028^c\ MSH2 - 0.009^c\ MSH3$
$- 0.005^c\ STC1 - 0.046^b\ STC2 + 0.002^c\ STC3$

$F = 30.182,\ R^2 = 0.5548$

Exhibit 9.5 (Continued)

B4: The turning points are 5% and 20% for both MSH$_t$ and STC$_t$

$MC = 7.74 + 0.00005^a\ A + 0.11^a\ RTD + 0.059^c\ UTD - 0.166^a\ MSH1 + 0.025^c\ MSH2 - 0.007^c\ MSH3$
$\quad - 0.056^b\ STC1 - 0.033^a\ STC2 + 0.004^c\ STC3$

$F = 30.33,\ R^2 = 0.5560$

B5: The turning points are 5% and 30% for both MSH$_t$ and STC$_t$

$MC = 7.76 + 0.00005^a\ A + 0.11^a\ RTD + 0.054^b\ UTD - 0.173^a\ MSH1 + 0.02^a\ MSH2 - 0.001^c\ MSH3$
$\quad - 0.06^b\ STC1 - 0.022^a\ STC2 + 0.009^c\ STC3$

$F = 30.932,\ R^2 = 0.5608$

---

[a] Significant at 99% confidence level.
[b] Significant at 95% confidence level.
[c] Significant at 90% confidence level.

Source: Ahmed Belkaoui and Ellen Pavlik, "The effects of Ownership Structure and Diversification Strategy on Performance," *Managerial and Decision Economics* 13 (1992), pp. 348–349. Copyright John Wiley & Sons Limited. Reproduced with permission.

CONCLUSION

Our results show a significant nonmonotonic relationship between performance and ownership structure and a positive direct relationship between performance and related and unrelated diversification. They indicate that the effects of ownership structure on performance are best examined and explained taking into account interfirm structural differences.

The significant nonmonotonic relationship between profit and market capitalization, on the one hand, and management stockholdings and stock concentration, on the other, is different from the one found by MSV. Our results are compatible with a dispersion of ownership and non-value-maximizing behavior by management for less than 5 percent ownership, a convergence of interests between managers and shareholders between 5 and 25 percent ownership, and an entrenchment of the management team as their stakes exceed 25 percent. Similarly, our results suggest the need for large stock concentration before shareholders can influence management decisions toward value-maximizing behavior.

The results on the impact of management stockholdings and stock concentration on performance are compatible with a model that views the interests of shareholders and managers as fundamentally in conflict over the issue of risk (Coffee, 1988). Managers may be wedded to their jobs, while shareholders have diversified their portfolios. Therefore, the managers will act in a more risk-averse manner than the shareholders and will be protective of their autonomy. Our results show that this "risk-aversion differential" between managers and shareholders and the resulting "excess earnings retention" are more compatible with high rather than low management stockholding and stock concentration. The higher level of management stockholdings allowed the kind of retrenchment and

Exhibit 9.6
Simple Linear Regression of 1987 Profit and Market Capitalization on Ownership
Structure and Diversification Strategy for 228 *Fortune* 500 Firms

| | Dependent variable | | | |
	Profit	Profit	Market capitalization	Market capitalization
Intercept	4.631	4.335	7.470	7.196
Total assets	—	0.000068	—	0.00006
	—	$(0.0000058)^b$	—	$(0.000005)^b$
RTD	0.1531	0.1521	0.1212	0.1201
	$(0.0629)^b$	$(0.048)^b$	$(0.0562)^c$	(0.0438)
UTD	0.1802	0.053	0.1226	0.0399
	$(0.0720)^b$	$(0.056)^c$	$(0.0637)^c$	(0.0503)
MSH	−0.008	−0.0015	−0.0118	−0.0049
	(0.007)	(0.0057)	(0.0065)	(0.005)
STC	−0.0172	−0.0124	−0.0153	−0.011
	$(0.0044)^b$	$(0.0034)^b$	$(0.0038)^b$	$(0.0030)^b$
F	6.917^b	36.815^b	7.483^b	38.520
R^2	0.1159	0.4671	0.1183	0.4645

[a] Numbers in parentheses are standard errors computed according to White (1980).
[b] Significant at 99% confidence level.
[c] Significant at 95% confidence level.
[d] Significant at 90% confidence level.

Source: Ahmed Belkaoui and Ellen Pavlik, "The Effects of Ownership Structure and Diversification Strategy on Performance," *Managerial and Decision Economics* 13 (1992), p. 350. Copyright John Wiley & Sons Limited. Reproduced with permission.

organizational slack on which earlier generations of managerial critics have focused. Takeover is the means by which the market may purge the modern corporation of this organizational slack. The results indicate that the timing of the takeover is more likely with higher than with lower levels of management stockholdings and stock concentration.

NOTES

1. The chapter has been largely adapted with permission of the editor from Ahmed Belkaoui and Ellen Pavlik, "The Effects of Ownership Structure and Diversification Strategy on Performance," *Managerial and Decision Economics* 13 (1992), pp. 343–352. Copyright John Wiley & Sons Limited. Reproduced with permission.

2. R. J. Normen and A. Downs, "A Theory of Large Managerial Firms," *Journal of Political Economy* 73 (1965), pp. 32–52.

3. R. Marris, *The Economic Theory of Managerial Capitalism* (London: Macmillan, 1964).

4. H. Demsetz and K. Lehn, "The Structure of Corporate Ownership: Theory and Consequences," *Journal of Political Economy* 93 (1985), pp. 1115–1177.

5. J. Gibbin and D. Leech, "The Effect of Shareholder Dispersion on the Degree of Control in British Companies: Theory and Measurement," *Economic Journal* 93 (1983), pp. 351–390.

6. C. W. Hill and S. A. Snell, "Effects of Ownership Structure and Control on Corporate Productivity," *Academy of Management Journal* 32 (1989), pp. 25–46.

7. R. A. Morck, A. Schleifer, and R. W. Vishny, "Management Ownership and Market Valuation: An Empirical Analysis," *Journal of Financial Economics* 20 (1988), pp. 293–315.

8. Demsetz and Lehn, "The Structure of Corporate Ownership: Theory and Consequences," pp. 1115–1177.

9. J. C. Coffee, "Shareholders versus Managers: The Strain in the Corporate Web," in J. C. Coffee, *Knights, Raiders, and Targets: The Impact of the Hostile Takeover* (Oxford: Oxford University Press, 1988).

10. A. A. Berle and G. C. Means, *The Modern Corporation* (New York: Macmillan, 1932).

11. H. Manne, "Mergers and the Market for Corporate Control," *Journal of Political Economy* 73 (1965), pp. 110–120.

12. E. F. Fama, "Agency Problems and the Theory of the Firm," *Journal of Political Economy* 88 (1980), pp. 288–307.

13. S. Shavell, "Risk Sharing and Incentives in the Principal and Agent Relationship," *Bell Journal of Economics* 10 (1979), pp. 55–73.

14. M. Jensen, "Agency Costs of Free Cash Flow, Corporate Finance, and Takeover," *The American Economic Review* 26 (1986), pp. 323–399.

15. Berle and Means, *The Modern Corporation*.

16. M. Jensen and W. H. Meckling, "Theory of the Firm and Managerial Behavior, Agency Costs, and Ownership Structure," *Journal of Financial Economics* 3 (1976), pp. 305–360.

17. H. Demsetz, "The Structure of Ownership and the Theory of the Firm," *Journal of Law and Economics* 26 (1983), pp. 375–390.

18. E. F. Fama and M. C. Jensen, "Agency Problems and Residual Claims," *Journal of Law and Economics* 20 (1983), pp. 327–349.

19. O. D. Hart, "The Market Mechanism as an Incentive Scheme," *Bell Journal of Economics* 14 (1983), pp. 366–382.

20. M. Jensen and R. Ruback, "The Market for Corporate Control: The Scientific Evidence," *Journal of Financial Economics* 11 (1983), pp. 5–50.

21. R. E. Hoskisson, "Multidivisional Structure and Performance: The Contingency of Diversification Strategy," *Academy of Management Journal* 30 (1982), pp. 625–644.

22. H. K. Christensen and C. A. Montgomery, "Corporate Economic Performance: Diversification Strategy versus Market Structure," *Strategic Management Journal* 2 (1981), pp. 327–343.

23. R. Amit and J. Livnat, "Diversification and the Risk-Return Tradeoff," *Academy of Management Journal* 3 (1988), pp. 154–165.

24. R. A. Bettis, "Performance Differences in Related and Unrelated Diversified Firms," *Strategic Management Journal* 2 (1981), pp. 379–393.

SUGGESTED READINGS

Amit, R., and J. Livnat. "Diversification and the Risk-Return Tradeoff." *Academy of Management Journal* 3 (1988), pp. 154–165.

Berle, A. A., and G. C. Means. *The Modern Corporation.* New York: Macmillan, 1932.

Bettis, R. A. "Performance Differences in Related and Unrelated Diversified Firms." *Strategic Management Journal* 2 (1981), pp. 379–393.

Christensen, H. K., and C. A. Montgomery. "Corporate Economic Performance: Diversification Strategy versus Market Structure." *Strategic Management Journal* 2 (1981), pp. 327–343.

Coffee, J. C. "Shareholders versus Managers: The Strain in the Corporate Web." In J. C. Coffee, *Knights, Raiders, and Targets: The Impact of the Hostile Takeover.* Oxford: Oxford University Press, 1988.

Demsetz, H. "The Structure of Ownership and the Theory of the Firm." *Journal of Law and Economics* 26 (1983), pp. 375–390.

Demsetz, H., and K. Lehn. "The Structure of Corporate Ownership: Theory and Consequences." *Journal of Political Economy* 93 (1985), pp. 1115–1177.

Fama, E. F. "Agency Problems and the Theory of the Firm." *Journal of Political Economy* 88 (1980), pp. 288–307.

Fama, E. F., and M. C. Jensen. "Agency Problems and Residual Claims." *Journal of Law and Economics* 20 (1983), pp. 327–349.

Gibbin, J., and D. Leech. "The Effect of Shareholder Dispersion on the Degree of Control in British Companies: Theory and Measurement." *Economic Journal* 93 (1983), pp. 351–390.

Hart, O. D. "The Market Mechanism as an Incentive Scheme." *Bell Journal of Economics* 14 (1983), pp. 366–382.

Hill, C. W., and S. A. Snell. "Effects of Ownership Structure and Control on Corporate Productivity." *Academy of Management Journal* 32 (1989), pp. 25–46.

Hoskisson, R. E. "Multidivisional Structure and Performance: The Contingency of Diversification Strategy." *Academy of Management Journal* 30 (1982), pp. 625–644.

Jensen, M. "Agency Costs of Free Cash Flow, Corporate Finance, and Takeover." *The American Economic Review* 26 (1986), pp. 323–399.

Jensen, M., and W. H. Meckling. "Theory of the Firm and Managerial Behavior, Agency Costs, and Ownership Structure." *Journal of Financial Economics* 3 (1976), pp. 305–360.

Jensen, M., and R. Ruback. "The Market for Corporate Control: The Scientific Evidence." *Journal of Financial Economics* 11 (1983), pp. 5–50.

Manne, H. "Mergers and the Market for Corporate Control." *Journal of Political Economy* 73 (1965), pp. 110–120.

Marris, R. *The Economic Theory of Managerial Capitalism.* London: Macmillan, 1964.

Morck, R. A., A. Schleifer, and R. W. Vishny. "Management Ownership and Market Valuation: An Empirical Analysis." *Journal of Financial Economics* 20 (1988), pp. 293–315.

Normen, R. J., and A. Downs. "A Theory of Large Managerial Firms." *Journal of Political Economy* 73 (1965), pp. 32–52.

Shavell, S. "Risk Sharing and Incentive in the Principal and Agent Relationship." *Bell Journal of Economics* 10 (1979), pp. 55–73.

White, H. "A Heteroscedasticity-Consistent Covariance Matrix Estimator and a Direct Test for Heteroscedasticity." *Econometrica* (May, 1980), pp. 817–838.

10

The Prediction of Corporate Reputation

INTRODUCTION[1]

The reputation of a firm is important for various decisions ranging from resource allocation and career decisions to product choices, to name only a few.[2] It is an important signal of the firm's organizational effectiveness. Favorable reputations can create favorable situations for firms that include (1) the generation of excess returns by inhibiting the mobility of rivals in an industry,[3] (2) the capability of charging premium prices to consumers,[4] and (3) the creation of a better image in the capital markets and to investors.[5]

With two exceptions, most previous empirical investigations have examined the relationship of earnings performance and social performance.[6] Two studies, however, investigated the relationship between reputation and various economic and noneconomic criteria that may be used by corporate audiences to construct reputations.[7,8] Although the signals used in these two studies show attendance by corporate audiences to different information cues, we propose that of most importance to these parties are signals about asset management performance. We therefore propose specific hypotheses relating assessments of reputation to various information signals about a firm's asset management performance, specifically using accounting and market signals, which indicate size of assets, market assessment of the value of the assets in place, asset turnover, and profit margin.

RELATED RESEARCH

Two studies have investigated the determinants of reputation building. Based on the thesis that an organization's social performance is an indistinguishable component of its effectiveness, one study[9] expanded the definition of social performance to include organizational effectiveness, and investigated the relationship between organizational effectiveness and economic performance. Following the ecological model, organizational effectiveness by constructs' reputational ranking of firms was used. The reputational rankings were found to be positively related to profitability, size, and price/earnings ratios and negatively related to systematic risk.

Using a similar approach, Fombrun and Shanley[10] found the same reputational rankings, for a different period and a different sample, to be related to the firms' risk-return profiles, resource allocations, social responsiveness, institutional ownership, media exposure, and corporate diversification. These are all signal constituents about firms' projects and generate reputations.

This chapter differs in terms of its focus on linking reputational rankings specifically to asset management performance, as this is the most salient issue in evaluating corporate performance.

REPUTATION BUILDING

Objective Function and Stewardship

This chapter hypothesizes that corporate audiences attend to different features of firms' asset management performance in constructing reputational rankings. The focus on asset management performance rather than other attributes of firm performance results from specific expectations of corporate audiences about the objective function of management and the nature of asset stewardship.

Organizations are social units deliberately constructed and reconstructed to seek specific goals. J. D. Thompson[11] differentiated between goals *held for* an organization and goals *of* an organization. The former goals are held by outside members of the organization that have a given interest in the activities of the firm, while the latter are the goals held by persons and/or managers who are part of the "dominant coalition" in terms of holding enough control to commit the organization to a given direction. The same distinction is made by Perrow[12] as official goals versus operative goals. The main difference between the goal arises when the official goals held by corporate audiences conform to a shareholder-wealth-maximization model and the operative goals conform to a managerial-welfare-maximization model.[13] The shareholder-wealth-maximization models holds that the operative goals are to maximize the wealth of stockholders. The firm accepts all projects yielding more than the cost of capital and therefore is interested only in an efficient use of the assets of the firm. The management-welfare-maximization model holds that managers run firms for their own benefit. It follows that corporate audiences committed to a shareholder-wealth-maximization view of operative goals will construct reputations on the basis of information about firms' asset management performance.

The stewardship concept is basically a feature of the principal-agent relation-

Exhibit 10.1
Model of Reputation Building under Conditions of Incomplete Information about Asset Management Performance

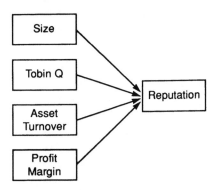

Source: Ahmed Riahi-Belkaoui and Ellen Pavlik, "Asset Management Performance and Reputation Building for Large U.S. Firms," *British Journal of Management* 2 (1991), p. 233. Reprinted with permission of the editor.

ship, whereby the agent is assumed to safeguard the resources of the principal. The stewardship concept has evolved over time. Birnberg[14] distinguished four periods: (1) the pure-custodial period, (2) the traditional-custodial period, (3) the asset-utilization period, and (4) the open-ended period. The first two periods refer to the need for the agent to return the resources intact to the principal by performing minimal tasks to fulfill the custodial function. The third period refers to the need for the agent to provide initiative and insight in using the assets to conform to agreed-upon plans. Finally, the open-ended period differs from the asset-utilization period by providing more flexibility in the use of assets and enabling the agent to chart the course of asset utilization. The third and fourth periods are more reflective of the contemporary conception of stewardship. It follows that corporate audiences holding these views of stewardship will construct reputations on the basis of information about firms' asset management performance.

Interpreting Ambiguous Signals about Asset Management

Based on the shareholder-wealth-maximization model for operative goals of firms, and the asset-utilization and open-ended use of assets for views of stewardship, corporate audiences are assumed to construct reputations on the basis of informational signals about firms' asset management performance. Asset management performance is perceived to be a combination of asset size, market assessment of the value of assets in place, and asset turnover and profit margin. Exhibit 10.1 presents the model linking reputation to these components of asset management performance.

Size. Large firms are more politically sensitive than small firms. If their profits are also large, they fear government actions. The amount and quality of information of large firms will be larger in response to the increased scrutiny. As a result it may be safe to assume that corporate audiences will better appreciate the information quality of larger firms and assign them a better reputation.

Hypothesis 1: The larger the firm, the better its reputation.

Tobin's Q. Tobin's Q, the market value of the firm divided by the replacement value of the assets, measures the market's assessment of the value of the assets in place and the company's future investment opportunities. It is a measure of managerial performance. It can also be interpreted as a measure of agency costs. Lang and Litzenberg[15] showed that a Q ratio below 1.0 is evidence of over-investment. Jensen[16] argued that overinvestment can be due to conflicts of interests between managers and shareholders over the use of free cash flow generated by the firm. As both a measure of managerial performance and a measure of agency costs, Tobin's Q can also be interpreted as a signal of asset management performance.

Hypothesis 2: The greater a firm's Tobin Q, the better its reputation.

Asset turnover and profit margin. A firm's efficient use of its assets is best reflected by its rate of return on assets. The rate of return on assets is in fact a composite measure depending on (1) the asset turnover as computed by sales over assets and (2) the profit margin as computed by profit over sales. The profit margin ratio indicates how much of net income is earned from each dollar of sales. The asset turnover ratio indicates how many times annual sales cover total assets. A firm's efficient use of its assets is best accomplished by securing higher values for both ratios or higher values for one of the ratios.

Hypothesis 3: The greater a firm's asset turnover, the better its reputation.
Hypothesis 4: The greater a firm's profit margin, the better its reputation.

THE MODEL

The four hypotheses may be expressed by the following model:

$$REP_{it} = \alpha_{0t} + \alpha_{1(t-1)} [TA_{(t-1)} - ITA_{(t-1)}] + [\alpha_{2(t-1)} - ITQ_{(t-1)}]$$
$$+ [TQ_{(t-1)} + \alpha_{3(t-1)}] [AT_{(t-1)} - IAT_{(t-1)}]$$
$$+ \alpha_{4(t-1)} [PM_{(t-1)} - IPM_{(t-1)}] + \varepsilon_{(t-1)}$$

where

REP_{1t} = Overall score of reputation

REP_{2t} = Score on quality of management

REP_{3t} = Score on quality of products/service offered

REP_{4t} = Score on innovativeness

REP_{5t} = Score on value as a long-term investment

REP_{6t} = Score on soundness of financial position

REP_{7t} = Score on ability to attract/develop/keep talented people

REP_{8t} = Score on responsibility to the community/environment

REP_{9t} = Score on wise use of corporate assets

$TA_{(t-1)}$ = Total assets for $(t - 1)$

$ITA_{(t-1)}$ = Average total assets for the industry for $(t - 1)$

$TQ_{(t-1)}$ = Tobin Q for $(t - 1)$

$ITQ_{(t-1)}$ = Average Tobin Q for the industry for $(t - 1)$

$AT_{(t-1)}$ = Asset turnover for $(t - 1)$

$IAT_{(t-1)}$ = Average asset turnover for the industry for $(t - 1)$

$PM_{(t-1)}$ = Profit margin for $(t - 1)$

$IPM_{(t-1)}$ = Average profit margin for the industry for $(t - 1)$

The model was run for both $t = 1987$ and $t = 1988$. The independent variables were adjusted for industry averages to control for industry membership.

THE DATA

Dependent Variable

The main dependent variable of reputation is the combined score obtained in an annual *Fortune* magazine. The *Fortune* survey covers every industry group comprising four or more companies. The industry groups are based on categories established by the U.S. Office of Management and Budget (OMB). Thirty-three industry groupings were included in the 1987 and 1988 surveys, covering 300 and 306 firms of different sizes. The survey asked executives, directors, and analysts in particular industries to rate a company on the following eight key attributes of reputation:

1. Quality of management

2. Quality of products/service offered

3. Innovativeness

4. Value as a long-term investment

5. Soundness of financial position

6. Ability to attract/develop/keep talented people

7. Responsibility to the community/environment

8. Wise use of corporate assets.

Ratings were on a scale of 0 (poor) to 10 (excellent). The score met the multiple-consistency ecological model view of organization effectiveness. For the purpose of our study, the 1988 and 1987 *Fortune* magazine surveys were used. They contain the overall scores for the firms' ratings in 1987 and 1986. The use of the overall score rather than a factor analysis of the eight scores is based on the facts that (a) it is the overall score that is published in *Fortune* magazine rather than the eight scores on the attribute and (b) it is then the overall score that is perceived by the readers as well as the respondents of the survey as the reputation index. From previous experience, the respondents know that the means of their scores on the eight attributes will be published as the overall score of reputation.

Besides the overall score, the eight individual scores on the eight key attributes of reputation were also used as dependent variables to evaluate their differential relations with asset management performance.

Independent Variables

The independent variables include firm size, the Tobin Q, asset turnover, and profit margin minus their respective industry average for the year. Size for 1986 and 1987 was computed as the total assets for each of these two years. The Tobin Q for 1986 and 1987 was computed as the market value of the firm, divided by the replacement value of the assets measures, for each of the two years. Asset turnover for 1986 and 1987 was computed as the total sales divided by the total assets for each of the two years. Profit margin for 1986 and 1987 was computed as the net profit divided by total sales for each of the two years.

Sample

To ensure the greatest sample of firms for which data would be available for all variables, the initial sample chosen was all the firms included in *Fortune*'s 1987 and 1988 studies of corporate reputation. Accounting data for these firms was obtained from Standard & Poor's Compustat industrial and business segment tapes. Replacement cost data was determined from the inflation data disclosures in the annual reports resulting from the application of Statement 33. The final sample amounted to 114 firms.

Exhibit 10.2 presents the basic descriptive statistics for all the variables in the model and the intercorrelations among these variables. The low intercorrelations among adjusted predictor variables used in the model gave us no reason to suspect multicollinearity, and various diagnostic tests run on derived regres-

Exhibit 10.2
Descriptive Statistics

Variables	Mean	Standard deviation	Correlations			
			1	2	3	4
Reputation	6.569	0.747				
Assets ($1000s)	276.609	620.790	0.150***			
Tobin Q	1.292	1.640	0.283*	−0.102		
Asset Turnover	0.064	0.067	0.345*1	−0.060	0.203*	
Profit margin	1.247	0.544	0.079	−0.136**	0.120***	−0.239*

*Significant at α = 0.01. **Significant at α = 0.05. ***Significant at α = 0.10.

Source: Ahmed Riahi-Belkaoui and Ellen Pavlik, "Asset Management Performance and Reputation Building for Large U.S. Firms," British Journal of Management 2 (1991), p. 233. Reprinted with permission of the editor.

sion models, where size was expressed as the logarithm of assets, confirmed that it was not a problem.

RESULTS

Exhibits 10.3 and 10.4 present the results of the regression coefficients for all the independent variables, using all the measures of reputation as dependent variables for both 1987 and 1988.

Hypothesis 1 predicts that asset size will positively affect reputation. With two exceptions, the results for both years corroborate the hypothesis that corporate audiences tend to assign higher (better) reputations to firms with bigger size as measured by total assets. The two exceptions are for reputation measured as quality of products/service offered and innovativeness for both years.

Hypothesis 2 predicts that the market's assessment of the value of the assets in place, and the company's future investment opportunities as measured by Tobin's Q, will positively affect reputation. With some exceptions, the results for both years corroborate the hypothesis that corporate audiences tend to assign higher reputations to firms with a higher Tobin's Q. The exceptions are for reputation as measured by quality of management in both years and as measured by responsibility to the community/environment in 1987.

Hypothesis 3 predicts that the asset turnover will significantly influence reputational judgments. With two exceptions, the results for both years indicate that corporate audiences tend to assign higher reputations to firms with a high asset turnover ratio. The two exceptions are for reputation as measured by quality of products/service offered and responsibility to the community/environment for both years.

Finally, *hypothesis 4* predicts that the profit margin will positively affect reputation. With no exceptions, the results for both years corroborate the hypothesis that corporate audiences tend to assign higher reputations to firms with a high profit margin ratio.

In short, the overall reputation of firms is positively related to the total assets, Tobin's Q, asset turnover, and profit margin of the firm after controlling for industry averages, as hypothesized. For the eight component scores of reputations as measured by value as along-term investment and soundness of financial position. The role of asset management in creating reputation is, however, present and significant to different degrees for each of the eight component scores and for each of the two years examined, showing a persistence for each score and for each year. The best performance by an independent variable is played by the significant role of the profit margin ratio for the total reputation score as well as the eight component scores for both years.

The subdimension regression also offers some interesting results. For example, the quality of management is highly related to asset size, showing an acceptance by external audiences of a managerial wealth-maximization technique used by managers, involving the maximization of size. This finding is also ver-

Exhibit 10.3
Explaining Corporate Reputation in 1987

Independent variables/ Dependent variables	Intercept	TA-ITA	TQ-ITQ	AT-IAT	PM-IPM	F	R² Adj.(%)
Overall corporate reputation '87	6.474 (94.6)	0.00001 (94.6)*	0.1322 (1.883)**	0.2889 (2.551)*	5.700 (3.797)*	8.345*	23.44
Quality of management	6.720 (78.3)	0.00001 (2.085)**	0.0974 (1.102)	0.3906 (2.734)*	5.864 (3.101*)	5.137*	15.74
Quality of products/ services offered	7.131 (105.87)*	0.000006 (1.296)	0.1140 (1.642)***	0.1697 (1.516)	3.095 (2.085)**	3.173*	10.34
Innovativeness	6.2367 (76.14)*	0.000001 (0.321)	0.1491 (1.766)***	0.2715 (1.993)**	2.8489 (1.677)***	2.954**	9.7*
Value as a long-term investment	6.19 (81.5)	0.00002 (3.863)*	0.1302 (1.662)***	0.2591 (2.051)**	7.731 (4.615)*	11.025*	28.62
Soundness of financial position	6.613 (75.8)*	0.00002 (4.411)*	0.2060 (2.292)**	0.4126 (2.845)*	6.82 (5.628)*	16.590*	37.63
Ability to attract/develop/ keep talented people	6.2917 (83.68)	0.00001 (3.619)*	0.1285 (1.658)***	0.3438 (2.750)*	5.8618 (3.536)*	8.212*	22.99
Responsibility to comunity/ environment	6.3058 (97.054)*	0.00001 (3.698)*	0.08866 (1.323)	0.1621 (1.501)	3.3274 (2.323)**	5.310*	16.18
Wise use of resources	6.208 (84.22)*	0.00009 (1.836)**	0.1411 (1.841)*	0.2060 (2.387)*	6.0246 (3.664)	7.310*	20.59

*Absolute value of t-statistic in parentheses. *Significant at $\alpha = 0.01$. **Significant at $\alpha = 0.05$. ***Significant at $\alpha = 0.10$.

Source: Ahmed Riahi-Belkaoui and Ellen Pavlik, ''Asset Management Performance and Reputation Building for Large U.S. Firms,'' *British Journal of Management* 2 (1991), p. 233. Reprinted with permission of the editor.

Exhibit 10.4
Explaining Corporate Reputation in 1988

Independent variables / Dependent variables	Intercept	TA-ITA	TQ-ITQ	AT-IAT	PM-IPM	F	R² Adj.(%)
Overall corporate reputation '87	6.553 (93.5)	0.000008 (1.7)***	0.2327 (2.640)*	0.2393 (2.120)**	6.2643 (3.968)*	11.535*	29.36
Quality of management	6.770 (22.2)*	0.000003 (2.513)**	0.1696 (1.543)	0.34053 (2.419)*	7.253 (3.686)*	7.871*	22.25
Quality of products/ services offered	7.147 (95.56)*	0.000001 (0.324)	0.2540 (2.707)*	0.1759 (1.465)	3.3936 (2.020)*	6.067*	18.57
Innovativeness	6.29 (71.30)*	0.000005 (0.840)	0.2453 (2.218)*	0.2400 (1.690)***	2.875 (1.452)	4.688*	14.56
Value as a long-term investment	6.360 (78.08)*	0.000001 (2.375)*	0.2123 (2.078)**	0.2126 (1.625)***	7.601 (4.155)*	10.70*	28.01
Soundness of financial position	6.73 (76.7)*	0.00002 (4.043)*	0.3456 (3.141)**	0.3335 (2.367)*	11.421 (5.797)*	22.49*	45.00
Ability to attract/develop/ keep talented people	6.35 (79.19)	0.00001 (2.451)*	0.2537 (2.519)**	0.2871 (2.226)**	6.667 (3.696)*	10.575*	27.77
Responsibility to community/ environment	6.36 (88.13)*	0.00001 (3.038)*	0.1857 (2.049)**	0.1039 (0.895)	3.667 (2.259)***	6.044*	18.02
Wise use of resources	6.35 (83.23)*	0.000006 (0.114)	0.1952 (2.039)***	0.1949 (1.690)**	6.877 (4.013)*	10.053*	26.85

*Absolute value of t-statistic in parentheses. *Significant at $\alpha = 0.01$. **Significant at $\alpha = 0.05$. ***Significant at $\alpha = 0.10$.

Source: Ahmed Riahi-Belkaoui and Ellen Pavlik, ''Asset Management Performance and Reputation Building for Large U.S. Firms,'' *British Journal of Management* 2 (1991), p. 233. Reprinted with permission of the editor.

ified by the highly significant relationship between wise use of resources and asset size. This points to an interesting congruence between management's objectives and external audiences' assessments.

DISCUSSION AND CONCLUSIONS

Both the shareholder-wealth-maximization model and the open-ended stewardship concept maintain that corporate audiences are very much concerned by managers' use of the assets of the firm. This study had hypothesized that, consequently, corporate audiences will construct reputational rankings on the basis of the asset management performance. More specifically, the results of an empirical study of 114 large U.S. firms supported the general hypothesis that corporate audiences construct reputations on the basis of information about a firm's asset management performance, specifically using market and accounting signals indicating size of assets, market assessment of the value of the assets in place, asset turnover, and profit margin. Given the potential that reputation rankings may crystallize the statuses of firms within an industrial social system, firms, through a thorough understanding of the informational medium from which corporate audiences construct reputations, signal these audiences about their asset management performance through both accounting and market signals.

NOTES

1. This chapter has been largely adapted with permission of the editor from Ahmed Riahi-Belkaoui and Ellen Pavlik, "Asset Management Performance and Reputation Building for Large U.S. Firms," *British Journal of Management* 2 (1991), pp. 231–238.

2. G. R. Dowling, "Managing Your Corporate Images," *Industrial Marketing Management* 15 (1986), pp. 109–115.

3. R. E. Caves and M. E. Porter, "From Entry Barriers to Mobility Barriers," *Quarterly Journal of Economics* 91 (1977), pp. 421–434.

4. B. Klein and K. Leffler, "The Role of Market Forces in Assuring Contractual Performance," *Journal of Political Economy* 85 (1981), pp. 615–641.

5. R. P. Bealty and J. R. Ritter, "Investment Banking, Reputation, and Underpricing of Initial Public Offerings," *Journal of Financial Economics* 15 (1986), pp. 213–232.

6. A. A. Ullman, "Data in Search of a Theory: A Critical Examination of the Relationship Among Social Performance, Social Disclosure and Economic Performance of U.S. Firms," *Academy of Management Review* 10 (1985), pp. 540–557.

7. C. J. Fombrun and M. Shanley, "What's in a Name? Reputation Building and Corporate Strategy," *Academy of Management Journal* 33 (1990), pp. 233–258.

8. A. Belkaoui, "Organizational Effectiveness, Social Performance and Economic Performance," *Research in Corporate Social Performance and Policy* 12 (1992), pp. 143–153.

9. Ahmed Belkaoui and Ellen Pavlik, *Accounting for Corporate Reputation* (Westport, Conn.: Quorum Books, 1992).

10. Fombrun and Shanley, "What's in a Name? Reputation Building and Corporate Strategy," pp. 233–258.

11. J. D. Thompson, *Organizations in Action* (New York: McGraw-Hill, 1967).

12. C. Perrow, "The Analysis of Goals in Complex Organizations," *American Sociological Review* 6 (1961), pp. 854–866.

13. A. Belkaoui, *Conceptual Foundations of Management Accounting* (Reading, Mass.: Addison-Wesley, 1980).

14. J. C. Birnberg, "The Role of Accounting in Financial Disclosure," *Accounting, Organizations and Society* (June, 1980), pp. 71–80.

15. L. Lang and R. Litzenberg, "What Information Is Contained in the Dividend Announcement?" *Journal of Financial Economics* 6 (1989), pp. 32–67.

16. M. C. Jensen, "Agency Costs of Free Cash Flow, Corporate Finance and Takeovers," *American Economic Review* 76 (1986), pp. 323–329.

SUGGESTED READINGS

Bealty, R. P., and J. R. Ritter. "Investment Banking, Reputation, and Underpricing of Initial Public Offerings." *Journal of Financial Economics* 15 (1986), pp. 213–232.

Belkaoui, A. *Conceptual Foundations of Management Accounting*. Reading, Mass.: Addison-Wesley, 1980.

Belkaoui, A. "Organizational Effectiveness, Social Performance and Economic Performance." *Research in Corporate Social Performance and Policy* 12 (1992), pp. 143–153.

Belkaoui, Ahmed, and Ellen Pavlik. *Accounting for Corporate Reputation*. Westport, Conn.: Quorum Books, 1992).

Birnberg, J. C. "The Role of Accounting in Financial Disclosure." *Accounting, Organizations and Society* (June, 1980), pp. 71–80.

Caves, R. E., and M. E. Porter. "From Entry Barriers to Mobility Barriers." *Quarterly Journal of Economics* 91 (1977), pp. 421–434.

Dowling, G. R. "Managing Your Corporate Images." *Industrial Marketing Management* 15 (1986), pp. 109–115.

Fombrun, C. J., and M. Shanley. "What's in a Name? Reputation Building and Corporate Strategy." *Academy of Management Journal* 33 (1990), pp. 233–258.

Jensen, M. C. "Agency Costs of Free Cash Flow, Corporate Finance and Takeovers." *American Economic Review* 76 (1986), pp. 323–329.

Klein, B., and K. Leffler. "The Role of Market Forces in Assuring Contractual Performance." *Journal of Political Economy* 85 (1981), pp. 615–641.

Lang, L., and R. Litzenberg. "What Information Is Contained in the Dividend Announcement?" *Journal of Financial Economics* 6 (1989), pp. 32–67.

Perrow, C. "The Analysis of Goals in Complex Organizations." *American Sociological Review* 6 (1961), pp. 854–866.

Thompson, J. D. *Organizations in Action*. New York: McGraw-Hill, 1967.

Ullman, A. A. "Data in Search of a Theory: A Critical Examination of the Relationship Among Social Performance, Social Disclosure and Economic Performance of U.S. Firms." *Academy of Management Review* 10 (1985), pp. 540–557.

11

The Prediction
of Capital Structure

INTRODUCTION[1]

This chapter employs a contingency perspective to examine the impact of the implementation of the multidivisional form (M-form) structure of a firm's capital structure given different corporate diversification strategies. Theories of corporate capital structure have often focused on the various roles of debt, including the tax advantage of debt,[2] choice of debt level to signal firm quality,[3] the use of debt as an antitakeover device,[4] the agency costs of debt,[5] and the usefulness of debt for restricting managerial discretion.[6] These theories and the related empirical work on capital structure have increased our understanding of the issues. There is, however, no consensus about which of the determinants have an impact on the capital structure decision or how they affect performance. We believe that Barton and Gordon's[7] suggestion to employ a strategy perspective will add to the understanding of the capital structure decision.

Specifically, we test whether implementation of the M-form structure is associated with a change in capital structure, and whether such changes vary over firms with different corporate diversification strategies. Williamson[8] discusses a theory of the firm's strategy for financing projects based upon the redeployability of the assets involved and the governance structure best suited to those assets. Both concepts are used in this study to motivate the differential capital structures expected from different diversification strategies. Three major categories of corporate diversification strategy are examined: vertical integration, related business diversification, and unrelated diversification.[9] Our central proposition is that the implementation of the M-form structure affects the capital structure decision differently depending upon which diversification strategy exists prior to M-form

implementation. We investigate the proposition by comparing the capital structure of large multiproduct firms before and after their reorganization.

The chapter proceeds as follows. The next section discusses the multidivisional form and its relation to firm performance. Hypotheses related to the impact of M-form restructuring and diversification strategy on capital structure are
presented. The third section details the sample, data collection, and the variables
used in the study. Our approach and empirical results are presented in the fourth
section. The final section contains a discussion of the results.

BACKGROUND AND HYPOTHESES

Implementation of the Multidivisional Form and Capital Structure

Extending Chandler's[10] work, Williamson[11] argues that as the size and diversity of centralized (U-form) firms increase, managers reach their limits of control
and may resort to opportunism, thereby threatening efficiency and profitability.
He suggests that the multidivisional form (M-form) of managerial structure can
reduce such opportunism. Since M-form implementation requires the firm to be
decomposed into distinct divisions, most operating decisions, and some strategic
decisions, are decentralized to these divisions. With effective decentralization,
middle-management opportunism can be reduced, since responsibility for operating budgets and cost management is shifted to division managers.

While the M-form may reduce middle-management opportunism, it offers less
to control top-management opportunism. One area where top-management may
display opportunism is in the misuse of free cash flow; namely, cash flow in
excess of that required to fund all projects that have positive net present value
when discounted at the relevant cost of capital. M-form implementation does
not prevent top management from investing free cash flow at below the cost of
capital, or wasting it on organizational inefficiencies.

M-form adopters may tend to have free cash flow. Population-ecology theory
suggests that as organizations age, they reach higher levels of performance reliability and move to a state of "structural inertia,"[12] which is characterized by
substantial free cash flow. Fligstein[13] uses population-ecology theory to explain
the adoption of the M-form.

Management that has been retaining free cash flow may be forced to release
it when seeking new financing. Jensen[14] theorizes that the capital market may
force firms to finance new capital with debt, rather than equity, in order to reduce
management misuse of free cash flow. He argues that debt reduces the agency
costs of free cash flow by reducing the cash flow available for discretionary
spending by top management. Increased debt financing would act to increase
the efficiency of organizations that have large cash flows, but few high-return
investments, by forcing them to disgorge cash to investors.

Two features of multidivisional form implementation suggest that additional financing may be needed by the firm. First, the evidence shows that the size and asset growth of firms increase after implementation of the M-form. Second, costly coordination and information-processing functions may be needed to realize the economic gains associated with the M-form. Following the implementation of the M-form, we expect that firms will seek new financing and be required to use an increased amount of debt to reduce opportunism in the use of free cash flow. Thus, we hypothesize:

H_1: The implementation of the M-form leads to an increase in the firm's debt/equity ratio.

Diversification Strategy and Capital Structure

Galbraith and Nathanson[15] trace the growth of firms in three major categories of corporate diversification strategy: vertical integration, related business diversification, and unrelated business diversification. Each strategy results in different economic benefits or costs and implies different management objectives. Transaction cost economics (TCE) suggests that the economic characteristics of the three diversification strategies may call for different types of financing.

TCE views project financing as a choice between alternative corporate governance structures and cash-flow requirements. Debt financing does not allow the debtholder voting power, but it imposes mandatory cash outflows for interest and principal on the borrower. Equity financing requires shared voting power, but does not involve mandatory cash flows. Since management is assumed to desire as little dilution of its voting power as possible, it will opt for debt financing so long as the project can generate sufficient cash flow. Thus, the choice of debt or equity funding for a project is related to the project specificity of its assets. If a project's assets are redeployable (less project-specific), they can be sold or put to an alternative productive use in the firm, and the cash-flow stream from these assets is less risky. Projects with redeployable (less risky) assets are thus suited to debt financing. Conversely, projects with less redeployable (more risky) assets are suited to equity financing, which has no mandatory cash outflow requirement. The implications of TCE for the three diversification strategies are discussed below.

Vertical integration offers the firm economies due to control of its supply/ output markets. The firm's value-added margin for a chain of processing is increased due to increased control over raw materials and/or outlets.[16] Further, market transaction costs, such as opportunistic action by traders or the drafting and monitoring of contingent claims contracts to ensure harmonious trading relationships, can be either eliminated or reduced.[17] Because up- or downstream integration provides cost savings to the firm, redeployment of these assets could tend to reduce the value of the firm disproportionately to their individual value.

Firms pursuing a strategy of related diversification can realize synergistic economies of scope through the joint use of inputs.[18] Exploitation of this synergy is achieved through both tangible and intangible interrelationships. Tangible interrelationships are created by such devices as joint procurement of raw materials, joint development of shared technologies or production processes, joint sales forces, and joint physical distribution systems. Intangible interrelationships arise from the sharing of know-how and capabilities. Redeployment of assets in a related diversified firm would again imply a disproportionate loss in firm value since synergistic economics could be lost.

A traditional argument for unrelated diversification suggests that the multi-product firm can realize financial economies. The risk pooling of imperfectly correlated income streams created by unrelated diversification is, in principle, assumed to produce an asset with a superior risk/return relationship.[19] The same risk diversification can, however, be more efficiently achieved by the investor with a portfolio of bond holdings.[20] Empirical evidence is also inconsistent with the idea that unrelated diversification reduces risk. Furthermore, unrelated diversification in itself does not imply the achievement of input/output market cost savings or the existence of managerial, technological, or operational synergies. While Williamson[21] contends that "conglomerate" firms may benefit from improved governance after the adoption of the M-form structure, assets (divisions) of unrelated diversifiers remain highly redeployable through spin-off or outright sale with little synergistic loss to the firm.

TCE argues that as assets become more redeployable, management prefers debt financing over equity financing. The previous discussion suggests that there is differential redeployability of assets among firms that follow different diversification strategies, with unrelated diversifiers holding more redeployable assets than related diversifiers and verticle integraters. In addition, Jensen[22] argues that firms that are generating large free cash flows (and are thus subject to the market discipline of debt financing) often diversify into unrelated areas. We hypothesize that the different diversification strategies employed by firms are associated with cross-sectional differences in capital structure between diversification strategies. More specifically,

H_2: Firms using related diversification or vertical integration strategies have lower debt/equity ratios than firms using an unrelated diversification strategy.

SAMPLE AND DATA COLLECTION

Previous research has identified 62 firms that adopted the M-form during the period 1950–1978. Our sample consists of these firms. Each firm was diversified at the time of its restructuring and was classified using a classification method. Firms were classified as having been in one of the three diversification classes—unrelated (16 firms), related (22 firms), or vertical (24 firms). Exhibit 11.1 lists the firms, their classification, and the year in which the restructuring occurred.

Dependent Variable

A longitudinal design was used to capture the effects over time of the implementation of a decentralized multidivisional structure. Data for the measure of capital structure, year-end long-term debt to common equity, was collected for years -5 through $+5$ (relative to the year of the restructuring). Financial statement data for each firm were collected from Compustat and, in cases where Compustat coverage was incomplete, from *Moody's Industrials Manual*. The data collected for the dependent variable were long-term liabilities (Compustat data item 9) and common equity (60).

Control Variables and Covariates

A control factor, early/late adoption of the M-form and three covariates (firm size, growth in total assets, and growth in GNP) are included to control for possible intervening effects. The control factor, early/late adoption of the M-form, is motivated by the belief that late movers learn from the experience of early movers and are thus able to restructure faster and more efficiently.[23] Early/late adoption is measured by the year of restructuring relative to the sample median. Firms adopting the M-form prior to 1967 are classified as early movers; those adopting in 1967 or later are classified as late movers.

Firm size, asset growth rate, and GNP growth rate are included as covariates. Their use is motivated by (1) the known relationship between leverage and size, (2) the suggestion that firms may sacrifice profitability in periods of growth, and (3) the need to control for changes in capital structure related to major external shifts in aggregate demand. Firm size is measured as the natural logarithm of average total assets; asset growth rate is measured as the proportional change in total assets. Data for year-end total assets were collected from Compustat (data item 6), or from *Moody's Industrials Manual* when Compustat coverage was incomplete. GNP growth rate is measured as the proportional change in GNP. Data for GNP were collected from the National Income and Product Accounts constructed by the U.S. Department of Commerce. Each of the covariates is measured over the same period as the dependent variable. Exhibit 11.2 gives the means, standard deviations, and correlations for the variables used in the chapter.

DATA ANALYSIS

A longitudinal design is used to capture the effects of overtime of the implementation of a decentralized multidivisional structure. Years -1, 0, and $+1$ relative to the year of the restructuring (year 0) were excluded from the analysis to avoid the potential confounding of capital structure measures with events during the transition. An analysis of covariance is used to test the overall relationship between (1) organizational structure and capital structure, (2) diversi-

Exhibit 11.1
Diversified Firms[a] Restructuring to the M-Form from the U-Form

Company Name	Diversification Strategy[b]	Year of Restructuring	Company Name	Diversification Strategy	Year of Restructuring
Aluminum Co. of America	V	68	CPC	R	67
BF Goodrich	V	53	Dow Chemical	R	63
Burlington	V	62	General Foods	R	52
City Service	V	66	Heinz	R	67
Continental Can	V	50	Honeywell	R	62
Crown Zellerbach	V	66	IBM	R	65
Getty Oil[c]	V	59	Ingersoll Rand	R	64
Goodyear	V	76	Monsanto	R	71
Hormel	V	66	Phillip Morris	R	67
International Paper	V	73	Procter & Gamble	R	66
Kaiser Aluminum	V	58	Quaker Oats	R	71
Kennecott Paper	V	66	Ralston Purina	R	68
Marathon Oil	V	63	R.J. Reynolds	R	70
Mobil Oil	V	60	J.P. Stephens	R	71
Occidental Petroleum	V	72	White Motor Co.	R	69
Phillips Petroleum	V	75			

Firm	Type	Value	Firm	Type	Value
Shell Oil	V	61	AMF	U	58
Standard Oil (California)	V	55	Borg Warner	U	70
Standard Oil (Ohio)	V	62	Brunswick	U	69
Standard Oil (Indiana)	V	61	Colt Industries	U	68
St. Regis Paper	V	69	Dart Industries	U	62
Sun Oil	V	71	Dayco	U	66
Union Oil	V	64	Esmark	U	70
Uniroyal	V	60	FMC	U	61
			Gulf & Western	U	67
Allied Chemical	R	72	ITT	U	68
Ashland Oil	R	70	Lear Siegler	U	62
Bendix	R	65	Ogden	U	69
Borden	R	68	Textron	U	60
Burroughs	R	66	US Industries	U	69
Celanese	R	63	Raytheon	U	59
Coca-Cola	R	68	SCM	U	62

[a] Firms in the study are drawn from the sample reported in Hoskisson (1987).

[b] V = vertically diversified, R = related diversification, U = unrelated diversification.

[c] "Before" variables for Getty Oil were constructed from data for years −4 to −2.

Source: Ahmed Riahi-Belkaoui and James W. Bannister, "Multidivisional Structure and Capital Structure: The Contingency of Diversification Strategy," *Managerial and Decision Economics* 15 (1994), pp. 267–276. Copyright John Wiley & Sons Limited. Reproduced with permission.

Exhibit 11.2

Means, Standard Deviations, and Correlation Coefficients of Variables by Strategic Type and Stage of M-Form Implementation (Three-Year Window Excluded)

Variables	Means[a]		Correlations[b]			
	Before M-form	After M-form	1	2	3	4
(A) *Vertically integrated firms*						
1. Long-term Debt/Total Equity	0.36 (0.07)	0.42 (0.07)	1.000	0.088	0.209	−0.393
2. Size[c]	6.77 (0.98)	7.32 (1.00)	0.054	1.000	0.585	0.019
3. Total Growth in GNP[d]	0.21 (0.06)	0.26 (0.07)	−0.058	0.330	1.000	0.223
4. Total Asset Growth[e]	0.29 (0.26)	0.28 (0.15)	0.339	0.224	0.324	1.000
(B) *Related diversified firms*						
1. Long-term Debt/Total Equity	0.25 (0.07)	0.46 (0.07)	1.000	−0.006	0.123	0.186
2. Size[c]	6.34 (0.69)	7.12 (0.67)	0.161	1.000	0.131	0.169

			1	2	3	4
3. Total Growth in GNP[d]	0.22 (0.04)	0.28 (0.04)	-0.014	0.161	1.000	-0.045
4. Total Asset growth[e]	0.30 (0.23)	0.42 (0.21)	0.145	-0.055	0.258	1.000
(C) Unrelated diversified firms						
1. Long-term Debt/Total Equity	0.59 (0.10)	0.70 (0.08)	1.000	-0.091	0.066	-0.351
2. Size[c]	5.19 (1.08)	6.37 (1.03)	0.075	1.000	0.526	-0.471
3. Total Growth in GNP[d]	0.21 (0.05)	0.28 (0.05)	-0.173	0.582	1.000	-0.147
4. Total Asset Growth[e]	0.65 (0.58)	0.62 (0.83)	-0.030	-0.396	-0.084	1.000

[a] Standard deviations are in parentheses.

[b] Correlations in the upper (lower) half of the matrices are from after (before) implementation of the M-form.

[c] Size is computed as 1n (Average Total Assets).

[d] Total Growth in GNP is computed as $(GNP_E - GNP_B)/GNP_B$, where B denotes the beginning of a period and E the end of a period.

[e] Total Asset Growth is computed as $(TA_E - TA_B)/TA_B$, where TA = total assets, B denotes the beginning of a period, and E denotes the end of a period.

Source: Ahmed Riahi-Belkaoui and James W. Bannister, "Multidivisional Structure and Capital Structure: The Contingency of Diversification Strategy," *Managerial and Decision Economics* 15 (1994), pp. 267–276. Copyright John Wiley & Sons Limited. Reproduced with permission.

Exhibit 11.3
Results of Analysis of Covariance for Long-Term Liabilities/Total Common Equity

Sources	F-Statistic	Pr. > F
Diversification strategy	6.59	0.002
M-form implementation	2.66	0.100
M-form x diversification strategy	0.65	0.526
Control variable Early/late adopter	2.85	0.094
Covariates		
Size	0.00	0.948
Total asset growth	0.17	0.679
Total growth in GNP	1.09	0.299

fication strategy and capital structure, and (3) the interactive effect of organizational structure and diversification strategy on capital structure. Early/late adoption is a control variable; firm size, asset growth rate, and GNP growth rate are covariates. The effects on capital structure of M-form implementation, diversification strategy and their interaction are first examined by an F test of the difference between variances after controlling for the effects of early/late adoption and the covariates.

Exhibit 11.3 presents the results of the analysis of covariance for long-term debt to total common equity for the 62 firms in the sample. The overall analysis of covariance is statistically significant (F [9,123] = 2.70, p = 0.007, and R^2 = 0.18). Further, nondirectional F tests for differences in variance indicate that (1) the implementation of the M-form leads to a different capital structure and (2) the different diversification strategies employed by the sample firms are associated with cross-sectional differences in capital structure. There is no interactive effect of organizational form and diversification strategy on capital structure. There is no interactive effect of organizational form and diversification strategy on capital structure. Directional tests of hypotheses related to the main effects are reported below.

Hypothesis H_1 states the implementation of the M-form is associated with an increased use of debt in the firm's capital structure. The impact of the M-form implementation on capital structure is further investigated by performing comparisons of mean debt/equity ratios before and after the M-form for the overall sample, and by strategic type. Exhibit 11.4 presents these results. In agreement

Exhibit 11.4

Mean Comparisons of Long-Term Liabilities/Total Common Equity by Strategy Type before versus after M-Form Implementation

Strategy type	Before the M-form	After the M-form	t-probability[a]
(1) All strategies	0.4010	0.5276	0.05
(2) Unrelated diversified firms	0.5879	0.7048	0.19
(3) Vertically integrated firms	0.3607	0.4173	0.29
(4) Related diversified firms	0.2542	0.4605	0.03

[a]H_1 predicts that the debt/equity ratio increases after M-form implementation; t-probabilities are one-tailed.

Source: Ahmed Riahi-Belkaoui and James W. Bannister, "Multidivisional Structure and Capital Structure: The Contingency of Diversification Strategy," *Managerial and Decision Economics* 15 (1994), pp. 267–276. Copyright John Wiley & Sons Limited. Reproduced with permission.

with H_1, the exhibit indicates that following the implementation of the M-form, firms in the overall sample significantly increased their debt/equity ratios. Further, the mean debt/equity ratio for firms in each of the strategy types increased. The analysis indicates, however, that the increase is statistically significant only in the case of firms employing the strategy of related diversification.

Hypothesis H_2 states that firms employing a strategy of unrelated diversification use more debt in their capital structure than do firms employing strategies of related diversification or vertical integration. The impact of diversification strategy on capital structure is further investigated by performing mean comparisons between type of diversification strategy. Exhibit 11.5 presents these results. As suggested by H_2, unrelated diversified firms have long-term debt-to-equity ratios that are significantly larger than those for vertically integrated firms and related diversified firms. Hypothesis H_2 did not make a projection about the relative use of debt and equity between vertically integrated firms and related diversified firms. A test indicates, however, that there is no significant difference in debt/equity ratios for firms following these strategies.

DISCUSSION

The central proposition of this study was that the implementation of a multidivisional structure is associated with different capital structures in firms that employ the different strategic diversification approaches of unrelated diversification, vertical integration, and related diversification. The results of this study support the contingency view of the relationship between capital structure and the implementation of the M-form.

Exhibit 11.5

Mean Comparison of Long-Term Liabilities/Total Common Equity by Strategy Type

Means for strategy types			t-probability[a]		
Unrelated diversifiers	Vertical integraters	Related diversifiers	U versus V	U versus R	R versus V
0.6463	0.3890	0.3574	0.0025	0.0026	0.6519

[a]U = unrelated diversifiers, V = vertical integraters, R = related diversifiers. H_2 predicts that unrelated diversifiers have higher debt/equity ratios than do related diversifiers or vertical integraters. Thus, the reported t-probabilities for U versus V and U versus R are one-tailed. H_2 makes no prediction about the relationship between R and V firms; the reported t-probability is two-tailed.

Source: Ahmed Riahi-Belkaoui and James W. Bannister, "Multidivisional Structure and Capital Structure: The Contingency of Diversification Strategy," *Managerial and Decision Economics* 15 (1994), pp. 267–276. Copyright John Wiley & Sons Limited. Reproduced with permission.

Hypothesis H_1 was confirmed, the sample firms increased the level of debt used in their capital structure. Although percentage debt usage generally increased for all diversification classes, within diversification classes only related diversified firms made a statistically significant change. An explanation for the general increase in debt is that the implementation of the M-form controls is associated with a reduction in the availability of free cash flow through debt creation. The reduction of opportunism implied as one of the goals of decentralization is further enhanced by the "control" mechanism of debt creation. The increase in debt level following the implementation of the M-form points to the role of debt in reducing the agency costs of free cash flow.

In regard to the significant increase in debt usage for related diversified firms, Hill and Hoskisson[24] suggest that, among the strategies of unrelated diversification, related diversification, and vertical integration, the strategy of related diversification requires higher costs of coordination and information processing to realize potential economic gains. A significant increase in debt level for the related diversified firms, rather than for the unrelated diversified or vertically integrated firms, supports their suggestion that extra funds may have been needed to achieve and exploit economies of scope, which require efficient interdivisional coordination.

The test of hypotheses H_2 also yielded statistically significant results, suggesting that, in agreement with Williamson's thesis, debt as a governance structure is more suited to projects where assets are highly redeployable and, therefore, that different diversification strategies with different asset redeployabilities are associated with different capital structures. Where the redeployability of assets is high, as in unrelated diversified firms, the use of long-term debt financing in the firm's capital structure is greater than for firms where redeployability of assets is lower, as in related diversified and vertically integrated firms. As a result, while increased costs of coordination may require a significant increase in debt for related diversified firms, the usage of debt in their capital structures after M-form implementation is still lower than in that of unrelated diversified firms.

These results show a link between diversification strategy, organizational structure and capital structure. At divisional level diversification strategies influence capital structure strategies. These results complement and add to the strategic-group paradigm.[25] Based on a firm's heterogeneous capabilities and resources, the strategic-group paradigm enables researchers and practitioners to map industrial firms into sets of similar competitors, the so-called strategic groups. While a more comprehensive review of the literature is provided by McGee and Thomas,[26] Thomas and Venkatraman,[27] and Barney and Hoskisson,[28] the results of this study indicate that the strategic linkages between the divisions of the firm and the rest of the firm need to be taken into account in the formulation of strategic groups. Better strategic groups could be identified by a simultaneous consideration of corporate diversification strategy and divisional strategy.

More research is needed to verify the results of this study and to test the questions that it raises. Replication needs to consider (1) using different data and multiple measures of leverage, (2) relying on recent periods, and (3) imposing a control group of firms not adopting the M-form. Until further research is completed, the results of the leverage effects of a historical shift to an M-form framework must be interpreted with caution.

APPENDIX: CLASSIFICATION OF DIVERSIFICATION STRATEGIES

A framework for the classification categories relies on three ratios: (1) the specialization ratio, (2) the related ratio, and (3) the vertical ratio. Each of the three ratios is based upon the proportion of revenues earned from various business activities. The specialization ratio is used to define firms into the primary categories of either single business, dominant business, related business, or unrelated business. The related and vertical ratios are then used to subdivide firms into finer classifications.

The specialization ratio (SR) is defined as the proportion of the firm's revenues that is attributable to its largest discrete product-market activity. The related ratio (RR) is defined as the proportion of firm revenues that are related to one another in some way. The vertical ratio (VR) is defined as the proportion of revenues attributable to all the by-products, intermediate products, and final products of a vertically integrated sequence of manufacturing operations.

The primary diversification strategies and their subcategories are: (1) single business; (2) dominant business as either (a) dominant vertical, (b) dominant constrained, (c) dominant linked or (d) dominant unrelated; (3) related business as either (a) related constrained or (b) related linked; (4) unrelated business as either (a) multi-business or (b) unrelated-portfolio.

A specialization ratio of less than 0.7 defines a business as unrelated. If 0.7 < SR < 0.95, then the firm is classified as a dominant business. The firm is classified as a single business if SR ≥ 0.95. A related ratio (RR) greater than 0.7 defines a related business. A vertical ratio greater than 0.7 defines a vertically integrated business.

A reduced classification system for the sample firms is used in this study. Each firm is classified as being in one of the three following categories:

1. *Primary dominant vertical firms*: vertically integrated firms (VR ≥ 0.7) producing and selling different end products, none of which contributes more than 94 percent of total revenues.

2. *Related-constrained firms*: firms with $0.7 \leq SR < 0.95$ and RR ≥ 0.7 which have diversified by relating new businesses to a specific central skill or resource wherein each business activity is related to almost all the other business activities of the firm.

3. *Unrelated business firms*: firms with $0.7 \leq SR < 0.95$ and RR < 0.7 that have aggressive programs for the acquisition of new unrelated business.

NOTES

1. This chapter has been largely adapted with permission of the editor from Ahmed Riahi-Belkaoui and James W. Bannister, "Multidivisional Structure and Capital Structure: The Contingency of Diversification Strategy," *Managerial and Decision Economics* 15 (1994), pp. 267–276. Copyright John Wiley & Sons Limited. Used with permission.

2. F. Modigliani and M. H. Miller, "Corporate Income Taxes and the Cost of Capital: A Correction," *American Economic Review* 3 (1963), pp. 433–443.

3. S. A. Ross, "The Determination of Financial Structure: The Incentive-Signaling Approach," *Bell Journal of Economics* 8 (1977), pp. 23–40.

4. M. Harris and A. Raviv, "Corporate Control Contests and Capital Structure," *Journal of Financial Economics* 20 (1988), pp. 55–86.

5. S. C. Myers, "Determinants of Corporate Borrowing," *Journal of Financial Economics* 5 (1977), pp. 147–176.

6. M. C. Jensen, "Agency Costs of Free Cash Flow, Corporate Finance, and Takeovers," *American Economic Review* 76 (1986), pp. 323–329.

7. S. L. Barton and P. J. Gordon, "Corporate Strategy: Usefulness Perspective for the Study of Capital Structure?" *Academy of Managerial Review* 12 (1987), pp. 67–75.

8. O. W. Williamson, "Corporate Finance and Corporate Governance," *Journal of Finance* 43 (1988), pp. 567–591.

9. J. R. Galbraith and D. A. Nathanson, "Role of Organizational Structure and Process in Strategy Implementation," in D. Schandel and C. Hofer, eds., *Strategic Management: A New View of Business Policy and Planning* (Boston: Little, Brown & Co., 1979), pp. 249–83.

10. A. Chandler, *Strategy and Structure* (Cambridge, Mass.: MIT Press, 1962).

11. O. W. Williamson, *Corporate Control and Business Behavior* (Englewood Cliffs, N.J.: Prentice-Hall, 1970).

12. M. Hannan and J. Freeman, "The Population Ecology of Organizations," *American Journal of Sociology* 92 (1977), pp. 929–1964.

13. N. Fligstein, "The Spread of the Multidivisional Form among Large Firms," *American Sociological Review* 50 (1985), pp. 377–391.

14. Jensen, "Agency Costs of Free Cash Flow, Corporate Finance and Takeovers," pp. 323–329.

15. Galbraith and Nathanson, "Role of Organizational Structure and Process in Strategy Implementation," pp. 249–283.

16. K. R. Harrigan, "Vertical Integration and Corporate Strategy," *Academy of Management Journal* 28 (1985), pp. 397–425.

17. C. W. Hill and R. E. Hoskisson, "Multidivisional Structure and Performance: The Contingency of Diversification Strategy," *Academy of Management Review* 12 (1987), pp. 331–340.

18. D. Teece, "Economies of Scope and the Scope of the Enterprise," *Journal of Behavior and Organization* 1 (1980), pp. 223–247.

19. W. Lewellen, "A Pure Financial Rationale for the Conglomerate Merger," *Journal of Finance* 26 (1971), pp. 521–545.

20. H. Levy and M. Sarnat, "Diversification, Portfolio Analysis and the Uneasy Case for Conglomerate Mergers," *Journal of Finance* 25 (1970), pp. 795–802.

21. O. W. Williamson, *Markets and Hierarchies: Analysis and Antitrust Implications* (New York: Free Press, 1975).

22. Jensen, "Agency Costs of Free Cash Flow, Corporate Finance, and Takeovers," pp. 323–329.

23. E. Mansfield "How Rapidly Does New Industrial Technology Leak Out?" *Journal of Industrial Economics* 34 (1985), pp. 217–225.

24. Hill and Hoskisson, "Multidivisional Structure and Performance," pp. 331–340.

25. M. Porter, *Competitive Advantage: Creating and Sustaining Superior Performance* (New York: Free Press, 1985).

26. J. McGee and H. Thomas, "Strategic Groups: Theory, Research and Taxonomy," *Strategic Management Journal* 7 (1986), pp. 141–160.

27. H. Thomas and N. Venkatraman, "Research on Strategic Groups: Progress and Prognosis," *Journal of Management Studies* 25 (1988), pp. 537–555.

28. J. B. Barney and R. E. Hoskisson, "Untested Assertions in Strategic Group Research," *Managerial and Decision Economics* 11 (1990), pp. 187–198.

SUGGESTED READINGS

Barney, J. B., and R. E. Hoskisson. "Untested Assertions in Strategic Group Research." *Managerial and Decision Economics* 11 (1990), pp. 187–198.

Barton, S. L., and P. J. Gordon. "Corporate Strategy: Usefulness Perspective for the Study of Capital Structure?" *Academy of Managerial Review* 12 (1987), pp. 67–75.

Chandler, A. *Strategy and Structure.* Cambridge, Mass.: MIT Press, 1962.

Fligstein, N. "The Spread of the Multidivisional Form Among Large Firms." *American Sociological Review* 50 (1985), pp. 377–391.

Galbraith, J. R., and D. A. Nathanson, "Role of Organizational Structure and Process in Strategy Implementation." In D. Schandel and C. Hofer, eds., *Strategic Manage-*

ment: A New View of Business Policy and Planning. Boston: Little, Brown & Co., 1979, pp. 249–283.

Hannan, M., and J. Freeman. "The Population Ecology of Organizations." *American Journal of Sociology* 92 (1977), pp. 929–964.

Harrigan, K. R. "Vertical Intergration and Corporate Strategy." *Academy of Management Journal* 28 (1985), pp. 397–425.

Harris, M., and A. Raviv. "Corporate Control Contests and Capital Structure." *Journal of Financial Economics* 20 (1988), pp. 55–86.

Hill, C. W., and R. E. Hoskisson. "Multidivisional Structure and Performance: The Contingency of Diversification Strategy." *Academy of Management Review* 12 (1987), pp. 331–340.

Jensen, M. C. "Agency Costs of Free Cash Flow, Corporate Finance, and Takeovers." *American Economic Review* 76 (1986), pp. 323–329.

Levy, H., and M. Sarnat. "Diversification, Portfolio Analysis and the Uneasy Case for Conglomerate Mergers." *Journal of Finance* 25 (1970), pp. 795–802.

Lewellen, W. "A Pure Financial Rationale for the Conglomerate Merger." *Journal of Finance* 26 (1971), pp. 521–545.

Mansfield, E. "How Rapidly Does New Industrial Technology Leak Out?" *Journal of Industrial Economics* 34 (1985), pp. 217–225.

McGee, J., and H. Thomas. "Strategic Groups: Theory, Research and Taxonomy." *Strategic Management Journal* 7 (1986), pp. 141–160.

Modigliani, F., and M. H. Miller. "Corporate Income Taxes and the Cost of Capital: A Correction." *American Economic Review* 3 (1963), pp. 433–443.

Myers, S. C. "Determinants of Corporate Borrowing." *Journal of Financial Economics* 5 (1977), pp. 147–176.

Porter, M. *Competitive Advantage: Creating and Sustaining Superior Performance*. New York: Free Press, 1985.

Ross, S. A. "The Determination of Financial Structure: The Incentive-Signaling Approach." *Bell Journal of Economics* 8 (1977), pp. 23–40.

Teece, D. "Economies of Scope and the Scope of the Enterprise." *Journal of Behavior and Organization* 1 (1980), pp. 223–247.

Thomas, H., and N. Venkatraman. "Research on Strategic Groups: Progress and Prognosis." *Journal of Management Studies* 25 (1988), pp. 537–555.

Williamson, O. W. *Corporate Control and Business Behavior*. Englewood Cliffs, N.J.: Prentice-Hall, 1970.

Williamson, O. W. "Corporate Finance and Corporate Governance." *Journal of Finance* 43 (1988), pp. 567–591.

Williamson, O. W. *Markets and Hierarchies: Analysis and Antitrust Implications*. New York: Free Press, 1975.

Index

About the Author

AHMED RIAHI-BELKAOUI is CBA Distinguished Professor of Accounting in the College of Business Administration, University of Illinois at Chicago. Author of more than 30 Quorum books and coauthor of several more, he is also a prolific author of articles published in the scholarly and professional journals of his field, and has served on numerous editoral boards.

ISBN 1-56720-164-4

HARDCOVER BAR CODE